UNEVEN JUSTICE

THE PLOT TO SINK GALLEON

RAJ RAJARATNAM

Post Hill
PRESS

A POST HILL PRESS BOOK
ISBN: 978-1-63758-281-7
ISBN (eBook): 978-1-63758-280-0

Uneven Justice:
The Plot to Sink Galleon
© 2021 by Raj Rajaratnam
All Rights Reserved

Cover photo by Martin Schoeller

This is a work of nonfiction. All people, locations, events, and situations are portrayed to the best of the author's memory.

Post Hill Press
New York • Nashville
posthillpress.com

Published in the United States of America
1 2 3 4 5 6 7 8 9 10

To all those who were wrongfully incarcerated

TABLE OF CONTENTS

PREFACE

In October 2009, I was arrested and charged with insider trading. I chose to fight the charges against me because I was innocent.

The prosecutors alleged that 0.01 percent of all my trades between 2005 and 2009 were illegal.

I understood that in the U.S., there is a 97 percent conviction rate (similar to China and Russia) and a punitive trial penalty for those who dare to go to trial. Empirical studies have shown that the trial penalty is just about double that handed to those who plead guilty. If a defendant agrees to become a cooperating witness, helping the government with testimony—regardless of the truth—to convict another defendant, the cooperating witness gets a much-reduced sentence and in many cases, just parole.

I understood the stakes. I chose to go to trial. Why? It's a question I've since been asked hundreds of times. Why? Why jeopardize everything? Because to my core, I believed I would get a fair hearing. And with a fair hearing and a rational exposition of the facts, the truth would have prevailed. Until my arrest, I had the highest regard for the Department of Justice (DOJ) and the Federal Bureau of Investigation (FBI). Until 2009, I believed that most Americans felt that way. Since then, of course, the American public has become jaded about the sanctity of these institutions due to multiple examples of overreach and excess. Certain DOJ and FBI sections operate, each attempting to further its own agenda, with no regard for Constitutional checks and balances. The terms "fake news," the "Deep State" are bandied about with almost wild abandon, humor, and satire. The public now assumes the existence of "fake news" alongside "authentic" news with little effort toward journalistic integrity. During the time of my arrest and trial, information from the media, DOJ, and FBI was absorbed with unquestioned "Trust," although some would argue that the Deep State had existed for many years. While I still believe that the vast majority of those who work for the DOJ and the FBI are people of integrity, this book is an attempt to shed light on the corrupt few who act with impunity and destroy lives and families to further their career ambitions.

From the moment of my arrest, the narrative of my story was recast with a precise agenda shaped to direct public attention away from the stark horror of the 2007–2008 financial crisis while promoting media idolatry of the publicity-hungry and ambitious rookie U.S. Attorney Preet Bharara, who became a demigod, the "Sheriff of Wall Street" riding into battle against me, a villain relentlessly personified as evil incarnate on the front pages of every major newspaper around the world. Wanton disregard for the law, acknowledged by the judge at my trial, allowed a corrupt element within the FBI, Agent BJ Kang, to falsify documents leading to my arrest and falsify testimony leading to my conviction. I faced prosecutorial misconduct at its finest. The overzealous media, feasting on a human story they could sell every day, also profoundly prejudiced any hope of gathering an impartial jury by the time of the trial. These three institutions, ostensibly guardians of the public interest, charged with impartiality and integrity, bore down in a concerted campaign to make me the face of the financial crisis. My arrest and subsequent trial, a two-year process, deflected attention from a glaring fact: not one major banker was held accountable for the 2008 global melt-down. No arrests. No searing prosecution. No jail time.

In the midst of a financial crisis that brought a multitrillion-dollar world economy to its knees, these three institutions, independently and collectively, targeted a tiny slice of the U.S. financial industry, hedge funds; honed in on a single hedge fund, Galleon; isolated only me, its CEO, who had recently become one of the few immigrants on Wall Street to be identified as a billionaire; and built a fabulous and intricate tale of "sex, drugs, and rock 'n' roll" to entertain the public and build their own reputations. Their two-year reality series was successful beyond measure.

Preet Bharara, then the U.S. attorney for the Southern District of New York (SDNY), used my prosecution to launch an unprecedented press campaign to promote himself. Bharara ran roughshod over the truth, standard DOJ protocols, and the office's own dignity in his extraordinary zeal to convict me. *Time Magazine* put Bharara on its cover, their headline proclaiming "This Man Is Busting Wall St." It was Preet's finest moment. Bharara did not touch the real perpetrators of the 2008 financial crisis: Wall Street's top bankers. In 2014, in a rare moment of sheepish public acknowledgement, both Bharara and the influential *New York Magazine* observed that the insider cases—"made our careers, but they (didn't) change the world."[1]

Bharara's impotent and poisoned approach to the nonprosecution of criminal activity on Wall Street—ranging from the mortgage bankers who precipitated the financial crisis (Goldman Sachs, Lehman Brothers), the money-laundering of drug cartels (HSBC), and the encouraging of tax evasion by U.S. citizens (UBS, CSFB)—is now the defining legacy of his tenure. Each of these firms settled civil charges by paying billions of dollars in fines using shareholder money, but not one single person was criminally charged or individually fined. Every one of the insider trader prosecutions was criminal. The towering hypocrisy remains startling.

The prosecution under Bharara's watch advanced a theory of trading to prosecute me and several others that the Appeals Court of the Second Circuit subsequently overruled, criticizing it for "doctrinal novelty." Soon after my trial in May 2011, then-Commissioner of the Securities and Exchange Commission (SEC) Mary Shapiro gloated that "the beauty of insider trading laws is the flexibility in interpreting them."

The lead prosecutor in my case, Jonathan Streeter, said in December 2012, "Insider trading cases are confusing to investment professionals." He went on to add, "There is incredible confusion on what is illegal and it's a real problem. The law is very complicated and the lines are a bit murky." A U.S. attorney, the prosecution in my trial, and the head of the SEC all acknowledged their reservations about a "murky" set of laws but had no "murky" reservations using them liberally in my case and at my trial.[2]

The FBI agent overseeing my case, Special Agent Kang, lied on his sworn affidavit to obtain wiretap authorization of my phone. Recognizing there had been government misconduct, Judge Richard Holwell, who presided over my trial case, issued a searing criticism of the wiretap application used by Agent Kang, reprimanding him for "reckless disregard for the truth with respect to both probable cause and necessity."[3] The judge went on to add that "false and misleading statements and omissions pervaded the affidavit [submitted by Special Agent Kang] so extensively that it was impossible for the authorizing judge to have the constitutionally required determination for the issuance of the wiretap…rather than provide a full and complete statement as required by the law, the wiretap affidavit made full and complete omissions and included literally false information."[4]

Kang did not stop at blowing through truth on paper. He menaced and threatened my family and employees with prosecution, frightened away crucial defense witnesses, and routinely leaked false information to the media, churning up an unabated feeding frenzy that shredded me in the court of public opinion. Kang took his cues from the playbook of publicly reviled former FBI Director J. Edgar Hoover. I was tried, convicted, and sentenced in the press even before I fully understood the charges against me. The atmosphere was so toxic that my lead counsel, veteran defense lawyer John Dowd, said "the prejudicial publicity orchestrated by the USA was so palpable in the courtroom…It was the most toxic atmosphere of any case I ever tried."

My defense team led by John Dowd, along with expert testimony from a former SEC legal counsel, repeatedly highlighted that all the information discussed in the wiretaps was already in the public domain. Every bit of information was in the public domain. It did not matter. No amount of truth could overcome the false testimony trained into the cooperating witnesses by Streeter, his team of prosecutors, and Bharara, who sat on the sidelines, waiting in eager anticipation for any opportunity for a press conference. Each of the cooperating witnesses had committed his own set of crimes unrelated to Galleon. Yet each chose to testify against me as an opportunity to reduce their probable and respective sentences. That they were perjuring themselves was irrelevant; the government coerced them into an immediate mandate to take me down. Even the government's star witness, Anil Kumar, offered damning testimony under oath in my case only to recant the very same sworn testimony three years later during the trial of my brother. My brother was subsequently acquitted as a result of the revised and opposite version of Anil Kumar's testimony. A few newspapers picked up on this gross disparity, but that was the extent of the reaction—the courts rejected our attempts at a formal hearing. The fact of perjury had no consequence. The cycle was vicious. "Innocent until proven guilty," the cornerstone philosophy of the American judicial system, was proving to be a farce.

I was convicted by a jury, sentenced to eleven years in jail, and paid fines of over $150 million. The irony is that even in setting the fines, the prosecutors working in tandem with the media kept up the unceasing drumbeat of punishment for the financial crisis. Never mind that I did not personally make any money from the alleged trades. And never mind that not one single investor sued me. Galleon went through an orderly process of closing down the firm and returned all investor funds including a gain of 22 percent. Not a single investor lost money. Most important to me, personally, was that not one single investor sued me.

In July 2019, I was released after serving seven and a half years of my eleven-year sentence under the First Step Act.

I wrote this book entirely in prison and by hand. I began by writing about an hour a day. Soon that increased to two hours. Then three. I am choosing to publish the book for two specific reasons: first, I want my peers, professionals who understand the nuances of managing money, to hear the facts of my case. I want them to judge me. It is my assertion that I was entrapped, framed, unlawfully wiretapped, surveilled, and then made to endure a brutal and very public media lynching.

Second, and more importantly, I want to begin a public discussion by creating awareness of how certain corrupt prosecutors and FBI agents are allowed to get away with criminal behavior. There are no checks and balances in our justice system. Recently there has been a lot of discussion as to whether the president should be above the law. The president is so closely scrutinized that doing anything against the law would ring alarms bells the world over. Instead, my assertion is that the focus should be on the corruption within the American judicial system, on a handful of corrupt U.S. attorneys who live their lives exempt from the law by which they control the lives of others and the rest of the country. In this book, I will show how ambitious prosecutors actively take advantage of murky laws and coerce testimony from government witnesses to obtain wrongful convictions. Winning at all costs, regardless of the truth, appears at every level to be an operative mantra. I realize there is only one book I can write to set the record straight. This is it.

My story is also about greed. In all its forms, greed boils down to avarice, hunger, power, money, ambition. All of these are readily available and identifiable in the financial industry, by definition. In fact, I would say that in the financial industry, greed is effectively a cliché with fear being on the flip side of a pair trade. Fear and greed are easy to communicate, and the media homes in on these aspects of Wall Street. But what I would like to do in this book is to home in on the excess and greed in the judicial system. Ambition in the judicial system also translates to power and money, a far more insidious and dangerous consequence to society because it goes unchecked. After I was convicted, the press had a field day speculating whether the new sheriff of Wall Street, Preet Bharara, was actually in line to succeed Eric Holder as the next U.S. attorney general when Holder stepped down. Although Bharara was at first coy about his intentions, he eventually made clear his goal to secure the job based on his work prosecuting Wall Street. He may have wanted the job but did not get it.

The same ambitions were true for the three government prosecutors in my case—all three left government shortly after closing out my case for higher-paying jobs as partners in leading law firms. They and their new employers spent considerable effort drumming up business on the heels of the skills honed during their time as former prosecutors to future defendants accused of insider trading. They had no problem making the transition from denouncing apparent "greed" in the financial markets to defending that same greed, switching sides in an effective demonstration of greed. As partners at leading law firms, they would be highly compensated. The "protectors from greed" sold themselves to the highest bidder, all under the trusting gaze of an unaware public. The door meant to separate and maintain a balance between the public and the private sectors revolves efficiently and profitably.

It is important to understand context of the time and the prevailing mood of the country in October of 2009, when I was arrested. In 2008, we had seen the near collapse of the financial system and the wiping out of trillions of dollars of home equity and life savings of the American middle class. The government was forced to bail out the major banks. An estimated $7 trillion in U.S. household assets were wiped out. The public was clamoring for blood and there was no blood forthcoming. From anywhere.

I had nothing to do with the housing crisis. I was an easy target for politicians, for prosecutors, for pundits, and for Bharara, who had just been handed leadership of the Southern District of NY, including a mandate for bringing Wall Street under control. I was a successful and expendable hedge fund manager who employed just 250 people. We obtained an overwhelming amount of information on a daily basis and my trading was 100 percent consistent with the written recommendations of my analysts. In *all* cases, I had a preexisting position in the stock before allegedly receiving the "tip." In 2009 and even today, insider trading laws are murky at best and often (intentionally) misinterpreted by prosecutors. The government painted our systematic, well-researched investing as being criminal. Theirs was an overreach of enormous proportions to show that Wall Street fat cats were being brought to justice. If I am guilty, then the entire investment business should be declared illegal.

As the *Wall Street Journal* noted insightfully,

> "Under standard rhetoric, the public is somehow cheated by all this, but the standard rhetoric is nonsense. The public isn't damaged because another party wants to sell or buy (and most hedge funds strive to make sure their trading doesn't affect prices anyway). But a cynic might note one thing: insider trading law provides a bottomless reservoir of (supposed) financial 'crime' for Washington to investigate whenever it needs a Wall Street prosecution to flounce in front of the press."[5]

As a child, having gone to boarding school in a foreign country at the age of eleven, I learned quickly and early to be a fighter, a scrapper. This is a blessing and a curse. Over the years, I have learned that you don't always have to fight. The kindness of many people has defanged and disarmed me to a large extent. However, when people try to take advantage of me, I have to respond. I don't back down. And I am fortunate to have been blessed with the mental fortitude and financial resources to fight for my innocence. Too many people do not have these things. They plead guilty to indictments they cannot challenge. In my experience, about 10 percent of the inmates at the prison in which I spent seven and a half years were innocent.

When I was researching the Justice Department while in prison, I came across a paragraph that struck a chord in me. Unfortunately, I did not write down the name of the author or the source. "Criminal punishment is the greatest power that governments use and wield against their own people. When employed justly and appropriately, it is vital to any safe and productive society. But when employed aggressively based on vague laws and personal agendas the criminal justice system unnecessarily destroys lives, livelihoods, and families."

Oddly, my experience of the law has left me without rage or a sense of victimhood. Although I would never say I am grateful for the experience, I can say with confidence that I like myself better because of it. When I finally broke through the wall of despair, I realized I had gained a sense of peace and awareness that had opened me up and cracked me free. I realized how incredibly strong the human mind is and that nothing can beat a person who refuses to be beaten.

Finally, I want to say that despite what happened to me as a result of a corrupt prosecutor, I love this country just as much as I did before I went to prison. I feel truly blessed to be one of the 5 percent of the world population who live in America. I do not see people lined up to immigrate to China, Russia, or Japan, for example.

As I reflect on my circumstances and my past, I'm confident that if God had arrived at my doorstep—with a crystal ball—when I was eleven and told me, "Raj, I will give you the wife and children you see here, these friends, ensure that both your parents live long and happy lives, and give you also the ability to help the less fortunate, but you need to sacrifice about seven years of your life," I would have taken that deal in a New York second.

I feel very fortunate.

I am very fortunate.

Raj Rajaratnam

CHAPTER 1

MY PERSONAL BLACK SWAN:
October 16, 2009

On Friday, October 16, 2009, I woke up at 5:30 a.m. as usual. It was still dark outside and I could see the mist on the East River. It was drizzling. The breeze coming off the river at this elevation was strong, making the windows rattle. My home was quiet; all were sleeping. Next door, my parents were also asleep, and it was a great comfort for me to have them right there. A wave of coziness passed through me. It felt so right and good. All was well, as it should be. It was going to be an overcast day. I love this time of the morning by myself.

I made my cup of coffee and went through all the emails I received overnight from our Asia analysts and brokers. By 6:15 a.m., I had sorted out my questions, made decisions, and sent off my replies. I got on the exercise bike. My goal was always forty-five minutes. Forty-five minutes of solitude before the day would come rushing in as it did every day. I watched the TV news on mute as I biked. The news continued to be about the financial market collapse a year ago, the newly elected President Obama, the routine mentioning of the prisoners at Guantanamo Bay, and the wars in Afghanistan and Iraq.

My day was packed. I was leaving on a weeklong business trip that evening. My son had become a teenager that week. The cake cutting was set for 5:00 p.m. After the cake cutting, he was going to see a Knicks game at

Madison Square Garden with a dozen of his friends while I headed to JFK to catch the last flight to London.

The next day, on Saturday, I planned to attend the London premiere of *Today's Special*, a film I had helped to finance. It was about a South Asian immigrant living his dream of becoming a chef in New York.

I was looking forward to the meetings planned for Monday when I would meet with bankers to discuss a long-held dream: to create a Sri Lanka country fund. After almost thirty years, the brutal ethnic war in Sri Lanka had ended in May 2009. In all those thirty years, I often thought of my homeland.

Throughout those thirty years, international investors had largely avoided the Sri Lankan capital markets. Now, with the end of the war, interest in the country's equity markets was surging. Through Galleon, we were planning to raise a $200 million fund to invest in equities, private companies, and fixed income. Our timing was particularly good for those who understood and wanted exposure to frontier markets.

My travels did not end in London. On Tuesday, October 22, I planned to fly to Geneva to meet with a few of Galleon's larger Swiss investors. Tuesday was also my wife's fiftieth birthday. She wanted to have a quiet dinner together in Geneva on a boat where, twenty-three years earlier, I had proposed to her.

I continued on the bike, lost in thought.

Suddenly, I heard a very loud knock on the door. I was alarmed. My wife ran out of the bedroom in her robe.

"Who's there?" I asked.

"FBI! Open up!"

I opened the door quickly.

An FBI agent, buzz cut and backed up by five other FBI agents, stood there blocking the entrance.

He growled, "Are you Raj Rajaratnam?"

Obviously. Yes.

Agent Kang: "Rajaratnam. You're under arrest."

"For what?" I asked.

Kang said he would tell me later.

He asked whether I had any guns or drugs at home—no—and told me to get dressed.

I went to my bedroom, got out of my exercise clothes, put on a pair of jeans, shirt, and a blazer. I asked my wife to contact the office at 8:00, an hour from then, and ask Galleon's chief financial officer to get me a lawyer. I also asked her not to cancel any of our upcoming flights—I was convinced there was a mistake. She looked at me. I stopped. I put my arms around her and told her everything would be okay.

Walking out of the bedroom, I realized that my two younger children were hiding under the blankets, their own terror overcoming concern for me, terrified of the bellowing voices. I did not want them to come out, but they did.

I would have recurring images throughout the day and the weeks and months that followed of their vulnerability and their exposure to the terror and danger of that moment.

I returned to the FBI phalanx, a blur of dark blue jackets, crew cuts, and cold.

"Hold out your hands," Kang barked. Again. I was handcuffed. I had no idea why.

On the way out, Kang said, "Take a good look at your son because you're not going to see him for twenty years." Then he looked at my wife and turned to me, "Your wife doesn't seem to be that upset. She must be thinking about all that money she can spend now."

I was shocked. And angry. There was nothing I could do about any of this.

The FBI later officially denied that Agent Kang made those statements. However, other defendants, including a portfolio manager at Galleon, cited similar heavy-handed experiences at the hands of Agent Kang. It was designed to traumatize my family and me. This was just the beginning. In fact, throughout my case, the FBI acted as if witness intimidation and outright lies were standard procedure. It would seem as if the FBI's once-reviled leader, J. Edgar Hoover, were still at the helm of their department.

We rode in a black sedan to the FBI offices in downtown New York in complete silence. My mind was racing. What in the world was this about? Nothing made sense.

I would later find out that the FBI typically makes their arrests early in the morning, hoping to catch their defendants groggy, still waking up, which increases the defendants' chances of incriminating themselves. Friday morning arrests were an especially effective FBI intimidation tactic: holding someone over the weekend without quick access to legal counsel was particularly useful in eliciting information.

At the FBI offices, I was taken to a room with no windows. The lights were bright and florescent, like in a hospital—night and day became undiscernible. There, I was asked to sit on a chair, in front of a table. Some of the officers who had arrived to arrest me were standing against the wall. Agent Kang tossed me the charge sheet. He told me I was accused of insider trading. Insider trading! I was shocked.

Agent Kang asked me to sign a waiver form and then began asking question after question. Among the first things he did was to play me a recording of my assistant answering my phones in the office. He had arranged this demonstration to show me my office phones were wiretapped. Then he played me various recordings of telephone calls and spent the next several hours asking me questions.

I answered all their questions.

Why would anyone answer even one question without a lawyer being present? To me, my innocence was obvious. I had no doubt this was all simply a mistake on the government's part. I replied as best and as honestly as I could.

Ironically, four months earlier, we had hired an ex-FBI agent-turned-consultant to the financial industry for an all-day seminar for Galleon employees. Our goal was to give employees a primer on FBI interrogation techniques to make their analysis of companies more effective. Their job and our daily work was to not just to ask questions but also to be able to differentiate an exaggerated reply or outright lie from an accurate reply. I had initially been very skeptical of the seminar; ultimately, not only did I approve it, I attended through most of that day. Throughout the morning with Agent Kang, I had flashbacks of that seminar. I was experiencing an actual interrogation. I recognized the techniques. Good cop. Bad cop. Threats. Intimidation. It could have been comical if it weren't unfortunately so real. The goal was not just to extract a guilty plea. Their goal was to generate an agreement to cooperate against other people. It was an attempt to generate an agreement to cooperate against my peers in the hedge fund industry.

I did neither.

It was clear to me that Kang and the FBI agents had no idea how hedge funds and investment firms operated. They were clueless, in fact, about the level of rigorous investment analysis, the careful portfolio construction, the continuous risk management, and fluid exchange of thoughts among portfolio managers. They had no idea. They were following a narrative that they were all engaging in insider trading.

Eventually, around 9:00 a.m., I was allowed to call my office. It took a few hours to arrange for an attorney. I had no personal lawyer, much less one who specialized in criminal law. Eventually the lawyer called. I had no idea who he was. He had no idea about me or Galleon. However, he gave me a single and immediate piece of sound advice: stop answering questions.

While I was being interviewed by the FBI, Preet Bharara, the U.S. attorney for the Southern District of New York, held a nationally televised press conference. He gathered the SEC and the FBI into the room. They all made a grand show of congratulating each other for the excellent work resulting in my arrest. The SEC issued a press release with the headline, "SEC charges Billionaire Hedge Fund Manager Raj Rajaratnam with Insider Trading." From then on, the tag "billionaire hedge fund manager" appeared to be permanently attached to my name.

Preet Bharara displayed several charts, each with me at the center of an "insider trading ring." The concentric circles included people I had never met nor even heard of. "This case should be a wake-up call to Wall Street and to every hedge fund manager," Preet Bharara proclaimed. "Greed is sometimes not good," he continued, turning on its head that iconic line by Michael Douglas's character Gordon Gekko in the 1987 film *Wall Street*.

Bharara loved the camera. It was clear. He was quite the showboat. I was the prize prop in his show.

"He is not the master of the universe," declared the SEC representative. "Instead, Raj Rajaratnam is a 'master of the Rolodex.'" It was verbal nitroglycerine, designed to detonate with the media and the general public.

Bharara did not tell the press that even if the charges in the initial sheet were all true, Galleon *had actually lost over $30 million on these so-called "insider trades."* That would not have made for very good press.

Then came the infamous "perp walk." Essentially, the prosecutor's office invites the press and television crews to watch as the defendant (even though at this stage he or she has not been proven guilty and is technically presumed innocent) walks, handcuffed, about fifty feet from the FBI office to the waiting police car, which will take him or her to the courthouse. It is also called the "walk of shame" and this staged process seems to be reserved for high-profile cases. It has only one purpose: publicly humiliate the defendant.

There appeared to be hundreds of people from the press. The television clips and photographs of my perp walk were shown all over the world. I was in a daze and yet outraged about being framed in guilt with no opportunity to understand the charges much less to rebut them. This would have been considered to be highly prejudicial in other countries. I was amazed that our American judicial system continues to allow these inflammatory and prejudicial practices.

Preet Bharara made the decision to put me through the perp walk. He had assumed the office just two months earlier, a relatively unknown lawyer who had served until then as the general counsel for New York Senator Charles Schumer. Hungry for celebrity, the limelight, political ambition, personal recognition, and publicity, Bharara would make mine one of his "signature cases." Interestingly, after October 16, none of the other insider trading defendants were subjected to the perp walk, even though one of the cases involved sums four times as large as the Galleon case. By the end of my trial, and because of it, U.S. Attorney Bharara would achieve his highly coveted wide recognition as the sheriff of Wall Street.

I had little sense of time. The FBI agents had not allowed me put on my watch. I had a sense from some of the comments that many of my family and friends had gathered at the courthouse in my support. Sometime midafternoon, I finally met my lawyer. He asked me a few basic questions about myself and any charitable work that I had done. As he began preparing for my bail, he instructed my brother Rengan to retrieve copies of my last five years' tax returns from the Galleon offices to show the judge the extent of my charitable work, which he did. Prosecutors would later claim that Rengan spent that time destroying files.

At the bail hearing, I learned that Anil Kumar, a former Wharton classmate and business associate, had also been arrested that morning. He appeared first before Judge Doug Eaton. He pled not guilty. The prosecutors agreed with the judge in granting him bail, secured by his house in California. Little did I realize that out of fear and FBI intimidation, Anil would change his plea, fabricate an elaborate and multifaceted story, and eventually testify against me.

It was my turn next. The prosecutors revved into high gear. They wanted me held in jail pending my trial. They claimed I had "substantial assets overseas" and had "enormous incentive to flee to [my] native Sri Lanka or elsewhere."

Judge Eaton looked at me. There are generally two reasons for a judge to deny bail: one, if the defendant is a threat to society; and, two, if the defendant is a flight risk.

Even the prosecutors could not argue I was a threat to society. They focused instead on my being a flight risk. Their rationale: My extensive travel and assets held abroad. *Blatant lies were not off the table.* They insisted to the judge that I had a sister who lived in South Africa. I have two sisters: one lives in New Jersey, the other then lived in Singapore. I assumed the prosecutors fabricated the South Africa story because that country has no extradition treaty with the United States, therefore strengthening the implication that I would flee there.

The South Africa gambit was the first of a series of inaccurate statements that the prosecutors would use to mislead the court throughout the trial. Winning at all costs was all they cared about.

I had never been in a courtroom before and believed that you could not tell a lie there, especially if you were a federal official.

If defendants or their attorneys lie, they can be prosecuted for perjury or disbarred. What about the prosecution? Do they get a free pass? It seemed that way to me.

Was this fair? Was this just? Would prosecutors cheat and lie in this way to get convictions? Were they accountable? To whom?

Judge Douglas Eaton set my bail at $100 million, secured by $20 million in assets and guaranteed by five other people. The bail was the highest in U.S. history. Even Bernie Madoff, who voluntarily admitted to a Ponzi scheme totaling billions of dollars, was granted bail of $10 million!

Among those who guaranteed my bail was Geoff Canada, head of the Harlem Children's Zone, which runs a chartered school, after-school organizations, and other support programs for the underprivileged. If I fled the country, he would lose everything. Geoff told the media, "I have not had a moment's doubt, knowing Raj and his character. I am not worried at all." He was right. I was not going to flee the country. I was going to fight for my innocence.

The context of the times and the prevailing sentiment in the country in October 2009 are important to understand: There had to be a fall guy and I was it. The US and global financial systems were reeling. Millions of Americans lost their homes and their life savings. Institutions including Lehman Brothers, Bear Stearns, Fannie Mae, AIG, and Freddie Mac either had filed for bankruptcy or lost over 90 percent of their market value. An estimated $7 trillion in U.S. household assets were wiped out, and things kept getting worse.

The SEC had ignored a decade's warnings about Bernie Madoff and his massive Ponzi scheme, the largest financial fraud in U.S. history, which resulted in widespread investor losses of more than $18 billion. Ironically, Madoff was actually *an insider*, having served as vice chairman of National

Association of Securities Dealers (NASD), the predecessor to the current FINRA, the largest securities industry regulator authorized by Congress. Bernie Madoff was actually once one of our top securities regulators.

The country was hostile to Wall Street, but not one single person from the big banks was prosecuted. Why? The administration fearing an economic domino impact eventually acquiesced to the notion that major banks were "too big to fail." Yet the public and the media were clamoring for blood.

Wall Street professionals (bankers, financiers, lenders, investors, and so forth) have historically been used as scapegoats by politically ambitious New York prosecutors, like Rudy Giuliani and Elliot Spitzer, who later became mayor and governor of New York, respectively. They built their reputations on supposedly bashing greed.

The current U.S. attorney, Preet Bharara, took a leaf from Giuliani's playbook in prosecuting the mob: charge the target; make him do the perp walk; threaten him with expanded superseding indictments; intimidate and charge family members; flip other defendants; offer plea bargains; use coerced testimony; manipulate the media with damaging leaks of information; and paint the defendant in the worst possible light. I was about to get a brutal lesson in how an ambitious US attorney could use everything at his disposal—ethical or not—to win at all costs. Although I was initially charged for insider trading in eight stocks, the indictment against me was expanded to thirty-four stocks, and during the trial, it was yet again arbitrarily reduced to nine stocks—this time adding Goldman Sachs.

Bharara was the master of playing the news media. Press leaks to friendly reporters were designed to inflame the public and weaken my resolve to resist. The public was reminded by the constant stream of leaks from "reliable government sources" or "people familiar with the government investigation." Week after week, reporters breathlessly reported how the government unearthed the largest insider trading ring with headline stories that read like prosecutorial briefs explaining to the public why I was guilty. These stories continued without interruption for several years, well after I had arrived in prison.

The prosecutors, with either the blessing or the blind eye of the press, were given carte blanche to take whatever action they deemed fit. The media simply looked on or compounded the prosecutions' messaging, become something of a hermetic cycle. The resulting mob hysteria only encouraged Preet Bharara to mount and then intensify the witch hunt, devastating many people's lives. A series of sensational and ill-founded prosecutions followed, with over eighty consecutive convictions or guilty pleas. To achieve these results, Preet Bharara found it expedient and was allowed a free pass to change the rules in the middle of the game, effectively and dramatically expanding the scope of criminal law to include harmless trading practices. Bharara routinely engaged in questionable ethical practices as he pursued victory at any cost.

A few weeks before the Galleon case, Preet Bharara hired a new head of public relations, Ellen Davis. She quickly expanded the public relations group of the U.S. Attorney's Office from three to fourteen professionals. With a long history in the television business, she used her producer's skills and well-honed sense of drama to the Justice Department's advantage.

This was no longer about justice; this was about creating a public relations win for the government, which was still reeling from criticisms about its handling of the economic crisis. Many in the press became tools of the government's prosecutorial efforts and propaganda campaign to distract public attention from the mortgage crisis, the Troubled Asset Relief Program (TARP), and the administration's lack of progress in addressing the systemic causes of the economic crisis.

A particular favorite journalist for the government's bully pulpit was Susan Pulliam of the *Wall Street Journal*. Pulliam spent the months leading to my trial writing a series of headline-grabbing articles on the Galleon case based on "sources close to the government investigation." She contacted many friends and colleagues during the early days but refrained from writing anything positive they said about me. She even had the temerity to leave messages on my phone, none of which I returned.

Other reporters who in theory act as watchdogs for the public seemed simply overwhelmed by the level of detail and unable to keep up with the deluge of information. For example, the indictment asserted that I had bought four hundred thousand shares of Hilton in the Galleon Technology Fund "whose stated mandate was to invest in the technology sector." There is only one obvious implication to be gleaned from that comment: my trades were illegal. However, even a casual reading of the Fund's prospectus would show that while the Fund's primary mandate was to invest in the technology sector, up to 25 percent of its assets could be invested in nontechnology as a diversification strategy. In fact, for the five years ending October 2009, between 15 and 20 percent of the Galleon Technology Fund's assets were invested in nontechnology stocks, including Pepsi Cola, Exxon Mobil, Pfizer, Amgen, JP Morgan, and the like. Not one reporter mentioned this; all chose, instead, to parrot the prosecutor's assertions and innuendos.

That first day was exhausting. Weariness had crept into my brain, my limbs, my veins. I finally returned home at about 7:00 p.m. There were no photographers hovering around at the court. There were no photographers waiting for me at home. It appeared that sensationalist news coverage had called it a day. I walked in through the door to the apartment and found it full of people—my parents, brothers, sisters, a few friends. All of them concerned for me. I had dinner, said goodnight, and went into the bedroom to begin to unravel the day's events and figure out what was going on.

As I read the indictment later that night, I felt that the government had deliberately blurred the lines between legitimate research and insider trading. I felt like I had been tried, convicted, and sentenced even before I fully understood what my alleged crimes were. Every trade in the eight stocks of the original indictment was supported by detailed written analyses by competent Galleon analysts. We were rigorous in our research. Even more insidiously and as importantly, the indictment showed the government to be cherry picking snippets from secretly wiretapped conversations to paint a picture that was radically removed from reality.

A particularly egregious example on the indictment was my comment on a recorded call to Danielle Chiesi, another portfolio manager to "keep it radio silent." Taken out of context, the implication from the prosecution that we were agreeing to keep information secret and even more insidious was that the information was not public. The reality could not have been more mundane: Dani called me late in the evening as I relaxed with my family to tell me she had heard from "her guy" that Akamai, a content delivery company, was going "to guide down." I told her that we already know that and had already accumulated a short position on Akamai. Typically, professional money managers hold information about their short positions close to the chest; I realized as soon as my words were out that I had made a mistake. It was in this context that I told Dani to keep it radio silent. A simple comment to gloss over my own error was seized upon by the prosecution and blown up as a flagrant example of my own criminality. My trading was based on the written, and therefore, transparent, recommendations of our analysts. In law, they say that documents do not have a character test. Prosecutors had access to all these documents and yet they chose to ignore them all.

In the blink of eye, my life had undergone an unexpected, seismic change—a black swan. I had no idea what the world had in store for me: the threats, the innuendos, the judgment.

CHAPTER 2

MY EARLY YEARS

I was born on June 15th, 1957, in Colombo, the capital of Sri Lanka, a teardrop-shaped island that drops off the southern tip of India into the Indian Ocean. I was the eldest son, but not the eldest child, in a loving rambunctious family of five children. We followed in the tradition and spirit of my father and my grandfather, both the eldest sons, which provided us all with a sense of obligation and responsibility.

My father was a self-made man. He graduated from the University of Sri Lanka and then earned a scholarship to study accounting in England. Five years later, he returned to Sri Lanka with my mother and just one month later, I was born. They made the journey from London during a particularly turbulent time when the Suez Canal was closed and the ship detoured around the Cape of Good Hope in Africa.

Hardworking and ambitious, my father quickly climbed the corporate ladder. By the time he was in his late thirties, he was CEO of the Sri Lankan operations of the Singer Company, an American multinational firm. In that era, the Singer sewing machine was ubiquitous throughout the world, especially in Asia. Many Asian families worked hard to buy a sewing machine. Almost every woman in this era learned to sew. Owning a Singer sewing machine was considered a sign of wealth and social status. Look into the family paraphernalia from the 1950s through the 1970s of any South Asian family and you would be sure to find a Singer sewing machine.

My father moved rapidly up the corporate ranks, retiring as regional head of the far east region for the Singer Company. He was remarkably confident, with a strong streak of independence. He lived a principled life that included a generous commitment to helping the underprivileged.

My mother went to college, which was somewhat of a rarity in those days, as South Asian families, like others around the world, sought marriage—not college—for their daughters. She majored in biology and zoology and was on course to go on to medical college. That was before she met my father. Things changed after they met and she put aside her academic aspirations when she accepted his hand in marriage and accompanied him to England to support his education in accountancy.

My mother considered learning to be one of her personal priorities. Education remained a key part of her outlook on life, and she transferred that passion to her five children. I have fond memories of her sitting with me for hours, explaining the intricacies of the human heart or helping unravel mathematical problems.

Education would dictate many of my parents' decisions for each of us. It was the cornerstone value in our lives, passed down from my grandparents. Living in a village in the northern part of Sri Lanka, my paternal grandfather had been the headmaster of the local boys' school, while my grandmother was the headmistress of the local girls' school. Their passion for education led them to encourage each of their six children to attend college, including their only daughter, a highly unusual choice at that time. Three of their children would become teachers, including their daughter.

Poignantly, perhaps ruefully, my grandfather told me once that he wished he had not educated just one of his children, for that way he would have had one child stay with him in the village, working as a farmer, and looking after him in his twilight years. Then he quickly let me know that he was "just talking," for his pride in his children and their accomplishments would always overcome the fleeting but real loneliness of age.

My grandfather's sentiments would later have a big impact on me. When my own parents were older and needed support, I made sure they lived with me in New York, in an apartment next door to my own. My father had the independence he could not live without, and I had daily access to my parents and peace of mind knowing they had everything they needed.

My maternal grandparents were landowners and farmers. They had three daughters, of which my mother was the eldest and first to go to college. Kind and caring, my maternal grandfather's great source of pride was that his three daughters had married well, a mark of achievement for Asian families at that time.

A fiercely determined and strong man, my maternal grandfather was very protective of his girls and once grabbed one of his sons-in-law, lifting him and hanging him over the balcony for yelling at his daughter. He bought his first car when he was in his seventies and got his driver's license at the age of seventy-seven after three attempts. Once when I visited him, he insisted on driving me to the bus stop in the town to catch a bus back to Colombo. It was such a wonderful gesture that I will always cherish, but also the scariest ride of my life! My grandfather's face was just a foot away from the wheel and my grandmother pointed out the cows and pedestrians randomly crossing the road and oncoming vehicles coming at us from the opposite direction.

As children growing up in Colombo, we would make the eight-hour trip to the north during the Christmas holidays to visit both our maternal and paternal grandparents. For months we would look forward to these trips. Once there, we would help with chores, milking the goats and collecting eggs from the chickens. We would head to the seashore early in the morning to buy the freshest catch from the night fishermen, who were just returning from the sea. We would have long conversations with our grandparents, and they would ask challenging questions, always encouraging us to be curious and thoughtful. I always enjoyed listening to stories about our ancestors and meeting other relatives who lived in the village. There was a quiet dignity about those in the village that I found admirable. Whenever I returned to Sri Lanka as an adult, I always made a point of visiting our grandparents, who all lived well into their eighties.

I have only the fondest memories of the Sri Lanka of my youth—the country was warm in spirits as was its weather. A small, teardrop-shaped island off the coast of India, Sri Lanka was a panoramic blend of beautiful sandy beaches, scenic rolling hills, and a variety of manicured tea plantations, coconut estates, rain forests, rivers, waterfalls, and more beaches. Marco Polo, on his way back from China, referred to the Island as "Serendip." Horace Walpole, the English philosopher coined the word "Serendipity" after reading Marco Polo's description of this beautiful country. The island was colonized over a period of three hundred years by the Portuguese, the Dutch, and the British, all of whom referred to the country as "Serendib," "Ceylan," and finally as "Ceylon."

Sri Lanka, which was formalized as the country's name in 1972 with the adoption of the constitution, has always been a multiethnic society, its people accustomed to integrating with foreigners throughout the past few centuries. The three main groups of people, the Sinhalese, Tamils and Muslims, the majority of whom all migrated from ancient India, historically lived through periods of harmony interspersed with periods of conflict.

It was during my teenage years that the turmoil between the majority Sinhalese and the Tamils began to grow. This turmoil, fanned by extremists on both sides, led to an almost thirty-year civil war resulting in over sixty thousand deaths. It wreaked havoc in the country during the 1980s, 1990s, and 2000s.

But this is not how I grew up. We were unaware of differences between the Sinhalese, Tamils, and Muslims. Whether people were Buddhist, Hindu, Muslim or not was irrelevant as long as they could play a pick-up game of cricket down the street. As children, we all played together and went to school together, and though we did have separate classes, the playground was the melting pot. At home, everyone was welcome to visit and stay as long as they liked. This early spirit of inclusion remains my foundation, the core of my values, and throughout my life, I have enjoyed friendships with people from all over the world.

The fabric of Sri Lankan culture is close-knit, with interwoven connections of family and friends, and it is very family-centric. The grown-ups would gather in the evenings to play badminton or to play cards on the veranda or simply to have a drink and chat; the children would be outside playing any game—cricket, marbles, tag, lizard-catching—until the sun set.

I loved my childhood. It was idyllic. We had a wide range of family friends and a large extended family. We lived our life at a leisurely pace, savoring time, enjoying friendships and family. The concept of racing from one adrenaline-filled rush of a day folded into another, as I later lived my professional life in New York, was never part of the lifestyle of my parents or my home in those days. We lived in a large colonial-style house with manicured lawns and beautiful gardens tended by my mother.

We also had mango, guava, and sour billing fruit trees in our back garden. If the fruit man did not come, we would go to the mango tree and pluck mangoes. If the mangoes were still green, we would cover the sour slices with salt and chili peppers. If the mangoes were too ripe, we would squeeze the flesh into pulp inside the skin, make a small hole, and drink the juice.

Sundays were beach days. My family and five others would all pile into our cars, trunks filled with food that had been cooked since dawn, and drive to the long, empty beaches outside Colombo, with coconut fronds to provide any protection from the hot sun. The mothers would set up umbrellas and sheets and settle in for a long day of chatting and card playing. The fathers would also join in the conversation, which would always involve gossip, ribald humor, and hearty laughter.

The twenty or so other children and I would largely ignore the grown-ups and spend the day playing our own games, whether it was cricket or sandcastle building. Every game would invariably end with our racing into the surf and diving, laughing, through the waves. With plenty of fun and food, we were all happy and relaxed.

It was those beach Sundays spent in the safety and comfort of family and friends, with the freedom to play for hours with other children, that left me with a deep and abiding love of water. On many occasions, having to deal with various life events, I would walk for long hours along the beach in an effort to gain clarity. As a young man, I was grateful that Sussex University was right by the sea; I proposed to my wife having dinner on a boat on Lake

Geneva; I got married on a boat that went around Manhattan; and my home in New York overlooks the East River.

Over the years, I have come to cherish this style of large family and friend get-togethers and have done my best to replicate them. When I had children of my own, we often vacationed in the Caribbean with other friends and family. Many weekends, our home was filled with friends and their kids, relaxing and laughing.

I also enjoyed the warm monsoon rain season in Sri Lanka. While other mothers would call their children indoors, my mother would encourage us to play in the rain. When we were drenched and had enough, we would come back inside to warm baths, for which my mother had already heated the water. While she was largely a traditional Sri Lankan mother, she had a quiet, independent spirit.

Night after night, my mother always told us stories; tales of our ancestors or old religious myths, legends that inspired us to find courage, be brave and stand upright. One of my favorites is called "Veerathai" ("Brave Mother") in Tamil. The mother in the story learns that her only son has been killed in battle. Refusing to wait until the body is returned to her, she rushes instead to the battle site to confirm just one thing: whether the arrow had penetrated his chest or his back. Finding that the arrow had pierced his heart, the mother is filled with tremendous pride: her son had not run away from battle.

As a young boy, I thought it odd that a mother could possibly be happy about the death of her only son. My mother would lovingly and patiently explain the moral until I finally understood that courage comes in many forms, including standing up and facing adversity with dignity.

There was another meaningful story from my childhood that I carried with me through that time. It was a story of a South Indian Tamil, King Kattabomman, an eighteenth-century ruler who was among the first to oppose British rule in India. When the British wanted him to salute them, he refused and was sentenced to death. Just before the execution, the British told him that if he saluted just *once* they would spare him, but he refused and was hanged. As a young boy, I wondered why he did not just salute. But over time, I learned more about his opposition to the British, and his principled and defiant spirit continues to resonate with me.

My parents stressed the importance of doing well in school and made sure we got the best education available. I was a good student, consistently among the top three students in my class. We had approximately thirty boys in our class and we were ranked one to thirty. As an adult, I now wonder how the boy who ranked thirty felt when he got his report card. The system was not always sensitive to children's feelings. The classes were segregated by language: I was with the Tamil boys, and there were classes for Sinhalese boys as well as those who spoke English.

Like all kids, we would eagerly await the midmorning recess. We would either play a quick game of cricket or organize wrestling matches. I enjoyed wrestling because I was taller and larger than most boys in my Tamil section. We would soon be joined by boys in the Sinhala, as well as the English sections. At the 10:30 a.m. morning break, pairs would be drawn between boys of similar size and heights. Then we'd draw a circle in the dirt and begin to wrestle, surrounded and loudly encouraged by our classmates. There were clear rules. No scratching or biting and no wrestling when one of the boys had crossed the crease. I learned early and well the value of a fair fight when opponents are suitably matched, and the rules are clear and fairly observed.

Listening to the radio was another source of entertainment in my childhood. Songs by Tom Jones, Englebert Humperdinck, Frank Sinatra, and Elvis Presley were particularly popular with the adults and played often in our homes. As a result, we knew most of the lyrics. The more tragic or melodramatic the song, the more it was loved.

Radio also brought us cricket commentary. Sri Lankans, like most South Asians, were and are crazy about cricket. Perceived as slow to many Americans, for those who know the game, cricket echoes the drama of life and follows a rhythm of play that is subtle and nuanced. Understand cricket and understand life! The thrills of victory, the details of each run, the courage of the batsman, the strategy of the bowler, all relayed through the voice of the commentator, helped us "see" the match. Sometimes the matches would last five days, and I would drop most things to stay close to the radio dial.

Unfortunately, childhood does not last. My own idyllic existence came to an abrupt end when my parents decided to send me to boarding school in India at the age of eleven so that I could study in English. In Sri Lanka, because both my parents were Tamil, it was mandated that I would study in Tamil. Children of Sinhalese parents were taught in Sinhalese, while Muslim children and those of mixed or European heritage were placed into English-speaking classes. Although I studied in English from the age of eleven, Tamil is the only language I speak without an accent.

My father's decision proved prescient. Three years later, in 1972, he was promoted to a regional post in Singapore and the whole family moved there with him. Thereafter, every three years or so, the family moved to a different country (United States, India, Thailand, and then back to Singapore) as my father was given increasing responsibility at Singer. There are specific times in everyone's life that are seismic events. Going to boarding school at so young an age and essentially learning to fend for myself was such an event.

From the onset, I did not like boarding school. I survived the first year by reliving stories and memories from home. I was just eleven years old. I missed my family, my relatives, and my friends. I missed the food, the music, and the beach. No more spicy chicken or meat curry, no more long hours on the beach, and certainly no listening to music; the teachers did not allow music in the dorm rooms. I even missed the smell of rotting fruit we knocked down from the trees in our backyard. I did not mind the sparse and drab living conditions, but I found the regimented routine at boarding school rigid and stifling, with too many rules and excessive supervision.

I persevered. I endured. And I never once complained to my parents. My mother may have understood how much I missed her because when I got ready to go back to school after any particular holiday, she would always say that of all her children, she was most confident in my ability to handle anything that came my way.

Eventually, like the children of many career expatriate families, I went to boarding school in England. A boarding school education in the United Kingdom remains a common choice among many Sri Lankan families, who prize education above all else. As a result, I spent most of my preteen to teenage years at boarding schools in India and England. For the entire time I was in boarding school, my mother wrote to me every week, no matter where she was in the world. Her enduring, thoughtful love was a source of strength for me.

After graduating from high school, I went to Sussex University. After the stifling daily regimen of boarding school and its pervasive and stuffy environment, Sussex and life at university was simply refreshing. I had learned to be disciplined on my own terms and loved the freedom and flexibility of campus life. Here I was, a normal college student, enjoying college life to the fullest. Sussex was one of the more left-leaning universities in the mid-1970s. As a result, the university attracted a liberal and international student body.

I had done well in mathematics and sciences throughout boarding school, and at Sussex, I majored in engineering. However, I soon realized that hard-core engineering was not my passion. There was no room for creative thought. I added operations research as a minor. Operations research is the science of applying mathematics to solving real-world business problems.

Socially, I flourished at Sussex. The group of international students at the university was large and diverse. I was surprised to meet a large group of Sri Lankans, most of whom had similar backgrounds to mine. Some of them remain my closest friends to this day.

Compared to boarding school, my daily life at Sussex was unfettered. I woke up just in time for lectures, which were always held in the mornings, leaving my afternoons free for long hours at the gym. I spent a lot of time playing racquet sports: badminton, squash, tennis, and especially table tennis. I enjoyed the one-on-one competition, and I began to represent Sussex University at varsity level table tennis. Our four-person team won the British interuniversity championship in each of the years that I was at Sussex.

In the evenings, we moved to the pub, where we would spend long hours discussing the stuff of college life: politics, current events, and sports. The conversations ranged from deeply philosophical to ridiculous and everything in between. The campus had seven or eight bars, and we frequented many of them. There was a lot to discuss in the England of the late 1970s.

The gay rights movement was growing, and apartheid was being challenged in South Africa.

Thursday and Friday nights found us at the campus disco, the Crypt. The movie *Saturday Night Fever* had come out a few years earlier, and many budding John Travoltas appeared on the dance floor. We fell in love; we won at love; we lost at love. I was in my element. It was magical, much like my early years in Sri Lanka, albeit with obvious differences.

Despite the freedom and enjoyment of Sussex, I experienced racism too. England in the 1970s was going through tough times, with stagnating wages and high unemployment. Many working-class Britons resented the fact that immigrants from South Asia were taking their jobs, a sentiment exploited by the ultra-right-wing National Front Party, whose platform proposed that all South Asians be deported. Gangs of Neo-Nazi skinheads roamed the streets, intimidating and beating up South Asians.

As a first-year student at Sussex, I visited my uncle, who was living in Greater London, in an area with lots of immigrants. While we were walking on the street, we were aggressively pushed aside by a group of skinheads. We stood, fought back intensely, but in the end, we were outnumbered and received a good old-fashioned beating. The skinheads ran away just as the local Pakistani and Indian shopkeepers in the area came out to help. The shopkeepers told me that this particular group of skinheads routinely harassed them and stole from their stores.

When I was a young boy in Sri Lanka, one of the neighborhood kids, a couple of years older than I was, would bully us all mercilessly. One day, I threw chili powder in his eyes and made him cry. From then on, he stopped bullying us. Years later, in London, I began to carry chili powder in my pocket to protect myself. Luckily, I never had to use it.

My father taught me never to throw the first punch, but if anyone else did, I should never back down. To this day, I have followed his advice.

By the time I graduated from Sussex University in 1980, there were signs of racial tensions in Sri Lanka between the majority Sinhalese and the minority Tamil communities. This would later turn into a brutal twenty-five-to-thirty-year war, which officially ended only in 2009 after more than sixty thousand people had been killed.

In 1980, going back to Sri Lanka and working as an engineer was not an option. By this point, I was interested in business and applied to do an MBA in the U.S. I was admitted to the MBA program at the Wharton School of Finance in Philadelphia. I thoroughly enjoyed my time at Wharton: the professors were excellent; the students were very smart and came from varied and interesting backgrounds; and the courses were challenging and exciting. I became fascinated by finance, particularly international finance and investment. I had found my passion. I did well at Wharton because I was really interested in the coursework. Although not as carefree as my Sussex years, my time at Wharton was intellectually very stimulating.

Over the decades, I have kept in close contact with about thirty or so classmates from Wharton. When I started Galleon and was looking for a trusted person to manage everything other than the investment side, I chose a flatmate from International House, a fellow Wharton MBA. Three other Wharton classmates have worked with me at Galleon, all as senior portfolio managers. I have invested in two start-up companies headed by classmates and invested in two real estate ventures as partners with other classmates. The Wharton connection has been very important.

In May, 1983, I graduated from Wharton with an MBA in finance and accepted a job with Chase Manhattan Bank, to start in the fall of that year. Taking advantage of my last long summer holiday, I returned to Sri Lanka. In July, a small incident between the army and the Tamils turned into an island-wide riot, leaving over two thousand Tamils dead. That day and night of inhuman rioting marked the beginning of a thirty-year civil war.

I was in Colombo at the time, staying with my uncle. On that one night at the end of July, Sinhalese gangs raged from house to house, looting and beating up Tamils. My aunt and younger cousins hid next door with a Sinhalese family while my uncle, a few male cousins, and I stayed back with sticks and knives, prepared to defend our home. Although the crowd attacked many Tamil houses on the street, our house was spared.

I left Sri Lanka in July 1983, sad that I felt unsafe in my own country. I did not return to Sri Lanka for ten years.

I returned to the U.S. and applied for citizenship. My deep love for the Sri Lanka of my early years would remain, but I was deeply grateful to be back in the U.S., where my family and I had been welcomed and were flourishing. In some ways, I would always remain an outsider here, but America was my home, and I was going to make my life in New York City.

New York has given me the same liberty it has afforded generations of immigrants: the freedom to be true to oneself. New York is defined as much by its newcomers as its natives, and I hoped to spend my life in New York. I started from nothing when I arrived in New York. My philosophy was to work hard, never give up, and learn to overcome the obstacles I would encounter along the way.

Despite all the contradictions of our island, I, like many Sri Lankans living abroad, feel a deep attachment to the country. There are volumes written about the origins of the ethnic and religious divisions in Sri Lanka and how these have played out through each generation. I will say just one thing: the politics of ethnicity and religion will always be fueled by two factors—ignorance and poverty.

Over the years, I have supported the development of orphanages, schools, and medical facilities in Sri Lanka. Two particular experiences stand out. Once when I was visiting a war-torn area of the country. I witnessed several children, each of who had only one leg, playing in a village. It was then that I understood firsthand the devastating impact of land mines on the civilian population. Children were particularly vulnerable as they walked to school and back. Because of the land mines, no area was safe for them to run around and play. With others, I helped provide funding to identify land mines using specially trained dogs from the U.S.

I established an annual scholarship for four or five students from less developed countries to study in America. After a thorough review of many applications by a third party, one of the first recipients was a very well qualified Sri Lankan student who happened to be Sinhalese. He arrived at Wharton from Sri Lanka and flourished. He did his summer internship at Galleon. After completing his MBA from Wharton, he returned to Sri Lanka to make important contributions of his talent and skills. The scholarship remains ongoing and has already supported the education of many talented students from less developed countries. Over the years, at least twenty college students of Sri Lankan origin from all three major ethnic groups have had summer internships at Galleon.

In 2004, I was vacationing with my family in the south of Sri Lanka when a tsunami demolished whole swathes of land, destroying homes and people in a horrific moment of total and unimaginable terror. Over forty thousand people lost their lives; I observed the destruction firsthand. Many fishermen were left homeless, and I was grateful that I could help them rebuild their homes, regardless of their ethnicity.

To this day, I feel like both an insider and an outsider in Sri Lanka. In the past two decades, whenever I have visited the country, I look down as the plane is about to land and feel a powerful connection to the place where I was born. I did not live in Sri Lanka during those key years of the war; I have no real firsthand understanding of what the people in the country endured. This has made me somewhat of an outsider. The Sri Lanka of my early years is a long-held memory. The land of my birth will always hold a special place for me.

CHAPTER 3

MY EARLY CAREER

By the time I graduated Wharton in May 1983, I wanted to work in the finance industry, with the goal of eventually moving back to Asia. I took my first step in that direction at Chase Manhattan Bank.

At Chase, all associates were inducted into the analytical process through an approximately nine-month credit training program. In the 1980s, this program was regarded as one of the best training courses in banking; the selection process was tough and mine was a diverse group. Essentially, the program was a full-time class, only we were paid to learn rather than the other way around. The Chase program was so well respected that as soon as trainees finished the program, headhunters would begin calling. We were first-round picks for jobs at other institutions. There were over one hundred students in my class, and I would guess that about 30 percent left the bank within a year or two of completing the program.

We were taken through rigorous financial and cash flow analysis, with the specific emphasis on applying these financial tools to understanding the credit worthiness of a business. The training was valuable and a perfect complement to the skills honed at Wharton. In business school, the emphasis was on viewing a business from a corporate, management standpoint—the fundamentals of running a business. Credit training taught us to drill into and analyze every number; as analysts, we were trained to peel away every layer of a company to get to as much granularity as possible. The mornings were focused on classroom training and the afternoons were devoted to hands-on credit analysis with a lending officer in the corporate bank. We got to see the result of our analysis in real time.

Credit training has changed over the decades; it's now considerably less rigorous. I am grateful for the opportunity to go through that level of learning, as it became another piece of my analytical skill set, which, combined with my engineering background, positioned me perfectly for my next role as a technology analyst.

One of the keys to analyzing any company is understanding the asset conversion cycle, the process of converting a company's proprietary asset into cash. Years later, as a security analyst and then a portfolio manager, I would often ask the CEO of a company what he viewed as his company's proprietary asset. Was the company efficiently converting that to cash? It made for a stimulating discussion.

At the conclusion of the credit training program, I joined the electronics division of Chase's corporate bank. In the '80s, commercial banks and investment banks had diametrically opposing business practices and cultures. Commercial banks tended to be staid with a leisurely pace, giving rise to the old expression "bankers' hours." On most days, the bulk of Chase's employees would leave the office by 5 or 5:30. We rarely worked evenings and never on weekends. The commercial banking culture was generally quite gentlemanly; investment banking was far more aggressive and demanding.

I was drawn to the more energetic and entrepreneurial environment of investment banking. And even more appealing was that the investment banking platform also had more direct access to the stock market. The intellectual challenge of using my analytical skills in the high-pressure, fast-paced world of Wall Street was very appealing.

NEEDHAM

Two years later, in September 1985, I left Chase to join Needham, a recently formed full-service investment bank. George Needham, the founder, was a well-respected senior investment banker who headed the technology practice at Credit-Suisse/First Boston. My job was to analyze the semiconductor and semiconductor equipment industries; publish reports on semiconductor companies that projected future earnings; and rate stocks as "buy," "hold" or "sell." Our reports were circulated to Needham clients, typically institutional money managers who would make their decisions to buy or sell a stock through Needham.

This was a dream job for me—engineering, finance, and my growing passion for the stock market. Semiconductors, typically made out of silicon crystals, are the foundation of modern electronics. In the mid-1980s, the industry was growing rapidly, driven by the widespread adoption of personal computers. Changes in the semiconductor industry were driving the miniaturization of all electronic equipment. Silicon Valley was booming. New companies were being formed. Many were going public, creating enormous wealth.

Our work at Needham could be very broadly grouped into two major buckets. In one bucket, we were maniacal in the application of our analysis to financial data put forth by companies as part of their reporting obligations. I spent the bulk of my day poring over financial statements; trying to figure out whether a company's inventories were bloated or their receivables increasing; doing cash flow analysis; or reading technical journals and newsletters. This is the core rigor of investing, understood by every true financial professional and ignored by every ambitious prosecutor.

The second bucket was predicated on the first. After digesting company and industry financials, we at Needham and our peers would meet with executives from the companies we followed. We did so openly in order to understand their strategies and pressure test them against the diligence that we had done.

I would travel to Silicon Valley at least once a month to meet with the senior executives of these semiconductor companies as well as their competitors, suppliers, and other firms in the value chain. I cross-checked everything in an attempt to verify what the executives told me.

Meeting with CEOs and CFOs of these public and private companies was one of my favorite duties. I learned so much from them every time.

I realized the importance of being a good and careful listener, which is also essential to being a competent portfolio manager. Although they have demanding schedules, most senior executives typically allocate time to meet with security analysts. I developed the discipline of spending time, an hour or two, with senior executives; it was impossible not to learn from these highly charged, extremely successful business people. It is also an opportunity that was neither extended to nor repeated for those who did not prepare diligently.

I was lucky to be meeting with senior executives so early in my career.

When I travelled to Silicon Valley, I would usually meet with four or five public and private companies a day or about twenty in the week. On Friday, I always tried to take the 3:30 p.m. flight to be home for the weekend. On the flight back to New York, I would write down everything I had learned during the week, noting what was specifically useful for my analysis or follow-up. This is a habit that I have maintained throughout my career. Even as Galleon expanded rapidly, I always noted my observations from each business trip on my way home.

It was just a great time to be in the middle of all this. Professionally, I was doing well. I was soon promoted to director of investment research, with overall responsibilities for all the research analysts at Needham. We were doing investment analysis in three key sectors: technology, health care, and consumer/retail, giving me valuable insights into the various companies and trends in these fast-growing areas. This would serve me well later when I would start my own investment firm/hedge fund investing in the very same sectors of the U.S. economy.

There were few layers of management. People wore multiple hats, rolled up their sleeves, and got involved in all aspects of the business. In those early days as we built our business, we had to create revenues and monitor expenses.

George Needham believed that 50 percent of the revenues should be allocated to employee compensation. In addition, he offered all employees an equity stake in the company, encouraging employees to think like owners. The Needham culture was not for everyone. Many who joined Needham from larger firms were not comfortable in the start-up culture. There were few places for a nonproducer to hide. If you produced, you got paid well. If not, you were not. In the early days, base salaries were capped at $60,000. The bulk of the compensation was bonus-based.

As a smaller, entrepreneurial firm, Needham's cash compensation was a good 25 or 30 percent lower than the Street for comparable jobs but was augmented with equity ownership. I was surprised by how many employees gave zero value to their equity ownership in the firm. They focused instead on current cash compensation reflective of the short-term culture of many on Wall Street. It was routine for them to jump to higher current, higher paying jobs.

Having worked with Silicon Valley companies, I appreciated the value of equity. I stayed at Needham for twelve years. George treated me fairly and I was given increasing responsibility. As a manager, one of my least favorite tasks was trying to retain someone who got a better offer elsewhere. When I appealed to their sense of loyalty, they would say, "Raj, I am a very loyal person, but first to my family. I owe it to them to get the best possible deal." There was not much I could say in response.

In 1992, about seven years after joining Needham, I was promoted to president. I was thirty-five years old. When I was appointed president, it became my responsibility to oversee the capital markets operations.

Sell-side investment banks like Needham had two distinct operations: the investment banking and capital markets. The investment banking group at Needham was led by George Needham. Capital markets, for which I was now responsible, involved sales, trading, and research.

The culture on the Needham trading desk was similar to that of any other trading desk on Wall Street: high testosterone and intense. One part gladiatorial, the other part sports locker room. The traders are born gamblers; they bet on sports, bet on horses, bet on everything, including whether someone could eat fifteen ice-cream bars in sixty seconds. In their off-hours, they were likely to go to Atlantic City or Las Vegas. During the workday, they were laser focused on the stock market, rarely leaving their stations even for food, preferring to eat at their desks. When the markets closed at 4:00, they usually left soon after.

Traders are tough to manage. I learned that it's best to let traders be traders. I was unlikely to make them polite and respectful. They were loud and opinionated. Yelling and screaming were commonplace because the pressure under which they operated was enormous.

It is this stereotype of traders that has been celebrated and caricatured in popular culture. The Wall Street greed and high intensity, the unprincipled trader, are a trope and a stock character in movies and television. And it would prove to be like catnip for prosecutors, a phenotype that was easy to exploit in front of a jury raised on Gordon Gekko and other such fictional characters.

This, however, was far from my experience. The traders I knew were aggressive, intense, and loved the competitive rush of the trading floor. They also overwhelmingly understood the rules of engagement and enjoyed success when earned. There was, contrary to popular opinion, a creed and principle behind their efforts, one driven by honest competitive spirit. I also found most traders were very generous in supporting charities, another characteristic that is not in the popular discourse on traders.

On the research side, I was responsible for hiring security analysts. They were generally quieter, studious, and enjoyed in-depth analytical work in a quieter environment. Their engagement added a counterpoint to the unceasing high energy of the trading desk.

I hired several South Asian analysts who were all well qualified and faced challenges when trying to break into Wall Street. In the mid-1980s and early 1990s, there were not many South Asians working on Wall Street. At one point, five of the fifteen research analysts at Needham were of South Asian origin. There began a quiet buzz in the firm that Raj hired only South Asians. When George asked me about these rumors, I pointed out that the entire corporate finance department were staffed with white, Anglo-Saxon protestant (WASP) men and a few women. Almost the entire trading desk was staffed with Jewish men, and not once had I thought about it. I asked him: "Which of the South Asian professionals at the firm does not carry his weight?" He was silent.

Overall, George was a good, pragmatic manager. He was prudent with expenses and worked as hard as anyone in the firm. I learned a lot from George: a strong work ethic and the "grit" the translated into a passion for building a sustainable and successful business. The results remain impressive. Today, some thirty-five years later, while many of its specialty investment banking competitors are no longer around, Needham continues to do well.

LEAVING NEEDHAM

I REALIZED THAT BEING A full-time manager was not fulfilling to me. I wanted to be a portfolio manager. Even though I had no direct experience managing money, I wanted to see whether I could make money consistently in the stock market. I proposed starting a hedge fund at Needham in which I could employ my investment analytical experience in the broader context of both investing and trading. In June 1992, we started a hedge fund with initial capital of $15 million, mainly from Silicon Valley executives whom I knew well.

The fund performed well and within four years, the assets had grown to $250 million.

Increasingly, my passion was investing. The daily challenge of identifying the useful pieces of information and distilling each to a single investment decision was very satisfying to me. The stock market was an organic entity requiring many, many data points to form a solid, thoughtful investment decision. The intrigue that fueled my early involvement in the market turned into a full-blown passion during my time at Needham. After almost twelve years at Needham, I decided to leave and focus solely on the investment management side. I was thirty-nine. The decision to leave was not an easy one. George and his company had given me an opportunity to enter Wall Street and had treated me fairly. But having worked closely with some of the most talented and smartest entrepreneurs in Silicon Valley, I was eager to become an entrepreneur myself.

In September 1996, I told George I would leave at the year's end to start my own hedge fund.

Below is the letter that George Needham wrote to employees announcing my departure.

Needham & Company
November 1, 1996

To: All Members of the Firm
From: George A. Needham

I greatly regret to announce that Raj Rajaratnam, my friend and partner, has decided to resign from Needham & Company at the end of this year. Raj plans to establish his own investment company based in New York City.

Raj joined us in 1985, soon after founding of the firm, from Chase Manhattan Bank, as a research analyst covering the semiconductor equipment industry. He has since served ably in, among other roles, Director of Research, Chief Operating Officer, President and as a Member of the Board of Directors of Needham & Company. Raj has also maintained throughout this period, relationships with a number of important clients. Raj is the finest research analyst I have ever known. His grasp of stocks and the market remains without peer. However, his capabilities go far beyond that; Raj has done an outstanding job in all his many capacities in assisting me in building the firm. Without his contribution, we would not have achieved the great success as a firm that we have over the past eleven years.

Raj has also been instrumental in building out asset management business over the past four years. Raj is the President of our mutual fund management company and is the managing general partner of Needham Emerging Growth Partners, Needham Emerging Growth International Fund and the Needham Omni Fund. Raj has found that his primary interest has, increasingly over time been with the investment management activities and has, therefore, decided to focus his entire efforts on that activity.

Raj has agreed to work closely with the firm over the next two months to execute a smooth transition of his responsibilities to other members of the firm. Raj will continue as a shareholder of Needham & Company.

I hope you will join me in thanking Raj for his contributions to our Firm and wish him great success in his new endeavor.

My experience at Needham shaped how I would manage Galleon. By the time I started Galleon, I had learned that to grow a thriving business, you had to pay your senior producers well and weed out the nonproducers. You also had to learn to listen. I let it be known to everyone that if there were something they did not like or wanted to change, they needed to discuss the issues professionally. I would always listen. But if they put a gun to my head—if they threatened to resign as a negotiation ploy—I would shake their hand, wish them luck, and move on. Heavy-handed tactics never worked well with me. This is something the DOJ would later learn, much to their surprise.

CHAPTER 4

GALLEON GROUP

Looking back to 1992, when I first started managing money at Needham, and then to launching Galleon in January 1997, I feel the same set of emotions like it was yesterday. Raw energy. Exhilaration. Gut-wrenching anxiety I could not share with anyone. Pure reward. I started Galleon from scratch. Three people joined me from Needham. We added six more. We had to buy paper, pens, computers, and desks. Many of us were trading a good steady salary for the unknown. A grand adventure. From day one, I had sole responsibility to meet the payroll for the ten employees who embarked on this journey with me.

I did not launch Galleon in a vacuum; I spent months analyzing the equity long/short hedge fund sector. Although it's common knowledge now, few people understood that the industry referred to an investing strategy of buying positions in stocks that are expected to increase in value ("going long") and selling positions in stocks that are expected to decrease ("going short"). I learned that successful hedge funds evolved around one of two business models:

1. Firms built on the premise of strong fundamental *research* with the trader functioning as an order taker, simply executing trades with no authority to make buy/sell decisions, and

2. Firms with strong capacity in short-term *trading* with analysts functioning primarily to chase down the latest market rumors affecting near-term stock movement.

At that time, few hedge funds combined strong research with active trading. The cultures, attitudes, and time horizons of analysts and traders are very different. Analysts typically look at time horizons of six to twelve months while traders function at five-minute to one-week time blocks. Six to twelve months would be a lifetime. There is a natural tension between the two groups. Traders believed you don't need analysts in bull markets and who needs them in bear markets? Analysts believed it was their work and reputations on the line in making recommendations while all the traders had to do was press a button on buy or sell trades.

I believed then as I do now, you can do both: combine strong, in-depth research and trading capabilities based on insights and research.

And that is exactly how we built Galleon, on the fundamental premise there were exponential synergies when you combined strong research with active trading around core positions. There would be one winner: investors.

Trading around a core position is now a common investment strategy that refers to buying and selling a stock around a targeted number of shares and price. For example, if you think a stock will increase in price from twenty to twenty-five dollars in six months, it is possible to make more than the five dollars during that time if you are a nimble trader who buys into the dips and sells in the rallies. For us, trading around a core position became one of our core competencies. Investors understood from the beginning that our research was intense and accurate and that our trading was disciplined and well founded.

In addition to trading around a core position, we also adopted an *event-driven strategy*—an investment approach that exploits share pricing inefficiencies that may occur before or after a corporate event, including earnings calls, bankruptcies, mergers, acquisitions, or spin-offs.

If there were an event coming up, we would increase the position in a stock—either on the long or short side—ahead of the event. Common on Wall Street, our analysts would write in-depth research reports, bullish or bearish, depending on the circumstances of the upcoming event. We would also receive a wide variety of investment reports from Wall Street. The analysts would spend time poring over each report, compile an analysis of the group, and weigh each against the other. In addition to an in-depth analysis of external research, Galleon analysts would do their own granular and independent research and arrive at an internal forecast of the whether the stock price would go up or down when the event was announced.

Galleon portfolio managers would review all the information and take positions based on these internally generated analyses as well as their individual views of the market. A firm's strength is measured by how well the firm analyzes and executes its investment decisions.

The level of analysis was rigorous and in-depth. On average, our between thirty and thirty-five analysts "interacted" with over five hundred companies every month, either attending conferences, traveling to company facilities, or conducting conference calls with senior managers. We gathered an enormous amount of information. The key was to connect the dots and determine an overall investment thesis.

To ensure that Galleon analysts and portfolio managers did not engage in insider trading, we maintained a compliance group. Every employee read and signed the compliance manual annually. By doing so, they were committing to comply with the firm's policies and procedures. The compliance officer at Galleon was an ex-SEC lawyer, well versed in the laws and regulations of the SEC. Research analysts, traders, and portfolio managers were instructed immediately to inform the compliance officer should they have had reason to believe the information they received were improper. The compliance officer would evaluate the information and make a determination whether it would be permissible to trade on this information. If it were not, the compliance officer would add the company and the information to a restricted list of stocks. The compliance officer's word was final. This list was updated and circulated weekly.

When the SEC interviewed over twenty Galleon employees in 2007, not a single one of these employees indicated or insinuated that there was any insider trading at Galleon. This would not prevent the SEC from citing an anonymous tip and moving ahead with its conjectures of apparent insider traders.

This insider trading policy was not just some useless set of rules that languished in a dusty binder on a shelf; it was an important part of our everyday work life. For example, when our software analyst called the investor relations representative at a company they covered—for example, Cognos—about rumors of the imminent sale, and if that person inadvertently said that they would take a bid in the low fifty-dollars-per-share range, this level of granularity of information immediately became a red flag. Such information was too specific and should not have been shared. The analyst promptly brought this to my attention and I passed it onto our compliance manager, who put the company on our restricted list, taking it off the table for trading. A few months later, Cognos was acquired by IBM at a significant premium.

In the effort to build a company integrating the intensity of traders and the considered, careful, and in-depth research of analysts, we anchored Galleon with a specific set of core beliefs that drove the hiring (or letting go) choices we made:

1. We would have as little bureaucracy as possible. The investment side had three types of professionals: analysts, traders, and portfolio managers. It was a flat organization. The goal was simple: to make money for our investors.

2. We would hire very competitive people. In this business, there is always one extra company to visit, one more research paper to write, one more annual report to read. The work was never done. Those who did not have the drive stagnated or were let go. Duration at the firm was irrelevant.

3. For highly technical sectors—technology or health care—we would hire specialists with technical or medical backgrounds. Many of our technology analysts were engineers who also had MBAs. It was easier to teach stocks to engineers than physics to MBAs. We also had a few medical doctors on our health care team to better understand the science of biotechnology and pharmaceutical companies.

A TYPICAL DAY

EVERY DAY BEGAN WITH A morning meeting. The meeting was mandatory for all investment professionals—analysts, traders, and portfolio managers. This meeting was our most important forum for communicating thoughts, research, and conclusions. The room was large, with a long conference table and plenty of chairs. The meeting lasted about an hour, from 8:25 a.m. to 9:25 a.m., ending just before the market opened at 9:30 a.m. About sixty or seventy investment professionals attended the meetings. We were serious about punctuality. We fined people twenty-five dollars if they were late by even one minute. When I was late, I, too, paid the fine. (The fines were periodically sent to a local charity.)

The meeting always started with the traders presenting their observations about the market from the previous day. They monitored the overnight market and reported on this as well. The analysts followed the traders, specifically about any salient developments in each one's sectors. The mandate for each was a solid and complete defense of their positions and recommendations. The portfolio managers would question both the analysts and the traders. There was no polite chitchat. Every day, we had a volume of information to get through in just one hour. Market hours meant business hours. There was no question in anyone's mind that this was business.

Our meetings were open to current and potential investors as well as friends and family who were curious about our operations. Although at many other hedge funds, meetings were closed to outsiders, we were transparent. People who observed our morning meetings were impressed by the quality of the analysis and the insights of the participants. The meeting broke up at 9:25 a.m. to allow us all to be at our desks for the market opening at 9:30 a.m.

Throughout the day, we communicated with each other, often digitally. Anything that was learned was input into a real-time chat room. Each investment professional had immediate access to the information. Everybody at Galleon understood that ours was a real-time business. Throughout the day, analysts and traders were encouraged to walk into my office and interrupt any meeting if they had money-making ideas.

My day began at 5:30 a.m. at home. I spent about forty-five minutes to an hour on my home office computer reading and responding to emails from our overseas analysts and catching up on the overnight news. After breakfast with the family, I was in the office between 7:30 a.m. and 7:40 a.m.

Up to the morning meeting at 8:25 a.m. I would take calls from the sell side, absorbing the stock recommendations of the various brokerage firms as well as getting ready for the morning meeting. Between 9:30 a.m. and 10:00 a.m., I met with my trader, developing a game plan for the day. During this time, my assistant knew to hold all calls. At 10:15 a.m., I would spend about thirty to forty-five minutes with the junior portfolio managers asking and answering questions and providing guidance. At 11:30 a.m., I met with our risk manager to determine whether we were comfortable with the overall market risk that the firm was taking. My morning was always intense.

To encourage a market-driven focus, we provided lunch for all employees. They ate lunch at their desks while continuing to work.

During the day, the analysts, traders, and portfolio managers were inundated with thousands of bits of information from sell-side analysts, traders, and other portfolio managers, as well as other industry specialists and consultants. The information was of varying degrees of usefulness, both public and nonpublic.

At about 3:30 p.m., my trader gave me a summary of all trades completed that day and his thoughts about the market. During the last half hour of the market, my assistant again understood I would not take any incoming calls. By 4:15 p.m. after the market closed, I'd get a real-time profit and loss report card as to how the firm did that day, including how every portfolio fared as well as our overnight risk profile. All administrative, managerial, and investor meetings were scheduled for after 4:30. On most days, I left the office by about 6:00 p.m. and took a ten-minute walk home in time to have dinner with the family at 7.00 p.m.

I found managing a hedge fund torturous but incredibly exciting. I got handed a report card every day. When we lost money, I went home with a pit in my stomach. My wife looked dowdy and my kids looked like little devils. When we made money, my wife looked gorgeous and my kids looked like little angels. You had to have courage—the courage to make the bet, the courage to win, the courage to get your butt whipped, and the courage to bounce back. It was life on the edge and I loved it. Managing a hedge fund was an all-encompassing commitment. You needed to be all in and everyone around you needed to be the same. It never really stopped. Stuff came up all the time, in real time.

GALLEON GROWS

EVERY MAJOR BUSINESS EXPANSION DECISION we made had to pass one key litmus test: Would it be additive to our investors? For example, in terms of locating offices, our first satellite office was in Silicon Valley. Over time, the manufacture of technology products moved to Asia, so we opened an office in Taiwan, followed by one in Singapore, to keep track of this outsourcing trend. Our analysts in Taiwan and Singapore frequently travelled to China and Korea to evaluate market activity there.

When we hired people at Galleon, their backgrounds did not matter much. We had men and women as portfolio managers and early on, a woman founding trading partner. At one time, I counted eighteen different nationalities working at Galleon. We tried to avoid hiring people who seemed entitled, preferring instead to hire those who had fire in the bellies. If the choice were between someone who was born with one eye and was angry at the world versus someone from a privileged background, my vote was always for the former. When John Gutfreund, the former CEO of Salomon Brothers, made his legendary comment that to succeed at his firm a person had to wake up every morning "ready to chew the ass off a bear," he was not far off. You cannot teach people motivation or drive.

The people who did well at Galleon were those who thrived in a competitive environment with constant pressure. There was a fierce competitiveness about everything we did. You stood up and took responsibility—or "manned up," as we would say—if you were wrong. On the other hand, if you believed you were right, you were encouraged not to back down.

The hardest managerial job I had at Galleon was to keep a balance between the traders, the portfolio managers, and the analysts. Sometimes it required a soft touch and sometimes a heavier touch—I provided both. I firmly believed that we had to work in unison for Galleon to thrive. Consequently, the analysts did not report to the portfolio managers but had a reporting structure that was clearly outlined in writing. They reported to a process. I had to be careful that the analysts were not bullied by the traders or the portfolio managers, for the analysts were in some sense the intellectual capital of our firm.

By 2008, Galleon had grown rapidly, and we were managing over $7 billion. We had built a full investment team (analysts, portfolio managers, and traders) in five major sectors: technology; health care; consumer and retail; energy; and financials. We had offices in Taiwan, Singapore, London, New York, and California. Our international fund was $1.5 billion and was based in Singapore, with a full cohort of portfolio managers, analysts, traders, and support staff. Annualized returns over the seventeen years since I first began managing outside funds was good. Investors who started with us in 1992 had doubled their money every three and a half years. Another way of putting it is that $1,000 invested with us in 1992 would have grown to $17,000 by the end of 2007.

The Galleon funds attracted a combination of corporate, individual, and institutional investors, including college and university endowments, charitable trusts, private and state pension funds, as well as some wealthy individuals. Galleon was not a fund that served only the rich. Many hard-working citizens of modest means invested in Galleon through such funds as the New York State and New Jersey State Employee Pension Funds. All these institutions performed extensive due diligence on Galleon before entrusting their money to us.

The stock market meltdown occurred in September and October 2008 on the heels of the Lehman bankruptcy. Our flagship fund (Galleon Diversified) lost 18 percent in 2008. This was in line with average losses at hedge funds in 2008. This was by far our worst year managing money. All investors in the market were panicking, and faced with a liquidity crunch, they were withdrawing large amounts from their hedge funds.

Many hedge funds, facing significant withdrawals, put in "gates," preventing investors from taking out their money. This was a gut-check moment for us. The question facing us was whether we should follow suit. I returned to our core litmus test: would it be additive to our investors? We chose not to put up gates. My belief was that it was the investors' money; if they wanted it, we would give it back to them. Faced with the inability to withdraw needed funds from other hedge funds, they increased the amount they withdrew from ours while applauding our stance.

In late 2008, with reduced funds under management, for the first time, we had to downsize our business. We had to let some good people go. This was hard. We concentrated our funds in the hands of our most experienced portfolio managers. We bounced back strongly in 2009—through October 15, our funds were up about 22 percent net of fees. Our investors had recouped their losses of 2008 and then some. Funds were flowing rapidly back into Galleon.

We were back to firing on all cylinders.

CHAPTER 5

RECALIBRATING

There are in life those events that are inflection points. The day of my arrest, October 16, was the quintessential example of such an event. And Saturday, October 17, the day after, marked the start of the next phase.

On that Saturday, I looked out my nineteenth-floor living room window and saw a throng of photographers with long lenses standing outside the building. I wondered about the economics of the independent photographer business model. Most of them had stayed for eight hours and had not gotten a single photograph. How did they make a living? How much did they get for a photograph sold to the media? Should I go outside and pose for them?

I was in uncharted territory.

The emotional detachment that got locked into me the tumultuous day before continued today: I focused on random thoughts to structure my thinking; nothing I was experiencing made any sense.

In addition to getting my head around all that had transpired in the past twenty-four hours, I had a series of significant decisions and considerations with which to grapple immediately. With respect to my legal defense, I needed to find quickly a good defense lawyer and arrange for the cash and security components of my bail, due in three days. With respect to my responsibilities as a leader of Galleon and its employees and a guardian of investor funds, I had to deal with the impact and fallout to Galleon.

And, most personally, I had to be mindful of and mitigate the impact on my family.

The first step was to understand what exactly were the charges brought against me. I still had no real idea of the charges against me. With the blur of the arrest behind me, I sat down and read closely the criminal complaint again. It offered no epiphanies, no aha moment.

Instead, the criminal complaint left me scratching my head. The document reflected the information that the government unilaterally provided to a judge to secure an arrest warrant. It was abundantly clear the prosecutors did not understand our business. The entire case appeared to turn on the reality of every financial professional in the investment business, both mutual funds and hedge funds. Our job was to ferret out *lawfully* whatever information we could to inform our trading. The apparent misperception of the financially unsophisticated prosecutors was that doing so was wrong.

We at Galleon were keenly aware of and careful to honor this line. From inception, I insisted that every Galleon employee sign a pledge committing to adhering to the law. The pledge included a proviso that they would not engage in receiving or transmitting inside information. We had rigorous protocols to document our research and the resulting analysis for each of our countless investment theses. We spent tens of millions of dollars on lawful and detailed industry reports and analysis and had a paper trail a mile long to document our trading.

As I read and more deeply processed the allegations, I felt better. We could readily explain all the trades that were in question in the initial indictment with the backing of the written work of our analysts.

In its criminal complaint, the government made not a single reference to the reams of analysis and research behind each trade in question. Instead, they relied exclusively on their shiny new toy—select wiretap recordings of my cell phone calls. As the government breathlessly shared with the press, their prosecution of me marked the first time in American history that a federal wiretap—a powerful investigative tool authorized by Congress to target the American mafia in the 1960s and used for other such violence-related crimes—was deployed in the financial industry. And, as will be discussed in further detail later, it proved an error-fraught adventure by the government that nearly—and should have—derailed their entire case.

On that Saturday, a full day after, many other things jumped out at me. First, I could not comprehend why they would approach me in this heavy-handed manner. I thought an ethical prosecutor would have appreciated the sophistication of our trading and sought explanations and insight from industry professionals. At the very least, they could have asked me to explain the conversations and provide some context to judge with greater accuracy what occurred and proceed with care. This was the norm in white-collar cases. Targets of investigations are routinely advised of concerns and engage with the government, providing information, making detailed and volumi-nous presentations, and arguing in advance of any charges the facts as each applied to the law. The white-collar bar throughout the country has evolved around this routine practice.

This protocol is not reserved for smaller cases. Remember Martha Stewart. Ms. Stewart was suspected of insider trading. She was not abruptly arrested with no opportunity to explain her conduct. On the contrary, Ms. Stewart retained Wachtell Lipton, one of the most revered Wall Street law firms, to represent her when these issues were brought to her attention by the government prior to any charges being lodged. Wachtell Lipton attor-neys spent hours explaining Ms. Stewart's position. And Ms. Stewart herself elected to meet with the government directly, flanked by counsel, to offer her view. Tellingly, Ms. Stewart was not ultimately charged with insider trad-ing. She was charged with lying to the authorities in these proffers. I never was offered any of these standard courtesies.

Second, and to my great surprise, my youngest brother Rengan was included in the initial indictment as an uncharged co-conspirator. The message was loud and clear. The government inserted Rengan into the complaint without charging him to use him as a pawn to pressure me into pleading guilty much as Rudy Guiliani had done with Michael Milken. The Guiliani playbook was just beginning. This would not be the last time the government threatened my family members to increase the pressure on me.

While I read the complaint quietly and processed my thoughts, the phone continued to ring off the hook with friends and well-wishers calling from around the world. The news of my arrest and footage of the infamous perp walk had been splashed all over the world through the internet, television, and newspapers. Many years later, during his podcast, Preet Bharara admitted that the perp walk was unnecessary for alleged white-collar crimes. But the damage was done.

Up until then, I had maintained a low profile. I avoided requests for interviews from newspapers, magazines, or television. For a couple of years, when Galleon was voted the best performing technology fund, I chose to send a Galleon representative to awards ceremonies. I largely avoided the New York black tie charity circuit, preferring instead to send a check or take a table and send others from Galleon. If the charity personally resonated with me, such as Harlem Children's Zone, the American Indian Foundation, or the South Asian Youth Association (SAYA), I made an exception.

Because of my low public profile, there was little about me in the public domain. The press was hungry for any information, fact or fiction. My photo and story were suddenly everywhere. I was unprepared for the onslaught. The prosecutors were interested more in scoring points with the public than in pursuing the truth. Everything moved at lightning speed.

CHOOSING A LAWYER

ARRANGING THE BAIL, SECURED BY cash and my home, was relatively straightforward. Selecting a lawyer was much more complicated. On the day of my arrest, the Galleon general counsel had called in a panic a well-known law firm to represent me immediately for my bail hearing. They did indeed secure bail for me, for which I am grateful. Afterwards, I thanked them profusely and advised them that I would need to interview other firms and make my own decision about counsel for this fight. I made my intentions to hire another firm clear and did not enter into any agreements with this firm. Eager for the inevitable business, they embarked on an elaborate effort to develop a pitch to lobby me further. Two weeks later, I confirmed I had chosen another firm. Remarkably, they handed me a bill for $800,000 for their additional and unauthorized effort. The legal money-making machine had been activated.

Many friends called and emailed to suggest legal counsel, and some of these candidates came to my home to meet me over the weekend of October 17 and 18.

Even though they claimed to be securities lawyers, many seemed unaccustomed to the world of hedge funds and their operations. Unprompted, several even estimated what my case would cost, giving me the uneasy feeling that what happened to me was irrelevant, as long as they were paid.

Strangely, even though I had lived in New York City for over twenty-five years and was active in the business world, I did not have a single lawyer friend. I called a nonlawyer friend who had gone through a big civil case and asked him for suggestions. He advised me to stay away from New York law firms, "They're all in cahoots with the prosecutors," he informed me. He was sure they would encourage me to plea bargain and cooperate with the government.

His point was not a matter of mere paranoia. The white-collar criminal defense sector in New York is dominated by former federal prosecutors from the Southern District of New York. Firms hire them at princely salaries specifically for their knowledge of the federal justice system and specifically for the strength of their relationships with the United States Attorney's Office for that district. The lion's share represent institutions, not individuals, and are trained to avoid trials on behalf of their client. In addition, many of their firms have numerous matters simultaneously with the U.S. Attorney's Office, resulting in a disincentive to press too hard for one client lest it compromise their relationships on behalf of other clients. Most white-collar lawyers have a good understanding of the federal prosecutorial system and the risks of going to trial. They usually embrace the system of plea bargaining and deal-making.

I desired neither. I wanted to prove my innocence.

My friend's first suggestion was the criminal defense lawyer, Brendan Sullivan of Williams & Connolly, a venerable Washington, D.C. firm.

Sullivan, however, was busy with a highly publicized Broadcom case and was unavailable. (The judge in the Broadcom case was a rare example of courage; he eventually dismissed the case, citing prosecutorial misconduct.) Sullivan in turn suggested John Dowd from the Washington office of Akin Gump Strauss Hauer & Feld. Dowd had represented Senator John McCain during the 1990–1991 Senate ethics investigation known as the Keating Five. McCain was cleared of wrongdoing. Dowd had represented Major League Baseball and other high-profile clients. Dowd sounded impressive, was not from New York, and came highly recommended.

On Friday, October 23, 2009, I met with Dowd in New York at the Galleon offices. Although gruff, Dowd had a certain old-fashioned southern charm. I had reservations. Dowd had no experience with securities law. He also did not understand what a hedge fund was or did. Indeed, he did not know the basics, such as the difference between the buy side and the sell side or a bid and an ask.

What Dowd did offer, unlike so many of the other attorneys I interviewed, was a source of strength. Dowd was not looking to make a deal and refused to countenance any suggestion of weakness. John Dowd was an ex-marine with a warrior's spirit and instinct that immediately resonated with me. I wanted and needed someone who would not back away from taking on a fight against the powerful, politically infused American justice system. I chose John Dowd.

John was also intuitively aware of the importance of my family. He was the only lawyer who asked about them, and he took the initiative of visiting my father. This simple gesture spoke volumes to me. Dowd seemed to recognize all the parts of my professional and personal life. Typical of most lawyers, on our very first meeting, he brought with him a pre-drawn engagement letter requesting an escrow of $10 million. Given the stress and intensity of the times, I did not question or analyze the request. I simply accepted the terms and signed the letter. John Dowd and Akin Gump became my defense team.

UNWINDING GALLEON

IN THEORY, THE AMERICAN JUSTICE is predicated upon the fundamental principle of innocent until proven guilty. On Wall Street, however, it does not work that way. Mere accusations and rumors can and do destroy firms.

Faced with these realities, I had to determine how best to protect the interests of our investors and our employees. A legal battle would clearly be long and time-consuming, and allowing the business to slowly hemorrhage would be bad for everyone.

When I interviewed lawyers, I asked each how much of my time this case would take. The answer was at least four or five hours a day for the next six months. I quickly determined that I could not spend this much time with lawyers and still effectively and responsibly continue as the managing general partner of Galleon.

I had no choice. I called a firm-wide meeting and told everyone of my decision to wind down Galleon. We would have to return all the monies to investors and provide for the orderly dismissal of our loyal, hardworking employees. There were many teary eyes in the room. When I looked around, I saw that most of the employees were in their twenties and thirties, with just a few in their forties. I realized how young and talented they were. It's an open secret that Wall Street employs the young; very few people enter Wall Street in their forties. Within a few days on October 22, I sent employees, investors, and other stakeholders a letter informing them of my decision to close Galleon and return their capital. At that point, through October 15, we were up slightly over 22 percent year to date. Nobody lost money at Galleon. No investor sued Galleon.

Dear Galleon Employees, Clients, and Friends,

> I have decided that it is now in the best interests of our investors and employees to conduct an orderly wind down of Galleon funds while we explore various alternatives for our business. At this important time, I want to reassure investors of the liquidity of our fund and assure Galleon employees that we are seeking the best way to keep together what I believe is the best long/short equity team in the business.

As many of you know we have built our business on the fundamental belief in rigorous investment analysis combined with active trading around core positions. We have encouraged and invited our investors to attend our daily research morning meetings. Many of you have done that and got a firsthand look at our process. This research process is the core of our investment and trading strategy.

The privilege of managing investors' capital is a responsibility that I have always taken very seriously. I want to reiterate that I am innocent of all charges and will defend myself against these accusations with the same intensity and focus I have brought to managing our investors' capital.

For those who have been my partners and supporters over the last 17 years, I sincerely thank you. I also want to thank you for the innumerable expressions of support I have received from you over the past few days.

Sincerely, Raj Rajaratnam

We moved quickly to liquidate our funds. By December 1, over 90 percent of the capital was returned to our investors. The rest was returned after the year-end audit. I waived the provision in the documents that the fund would pay my legal expenses. I opted to pay for it myself. The total cost of my legal battles would eventually be over $50 million, but I was determined to do right by our investors.

This was a very conscious and easy choice for me, but not an obvious one. Hedge funds are careful to place conditions by which investors can seek "redemptions" or a return of their investment plus any increase in value. In particular, funds can "gate" invested proceeds and release them only on a predetermined schedule. In the interim, while these gates are down, the fund would continue to earn its management fee of 2 percent of the assets under management. The same was true for Galleon, which at the time had several billion dollars under management; the potential management fee had we asserted our gating rights would have totaled approximately tens of millions of dollars. I never considered gating these funds. My investors believed in Galleon. I felt duty bound not to drag them into my fight.

Through the painful and sad process of unwinding Galleon, I took great pride that not one investor lost money or complained about the process in any way. Not a single investor sued us. They were very satisfied with our management of their capital over the years, and that their funds were promptly returned to them.

Shortly after my arrest, we instructed employees not to destroy any documents. We removed all the shredders in the office. Employees were asked to return their laptops in order to make them available as evidence. *We had nothing to hide.* Everyone except Adam Smith, a technology portfolio manager, returned the laptops. Adam said he had lost his, and I had no reason to doubt him. Later on, Adam would admit in court, under oath, that he had engaged in other wrongdoing and deliberately destroyed his laptop. (More on Adam Smith in Chapter 14.)

I naively thought that if we presented the facts, the jury as well as the media or anyone following my case would understand our consistent methodology for buying and selling stocks. A simple exercise of looking through Galleon's extensive database of research would make it obvious that our practice did not include breaking any laws. Rather than chase facts, the U.S. attorney's office was intent on selling its story to a public angry at Wall Street and the financial system that had triggered the economic collapse and recession.

The first weekend after my arrest, the FBI went unannounced to the homes of three Galleon professionals and tried to flip them. The message to each was identical. The "big guy" (Raj) was cooperating with the government, so it was time to get on the train or it would be too late. Of course, this was not true. Their deceit got them nowhere. They made no headway. Not one Galleon employee provided any incriminating information because there was none to give.

It surprised me to learn as a part of my crash course in the American justice system that the government is in fact permitted under law to deceive affirmatively and create artificial pressure on witnesses to cooperate as part of their investigation. As I would soon learn, their chicanery permeated every aspect of their investigation and prosecution of me, both before and after my arrest. Simply put, the government, whose investigative team was led by Agent Kang, did not let facts or laws stand in the way of their career case.

THE DEFENSE TEAM

AT AKIN GUMP, THE THREE senior lawyers in my case were John Dowd; Terry Lynam; and Patricia Millett, Akin Gump's head of the appellate practice. When I first met Dowd in October 2009, he was sixty-eight years old. He was a lumbering man. I worried about his stamina. He was a traditional old-school lawyer and I initially found some of his old-school habits charming. He always referred to his wife as "Mrs. Dowd." When I first went to Washington to meet with him and his team, he gave me a ride back to the train station, and as he started his SUV, a devotional Christian song began playing on the CD. I gathered he was a religious man, and this gave me some comfort that I was in good hands. Like many people in life-critical situations, I found solace in some of the smaller characteristics of people and their actions.

This was by far the biggest and most complex case John Dowd had ever handled. In fact, it was the biggest criminal case in the United States at the time. His last significant criminal case, had been about seventeen years ago. On reviewing all the written evidence connected to my trading, he told me he could win the case even though the road ahead was going to be tough because the prosecutors are allowed to play with a stacked deck and the FBI is allowed to lie, as Kang had done when he told Galleon employees that I was cooperating with the government. Dowd preened in his moment in the sun, delighting in the countless lawyers who showered him with praise, many if not most who were seeking to have Dowd "refer" witnesses to them and therefore profit commercially from my case. But above all else, Dowd thrived in the attention he received and his own newfound celebrity in New York and elsewhere.

Terry Lynam was the second most senior lawyer on the team. Like Dowd, he was experienced and capable. Unlike Dowd, Lynam had tried cases involving the SEC and was somewhat familiar with the workings of the stock market and maintained a studiously low profile. Terry Lynam and I worked well together. He always listened to my point of view, and if he disagreed, he would tell me why, which is how I operate. Smart and agile, he was able to think on his feet, be it in the middle of the conference room or in the well of a courtroom during trial. I had great respect for Terry as a lawyer and as a person. In my opinion, he was the best trial lawyer on our team. My only criticism of him was that he deferred to John too much. One day in the middle of the trial, John yelled at Terry in the private room adjacent to the court that was reserved for the defense team. Terry just walked away. I pulled Terry aside and asked why he did not stand up for himself, and Terry just shrugged and said "that's John." John Dowd's hair-trigger temper caused unnecessary tension on the defense team. The junior lawyers and associates who worked for Terry loved working for him. While preparing for the trial, I heard many complaints from junior lawyers about working with John.

Patricia Millett was in my mind a superstar. In this case, my intuition was spot-on. Pattie had argued more cases before the United States Supreme Court at the time than any woman in history. After my case, she was named by President Obama to the prestigious District of Columbia Circuit Court as a judge and shortlisted publicly to fill Justice Scalia's seat after his death. Personable, knowledgeable, and insightful, I enjoyed working with her.

Pattie was not a trial lawyer and Dowd, who was threatened by her intellect and confidence, used this as an excuse to marginalize her. This was a mistake. Pattie was that rare appellate specialist who, as I later learned, would have been invaluable in the development of a trial strategy and policing the government's conduct and misconduct throughout the trial to make and preserve legal challenges. Dowd, however, limited Pattie's role to working on the challenge to the wiretap charges with the New York-based lawyers who had experience on those issues.

The Akin Gump team, together with the Galleon team, did a great job of assembling and analyzing the information. The rigorous work at Galleon in developing and supporting our investment strategies provided to be a treasure trove for our defense. In every single case of trading in question, we had hard, documented evidence that what the government claimed to be confidential information had appeared in popular financial newspapers or the media, as well as in the Galleon analysts' reports, weeks and months before any alleged tip. We had evidence to show that the confidential or secret information that the prosecutors were claiming was in fact public information that was well circulated on Wall Street and available to anyone who did the work. The Galleon analysts' reports were done in real time by the analysts. Under the Galleon system, these records could not be destroyed or manipulated. They were maintained by a third-party vendor.

Unfortunately, soon there was turmoil on my Akin Gump criminal defense team. Cracks began to appear. We began with four senior partners (two in New York and two in Washington) in addition to Pattie. John had initially advocated adding the two New York partners because both had worked as prosecutors in the Southern District and accordingly understood its inner workings and in particular the wiretap laws.

John was the established lead attorney. He mandated total control. All correspondence and conversations from me to the lawyers had to be routed through him. There was a lot of ground to cover with what eventually became thirty-four stocks, and everything email needed to be funneled through John. Given the complexity of the case, this became cumbersome, but John remained resolute. We all had to adhere to this process. John would sign his emails *Semper Fi*, a common term among Marines meaning "always loyal." On one occasion, I asked John about his combat experience. He deflected the question. I later found out that he was in fact a JAG lawyer in the marines. Marine Corps JAG lawyers never saw combat.

As it turned out, John had a quick and volatile temper. In one meeting, he blew up at one of the partners from New York. The explosion took place in front of me as well as other junior lawyers. I was embarrassed for that partner, who was dropped from the team a few days later. A few months after that, the other New York partner on the team was also dropped. John explained that the two New York partners were "too close" to the prosecutors in the Southern District, which made him uncomfortable. Not familiar with the legal system, I deferred to him, although it seemed illogical to fire the very team members who knew most about the workings of the department in the venue in which I would be tried.

At one point, I was also the target of one of John's tantrums. I rose up out of my chair and told him that if he ever spoke to me like that again, I would fire him. He was quick to apologize. Looking back, I realize we were in the middle of the battle, and when you're in the thick of the action, you learn to adjust to each other's personalities and styles in order to stay focused on the end goal—proving my innocence.

John's overall strategy was to show that everything the prosecutors alleged to be confidential information was already in the public domain. He believed the concept was a simple one to convey and therefore, would be equally simple to grasp, to understand. In retrospect, his assessment of a jury with no experience with the financial industry was overly optimistic.

Even now, I remain surprised by how challenging it was to explain the securities business to John and the attorneys. If John and his team, experienced and intelligent as they were, had a hard time initially grasping the implications of the myriad information, how could a jury of laypeople not be baffled and confused? I was concerned about how John and his team would simplify and explain securities trading to a jury.

That was key.

MAKING SENSE OF MY INDICTMENT

AT THE SAME TIME, I assembled a small team of Galleon analysts to pull out Galleon and Wall Street research on all the stocks named in the indictment. We searched through a wealth of documentation in the Galleon chat rooms for specific discussions on each company. I was pleased with what we uncovered. With all the in-depth research we had done, I believed we could conclusively prove my innocence.

In every instance, we compiled many, many emails sent to me before the alleged tip. Each of these emails supported the trades in question. In almost all instances, I also had a position in the stock before the alleged tip. Our highly experienced analysts had closely followed each of the stocks and wrote well-researched briefs supporting all our trading positions. There was not a single stock among the government allegations for which we did not have research coverage. We believed research was the basis of our DNA and would conclusively prove that I did not engage in insider trading.

Prosecutors have built many a criminal case on perpetrators' surreptitious actions and secret use of coded language in intercepted conversations. This, they argue, is indicative of criminal activity. The wiretaps collected in my case revealed normal conversations that professionals in the investment business have every day. There was no secret information exchanged in hushed tones; there were no secret codes. Because I had nothing to hide, I hid nothing. The prosecutors had to get creative, and therefore, began characterizing my conversations as "brazen." The media strategy continued its successful march as the reporters now mindlessly began using that adjective in their pieces, as if they had all just discovered that I was "brazen" in addition to all the adjectives they had been spoon-fed.

The initial charges involved eight stocks zeroing in on total profits of $18 to $20 million over a five-year period from 2004 to 2008. In reality, the alleged trades amounted to losses of over $50 million, making the net loss approximately $30 million in the same five-year period.

As part of the discovery process, the prosecutors turned the wiretaps over to us. We had to listen to all 1,300 of them, get them transcribed, and then choose the phone calls that we thought the prosecutors would probably use in court. In the original charges, the government had taken snippets of wiretaps or emails and interpreted them in the worst possible way. They were looking through a dirty peephole. We were hoping that putting these excerpts in accurate context would exonerate me. After having reviewed the wiretaps, we learned that there were no revenues, earnings, merger or acquisition information exchanged, *period*.

Everything that was discussed on the wiretapped calls was either public information or the work of a Galleon analyst. Furthermore, the prosecutor's charges represented trades that were less than 0.2 percent of my trades between 2003 and 2008: two tenths of one percent. During this period, I personally did over thirty-six thousand trades. In the five-year period between 2003 and 2006, the total value of my trades was a staggering $172 billion: a yearly average of over $34 billion or about $150 million a day.

Initially, Anil Kumar and Rajiv Goel—both my former Wharton class-mates—declared their innocence and had no intention of pleading guilty. As a result, the early plan was to work with their respective lawyers to form a joint defense.

The last contact I had with Anil Kumar was at our bail hearing on October 16, 2009. Immediately after our arrests, he contacted two of my New York friends, a couple, who twice had him over for dinner in December 2009. Anil calmly discussed his options. He said he could fight or cooperate in the hopes of benefiting. He estimated it would take $25 million to fight the charges. Then he made a strange request to the wife—that she buy a prepaid phone so that he could communicate with her securely. She was puzzled by the request and did not comply. Later on, at trial, he would claim that I had wanted him to buy a prepaid phone!

Ultimately, both Anil Kumar and Rajiv Goel, faced with potential federal charges for tax evasion, chose to take a plea. This meant that they would plead guilty to the insider trading charges and agree to cooperate and testify against me so that they could get a reduced sentence and have their tax evasion charges dismissed.

The American justice system relies on plea bargaining: 97 percent of criminal cases are decided by having the accused admit to a lesser charge and forgo a jury trial. Often, the accused avoids a long sentence by giving evidence against someone higher up. That is what happened here. I was to learn firsthand about the terrible consequences of this common coercive tactic of plea bargaining so readily used in the American justice system. The prosecutors were not interested in Anil or Rajiv's tax evasion, only in targeting me, the more high-profile target, at any cost, regardless of the truth.

Equipped with both mental fortitude and financial resources, I was determined to fight for my innocence. As a result, the prosecutors decided to up the ante and file a superseding indictment, expanding the allegations to thirty-four stocks from the initial eight. This time, my other brother, RK, was also named as an uncharged co-conspirator. The prosecutors were tightening the screws. Once again, this was eerily similar to Giuliani's strategy with Michael Milken. Giuliani went after Milken's family members and threatened to file superseding indictments. Under enormous pressure, Milken finally capitulated and pled guilty.

I was troubled by the notion of prosecutors using family members as bargaining chips. It did not seem like the fair-minded America I had grown to respect and expect. I chose not to back down. I was convinced that both a judge and jury would see the truth.

In the early days, despite his temper issues, John Dowd was a tower of strength. He believed we would win the case, and this belief sustained me as well. The task was now to process all the material on the thirty-four alleged stocks. This was a time consuming and expensive project. Some twenty lawyers and paralegals from Akin Gump and a team from Galleon painstakingly gathered all the relevant documents and put them in large binders. The legal team was divided into three groups, with each group responsible for the defense strategy of about ten to twelve stocks. Every single communication within Galleon and with our outside brokers, including emails, instant messages and weekly reports, was obtained and organized. Early on, we shared portions of Advanced Micro Devices (AMD) chronologies with Anil Kumar's lawyers and portions of the Clearwire chronologies with Rajiv Goel's lawyers, as part of the joint defense agreement.

MEDIA STRATEGY

IT WAS BECOMING EVER MORE apparent that we had to come up with a strategy to deal with the press. The news coverage resembled a public crucifixion, with the press eagerly applauding the latest assault on "greed and corruption." There was no informed analysis; reporters were eager to mindlessly jump on the government bandwagon. If the media had examined the allegations dispassionately and done the arithmetic, they could have determined that the alleged inside trades on the original indictment had actually lost money cumulatively. But no reporter was up to the task.

I was surprised that even the financial press mindlessly parroted the Justice Department, with no independent research or critique. The news media are supposed, in part, to be a government watchdog, but by and large it is more concerned with generating profits from sensational journalism than in seeking the truth.

Because greed was the central theme of the news coverage, we briefly considered an aggressive PR strategy to tell my side of our story, including a discussion of my charitable activities. Interestingly some of the foreign press actually went to Sri Lanka and saw firsthand the houses we had built after the tsunami hit Sri Lanka. Ultimately, we decided against hiring a major PR firm, concerned that the effort might backfire, with the press denouncing us for trying to manipulate public opinion. In hindsight, we should have been watching the press strategies of the U.S. attorney's office and matching them with the same level of firepower.

Eventually, we hired a professional public relations expert who would coordinate with John Dowd to respond to questions from the press and work behind the scenes to try to correct some of the inaccuracies. We also started a website so that the public could more accurately follow important developments in the case. It was a defensive, rather than an offensive strategy. As a result, the prosecutor was able to define me and control the narrative from the very beginning.

On the heels of the Galleon case, the government charged and indicted several other people involved with hedge funds. They managed to convince the press that all this was somehow related to the Galleon case. I had never heard of some of these individuals, but when they were charged, they were referred to as "Galleon figures." Once again, the U.S. attorney had created a bigger narrative than really existed.

One of the larger cases involved Primary Global Research (PGR), a consulting firm that connected hedge fund analysts with company employees for a fee. There are a number of firms that legitimately provide this service. However, some of these firms have had their employees recorded giving revenue and earnings information to a hedge fund analyst: an unmistakable violation of securities laws. Although PGR had approached Galleon and wanted to do business with us, we were not comfortable with them and declined. We were never their client, but PGR was now deliberately and erroneously linked with Galleon as a result of the prosecution's spin machine.

The government was constantly leaking information to an uncritical press. The U.S. attorney launched a media blitz, appearing on television, giving interviews to news magazines, saying that greed and corruption was prevalent on Wall Street. I was determined not to let the negative publicity wear me down, but I found my world was shrinking. I was living a life in retreat.

After spending my days with lawyers and poring through documents, emails, and internal records, I would spend my evenings alone, thinking about the case. My wife was concerned about me and suggested that I see a therapist. I was reluctant because I had never seen one in my life. My brother-in-law, who is a psychiatrist, also recommended counseling. I relented. Therapy did not come naturally to me. Men in our family do not hug each other. We do not talk about feelings with strangers. The first session was the last. I did not go back.

I went through a period of soul-searching. Why was this happening to me? Ultimately, I realized that I had to fight for my innocence and resolved to fight the battle to the finish. I tried not to think of the past. I realized the weeks and months ahead would be the greatest test of my life.

The support and encouragement of my family and close friends were unparalleled. I was nourished by their boundless compassion, solidarity, and goodwill. During the pretrial period, I worried endlessly about the impact of the case and the media onslaught would have on my children and wife. I am deeply fortunate to have been raised in a strong, tight-knit family, and my parents, brothers and sisters quickly and quietly stepped in to support me. I was determined that my family would have as normal a life as possible under the circumstances. Friends from around the world visited me; others wrote to me regularly. The support and value of family and friends is something I feel very fortunate to have—and will always cherish.

CHAPTER 6

JUSTICE SYSTEM

The U.S. has 5 percent of the world's people, but 25 percent of the world's prison population. There are approximately 2.3 million prisoners in the U.S., with several hundred thousand more incarcerated every year. In the past thirty years, the U.S. prison population has increased by an astounding 800 percent. Today, the incarceration rate in the U.S. is between six and twelve times greater than that of other western democracies such as the UK, Canada, Germany, France, and Australia. The U.S. incarceration rate is also about twenty-four times greater than that of India, the world's most populous democracy. This proclivity for incarceration cost the American taxpayer over $80 billion a year. This does not include the vast indirect costs inflicted upon the incarcerated, their families and communities. These are some of the startling facts I learned about the U.S. justice system after my arrest.

Although I have lived in the U.S. for over thirty years and have enjoyed discussing many social and political issues with people from all walks of life, I do not recall having a single serious discussion about the U.S. legal system. Like many people, I had blind, naive faith in the integrity of law enforcement professionals, prosecutors, lawyers, and judges. Although there are undoubtedly very many fine, capable, and honest law enforcement professionals, lawyers, and judges, there are some power hungry, corrupt, and greedy prosecutors who focus disproportionately on high-profile cases in a blind pursuit of winning at any cost regardless of the facts or the consequences. Winning leads to promotions.

I learned as I went through my arrest, trial preparation, and trial that there are few prosecutorial checks and balances. This oversight allows corrupt prosecutors to pursue their own ambitions with a nonchalance that comes at the expense of justice. They are not held accountable and their prosecutorial overreach has wrecked many innocent lives.

Prominent legal scholar and Harvard professor Alan Dershowitz noted that "prosecutors can easily succumb to the temptation of first picking the man and then searching the law books or putting investigators to work to pin some offense on him." Dershowitz also notes that the current US justice system is eerily similar to that of the former Soviet Union. "Every Soviet citizen committed at least three felonies a day, because the criminal statutes were written so broadly as to cover ordinary day-to-day activities. The Communist Party decided whom to prosecute from among the millions of possible criminals. They picked dissidents, refuseniks and others who posed political damage to the system."[6] In Stalin's Russia, KGB head Lavrentiy Beria was infamously quoted as saying, "Show me the man and I'll find you the crime."[7]

Today, there are over 4,700 federal laws in the U.S., and the average citizen is completely unaware of most of them. Although some are clearly essential to keeping law and order, many laws border on the ridiculous, such as a 2013 law mentioned earlier that bans people from unlocking their own smart phones, a federal crime punishable by prison time and a fine of *half a million dollars.*

Traditionally, to convict someone of a crime, prosecutors had to show convergence of harmful conduct (known as actus reus) and a culpable state of mind (mens rea). The basis of this reasoning is that nobody should be convicted of a crime without the government having proved that they knew they were doing something illegal. However, today many criminal laws make it possible for the government to convict a person even if he acted *without* criminal intent.

Harvey Silverglate, a prominent criminal defense lawyer, has argued extensively that federal prosecutors are abusing their power by expanding the number of criminal laws, many of which are vague, to prosecute Americans who have no idea they are even committing a crime. Especially problematic is when overzealous prosecutors threaten junior people or underlings with prosecution for these supposed "crimes"—unless they cooperate against the real target. Because federal laws carry outrageously high sentences, often with mandatory minimums, the prosecutorial threats are terrifying. They turn friends into enemies, family members into government witnesses, and employees into stool pigeons.[8] Statistics show that 97 percent of defendants plead guilty and do not go to trial.

I was one of the exceptions. I went to trial because I was not prepared to plead guilty for something that I did not do, no matter what the ultimate cost.

There are some unique aspects of the U.S. justice system that tilt the scale in favor of the prosecutors. The grand jury and plea-bargaining systems are two of the most important ones.

The grand jury system is the process whereby the government charges defendants. Currently, the U.S. is one of the very few countries that still use grand juries. Most countries employ some other type of preliminary hearing to charge an individual. In the U.S., grand jury proceedings offer only the prosecution the opportunity to present evidence against a defendant, often with the assistance of a cooperating witness who usually has plenty of incentive to do the prosecutors' bidding. Unlike during a trial, in a grand jury proceeding, defendants and their attorneys do not have the right to appear. As a result, the grand jury proceedings become a negative, accusatory investigative forum with incomplete and often-biased evidence. The balance tips so dramatically in favor of the prosecution that it has been noted time and again that "a good prosecutor could get a grand jury to indict a ham sandwich."

In a plea bargain, someone who is accused of a crime agrees to plead guilty (sometimes even before indictment) to a particular charge without going to trial in exchange for a concession from the prosecutors. There are a number of reasons why a person may accept a plea bargain, including:

a lesser charge; a lighter sentence; more control over the results (trials can be unpredictable); less financial expenditure; and less publicity. Prosecutors often offer lower sentences or even probation if the accused agrees to testify on behalf of the government against another person, thus perpetuating the vicious cycle of plea bargaining.

In November 2013, the Missouri state appeals court overturned the murder conviction of Ryan Ferguson, who was imprisoned for nearly a decade based on the false testimony of a friend who accepted a plea bargain and agreed to testify against Ferguson in return for a lesser sentence. The friend later recanted his entire confession and testimony, but an innocent man spent almost a decade in prison. Plea bargaining when used to intimidate people to testify falsely is evil and corrupt and cannot be reconciled with the traditional notion of American Justice.

It is so important for prosecutors to play fair that this obligation was embodied in the 1963 Supreme Court ruling *Brady v. Maryland,* which required prosecutors to provide the defense with any exculpatory evidence that could materially affect a verdict. More than fifty years later, too many prosecutors fail to fulfill that constitutional duty—and rarely do courts hold them accountable. In December 2013, Chief Justice Alex Kozinski of the U.S. Appeals Court of the Ninth Circuit wrote, "There is an epidemic of *Brady* violations in the land and only judges can put a stop to this." He further noted, "Some prosecutors don't care about *Brady* because the courts don't MAKE them care."

Today, we have a judicial system where the prosecutor sits at the top of the food chain with unmatched power that is significantly greater than those of the defendant or the defense lawyers.

CHAPTER 7

INSIDER TRADING

*For too long, insider trading law has lacked clarity, generated confusion, and failed to keep up with the times. Without a statute specifically directed at insider trading, the law has developed through a series of fact-specific court decisions applying the general anti-fraud provisions of our securities laws across a broadening set of conduct. As a consequence, the law has suffered—and continues to suffer—from uncertainty and ambiguity to a degree not seen in other areas of law, with elements of the offense defined by—and at times, evolving with— court opinions applying particular fact patterns. The rules of the road have been drawn and redrawn around these judicial decisions, and not always consistently across the country or over time. **Although there have been attempts in the past to codify the law to bring greater certainty and clarity to the offense of insider trading, none has succeeded.** This has left market participants without sufficient guidance on how to comport themselves, prosecutors and regulators with undue challenges in holding wrongful actors accountable, those accused of misconduct with burdens in defending themselves, and the public with reason to question the fairness and integrity of our securities markets.*[9]

So says the executive summary of a January 2020 report prepared by a task force on insider trading. The task force was composed of a "blue-ribbon working group of experts on insider trading." Over the course of twenty-two meticulously researched pages, replete with citations to key cases and academic writings, the task force laid bare the weakness and lack of clarity in insider trading law. The report culminates with a clarion for Congress to repair the broken jurisprudence.

The chair of the task force? None other than Preet Bharara, the very same former U.S. attorney who oversaw and publicly celebrated my prosecution, conviction, and incarceration under the very same laws his task force now assailed. Bharara was not just the chair of the task force—consistent with his notorious hubris, he dubbed this effort that he organized as the "Bharara Task Force." I kid you not. (See Chapter 18)

Bharara was not alone on this task force of hypocrisy. The vice chair was Joon H. Kim, who served as Bharara's right-hand man in pursuing my prosecution. The Bharara Task Force included Joan McKown, the chief counsel of the SEC's division of enforcement who led the SEC's civil litigation against me. And to cap it all off, the Bharara Task Force featured the Honorable Jed S. Rakoff, the federal district court judge who imposed an unprecedented $93 million discretionary civil penalty against me despite unrebutted evidence that the *potential* gain to me personally from the miniscule fraction of a sub-1 percent of my trades at issue was $3.6 million. Rakoff imposed this penalty despite knowing that I was fined $63 million as a criminal penalty. The other members of the task force were all former DOJ or SEC officials with the exception of a sole academic and the complete exclusion of any market participants.

Part of me admires the sheer brazenness of Bharara. He crowed incessantly while serving as the U.S. attorney for securing consecutive convictions of eighty-one individuals for violations of insider trading from 2009 to 2014. One accused portfolio manager committed suicide. Bharara asked the federal judge to sentence me to twenty-four years despite believing the laws were murky.

And having been fired from his position by the incoming Trump administration, Bharara pivots and questions the validity of the very same laws upon which each and every one of these convictions was based. Neither Bharara, Kim, McKown, nor Judge Rakoff voiced any of their apparently deep-seated questions about insider trading law while respectively seeking and imposing historic criminal sentences of incarceration and ruinous criminal and civil sanctions predicated on the same law. Nor did any of these members of the legal watch group speak up when SEC Commissioner Mary Shapiro gloatingly stated in May 2011, shortly after my trial, that "the beauty of insider trading laws is the flexibility in interpreting them." She might as well have said that they could indict any investment professional they wanted to at any time.

The hypocrisy was not, unfortunately, limited to the clubby world of prosecutors, regulators, private defense lawyers, and even the bench, as best exemplified by the Bharara Task Force. Although the DOJ and SEC in particular targeted insider trading in the hedge fund space in response to the 2008 economic crisis, they turned a blind eye to blatant trading improprieties by members of Congress. During the crisis, then Speaker of the House John Boehner, Minority Leader Nancy Pelosi, and other members of Congress were routinely attending top-secret briefings given by Treasury Secretary Hank Paulson. A journalistic expose by the *Washington Post* revealed that "Boehner is one of 34 members of Congress who took steps during the financial crisis to recast their investment portfolios after phone calls or meetings with Paulson, his successor Timothy Geithner, or Federal Reserve Chairman Ben Bernanke. These 34 members (19 democrats and 13 Republicans) changed their positions a total of 166 times within two business days of speaking or meeting with administration officials."[10]

Much later, I was shocked to learn of this. While I was being arrested for insider trading, it was perfectly legal for members of Congress to trade on inside information—and not just one or two trades, but an active series of often daily trades, all designed to protect and enrich themselves and their financial lives. Not one of the thirty-four members were held accountable by any policing or regulatory body. Most ethics experts maintained, however, that these legislators should have refrained from making changes in their financial portfolios when they knew more than the public they represented. "They shouldn't be making these trades" said Richard W. Painter, who had served as the chief ethics lawyer for President George W. Bush. "If this were going on in the private sector or in the executive branch, the SEC would be investigating."[11]

Another study showed that between 1993 and 1998, U.S. senators' average portfolio performance beat the market average by approximately 12.3 percent, a result that would have pleased even top tier hedge fund managers.[12]

The public were largely unaware of any of this until November 13, 2011, when the high-rated TV show *60 Minutes* cast a searing light on the many ways members of Congress took advantage of inside information. One of them, former U.S. Representative Spencer Bachus of Alabama, went so far as to short the market the morning after meeting with officials, and then cashed in his profits within a week. The news segment appeared at a moment when DOJ was intensifying its pursuit of insider trading among hedge fund managers and delivering crushing prison sentences. The report magnified the already intense public media outrage, leaving an embarrassed Congress to pass the STOCK Act of 2012 a few months later. Lawmakers, their staff, and top executive branch officials were banned from knowingly using confidential information gleaned from their legislative roles.

However, the STOCK Act was largely a ruse. It did not specifically prohibit lawmakers from trading stocks in companies whose representatives appear before them. It also did not prohibit them from restructuring their portfolios after briefings with senior administration officials. Congress gave itself yet another free pass. (In fact, even nearly ten years later, lawmakers are actively trading stocks on information that they received in their legislative capacity for personal gain in the middle of a nation-crippling pandemic.)

As laid bare by the Bharara Task Force too, it is an insider's game with one set of rules for lawmakers and a diametrically opposite set for the public they were elected to govern.

THE EVER-CHANGING AND INSTABLE LAW OF INSIDER TRADING

IF YOU ARE NOT A member of Congress—namely, the rest of us—insider trading laws prohibit investors from trading on material nonpublic information (MNPI) in instances where the recipient of MNPI either knew or should have known that an insider breached a fiduciary duty in disclosing the information for a benefit. The problem is that there are no clear or specific definitions of MNPI or the benefit requirement.

Neither the DOJ nor the SEC have taken steps to articulate a clear definition of insider trading—well, at least not when any of the DOJ or SEC officials were actually in power. In fact, they have actively resisted attempts to do so, routinely challenging any of the countless requests by defendants and their attorneys to challenge the legal ambiguities. Why? Murky laws allow prosecutors and regulators maximum flexibility to charge whomever they want using broad interpretations of relatively obscure language.

The ambiguity of insider trading law is a perfect mismatch for the lawful work that hedge fund professionals engage in on a daily basis. It has been a long-standing and accepted precedent that financial professionals are permitted, if not encouraged, to "ferret" out information about publicly traded companies in order to inform trading strategies. Security analysts from both the buy and sell sides routinely talk to corporate officers and other insiders as a normal part of their everyday business. This is not done in secret—on the contrary, the interaction between corporate officers and other insiders and financial professionals is aspirational for most insiders. It is a way for them to share information with the marketplace and encourage investment through the stock market and otherwise in their companies for the benefit of their shareholders; it is consistent with their fiduciary duties. The information may include "nonmaterial nonpublic information" as well as public information to which hedge fund professionals then apply their own analytic ability in order to develop investment thesis and strategies. This is called the "mosaic theory"—it is permissible under the law and the foundation of our publicly traded securities market.

The securities space has evolved with the times and the explosion of information that permeates our broader society. Some thirty years ago, when I began working in the industry, the sources of information were limited.

Times have changed. Public attention to the markets has skyrocketed and the advances in computer and mobile technology have increased the availability of information which, in turn, has spawned a slew of quasi-investment professionals and day traders. In response, a flurry of news items, varied company disclosures, rumors, and disinformation has flooded the once serene and measured marketplace of investment information. Countless televised financial channels including CNBC and Fox Business News routinely discuss rumors relating to public companies. These broadcasts are accessible to all and often feature elaborate detail.

In response, public companies have greatly tightened up their compliance programs. Company executives and employees with access to MNPI are given rigorous training on their fiduciary duties to prevent unwarranted leaks. Lawyers both within the company and from expensive, white-shoe firms police the dissemination of information—MNPI and otherwise—to ensure that no improper information is disclosed. And public companies trumpet these rigorous efforts both to guide their executives and employees and to reassure the marketplace that information being provided by company insiders has been vetted for use by investment professionals.

These steps taken by corporate America to increase compliance were not in any way intended to stifle participation and trading in the stock market. To the contrary, they were taken to increase participation and free insiders to communicate with investors. These steps permitted sophisticated investors to speak freely with insiders with a comfort that the insiders understood their obligations. And this process allowed investors to continue with their lawful work of ferreting out information from as many sources as possible to develop a thesis and pursuant an investment strategy, with greater comfort that information put into the stream of commerce by company insiders was appropriate.

This, of course, does not address rumors in the marketplace about publicly traded companies. Rumors pervade the investment space—they always have and they always will. And investment professionals listen to rumors as additional data points in crafting an investment thesis. Successful professionals can sort the wheat from the chaff; short-lived investment professionals are unable to do so. In this age of information, news and rumors become commodities. These rumors come from all sources—market-focused television programs, investment websites, newsletters, and individuals in the market trying to make a name for themselves.

I, like every other hedge fund portfolio manager, did not turn away information. I listened, considered the source, and considered the logic behind the substantive information. This was how I ferreted out information to create a mosaic. All are strategies squarely endorsed by the federal courts as lawful. Well within the law. I also had an additional advantage—I had the power of my team at Galleon, which conducted rigorous and detailed analysis to pressure test the incremental information that I and others would hear in the course of the day. This was by no means a fly-by-night support staff—I spent approximately $40 million to $50 million per year paying analysts to construct and support investment thesis and work closely with me and the rest of the traders.

We at Galleon were prolific traders, like other similarly driven and strategy-based hedge funds. We made investment decisions based on our long-term prognosis of companies that we studied. We also conducted event-based trading, shaping our positions around quarterly earnings releases and other disclosures or rumors by issuers. We trusted the information that came to us and that we sought out as being lawful. When we learned information from an insider, we presumed that they were authorized by their compliance departments to share. When we were told information by third parties, we assumed that they were either advancing their own thesis (including with some puffing at times) or learned the information legally. Our trades were successful sometimes; other times they were not. But we did not cheat.

The lead prosecutor in my case, Jonathan Streeter, admitted during a Bloomberg Hedge Fund Summit panel discussion on December 5, 2012, (well after my case) that "insider trading laws are confusing to investment professionals. There's incredible confusion on what is or not illegal, and it's a real problem. The law is very complicated and the lines are a bit murky."[13]

A year later, Jonathan Streeter was a partner at a prestigious law firm in New York City.

Back during the early 1980s, Rudy Giuliani, the ambitious U.S. attorney for the Southern District of New York, was quick to see the opportunities to further his career by capitalizing on the public's distrust and envy of financiers. He initiated a series of sensational prosecutions using murky laws and aggressive tactics that led to the demise of investment bank Drexel Burnham Lambert (1990) and the incarceration of junk bond pioneer Michael Milken (1989). But despite the legal concerns about his unethical tactics, the die had been cast and the Giuliani playbook became a blueprint for other ambitious prosecutors to catapult their careers using Wall Street as their launch pad. Examples of cases following this playbook by U.S. attorneys include the prosecution of Martha Stewart (2003) and the public lynching of Frank Quattrone (2002, 2004).

Here's the Giuliani playbook:

O Identify a high-profile target

O Take advantage of murky or confusing laws to craft charges

O Threaten selected colleagues or juniors with prosecution unless they cooperate and agree to testify against the target

O Hold a highly touted and sensational news conference to demonize and humiliate the target well before the defendant has a chance to review the accusations

O Threaten family members with prosecution unless they cooperate

O Constantly leak damaging news about the defendant to the news media

O Threaten the defendants with further charges if he does not capitulate

O Adopt a win-at-all-costs strategy with no regard for facts or the law

Milken assembled a world-class legal team, had unlimited resources, and initially was fully prepared to fight the charges. But even he buckled under the relentless pressure and intense media scrutiny. Eventually he pled guilty to acts that many felt were not criminal.

In 2009, the relatively new and unknown U.S. attorney for the Southern District of New York, Preet Bharara, saw an opportunity to take advantage of the public anger and frustration with Wall Street after the 2008 mortgage crisis. Riding a populist wave against all aspects of corporate life, he went on a crusade against the hedge fund industry.

Inexplicably, he shied away from bringing any criminal cases against the big banks, financial institutions, or their executives—the ones most responsible for the financial crisis of 2008. Instead, Bharara adopted a strategy of attempting to levy heavy fines against these big banks without requiring any acknowledgement of wrongdoing. Business columnist Mike Taibbi focused media attention on the strategy, stating that "Not a single executive who ran the companies that coked up and cashed in on the phony financial boom of an industry-wide scam that involved the mass sale of mismarked fraudulent mortgage securities—has ever been convicted. Their names are, by now, familiar to even the most casual middle American news consumer: AIG, Goldman Sachs, Lehman Brothers, JP Morgan, Bank of America, and Morgan Stanley."[14]

For example, HSBC was accused in facilitating money-laundering schemes valued at almost a trillion dollars of drug trafficking profits. They were allowed to settle with fines of $1.9 billion. Although many of these banks were fined billions of dollars, the management does not pay these fines; the shareholders do. Federal Judge Jed Rakoff, who presided over some of these proceedings, said "if the allegations in these settlements are true, management is buying off cheap from the pockets of their victims."[15]

Although he ignored the complicity of major banks in the financial meltdown, Preet Bharara showed no hesitation bringing criminal charges against the hedge fund industry. Bharara referred to insider trading as if it were capital murder committed by white-collar defendants. He misled the general public and issued over eighty criminal indictments. Why? Why did he do this? The answer is easy: the hedge fund industry is small, employs far fewer people, and has little or no political constituency to defend it.

There appears to be no rhyme or reason why prosecutors go after some with criminal charges and others with civil charges. I never understood the rationale to target 0.01 percent of my total trades as the foundation for an alleged criminal conspiracy. What could justify taking me and therefore Galleon down on criminal charges while other larger hedge funds with larger profits were civilly charged and simply fined?

In the Galleon case, Preet Bharara not only followed the Giuliani play-book, he went well above and beyond. He orchestrated the perp walk, a humiliating experience televised all over the world; used wiretaps for the very first time in a white-collar investigation; and constantly leaked damaging false information about me to the press. I have no issue with law enforcement using wiretaps; however, I believe their use should be justified within the law. In putting together their case against me, the FBI lied multiple times on their sworn affidavit to obtain the wiretaps and then the prosecutors knowingly took snippets of conversation out of context to win rather than as a tool to ferret out the truth (see Chapter 9: Wiretaps and "Reckless Disregard for the Truth"). Judge Richard Holwell characterized the sworn FBI wiretap applications as an affidavit showing "a reckless disregard for the truth," which, in plain language, means "full of lies."[16]

Bharara understood the fine art of manipulating the media to further his political ambitions. He assembled and actively used a well-established PR office. He was ever-ready for multiple appearances on TV and news shows expounding the greed on Wall Street. He was ubiquitous and effective in the short run. He was dubbed the Sheriff of Wall Street. He was hailed as a hero, a savior of the "truth." Bharara's marketing machine was unparalleled. The Justice Department website and the government presentation had been transformed from traditional and staid, a conservative representation of legal business and U.S. attorneys, to an eye-catching clone of MTV. A more ethical prosecutor would have the justice system work in a more dignified and conservative manner. Not Preet Bharara. Bharara held sensationalistic press conferences for just about every Wall Street case even before the defendant had a chance to respond. Bharara won a string of almost eighty convictions with his own novel interpretation of insider trading and found equally novel ways of feeding the media false information. However, it was only a matter of time until sanity began to prevail. With the government's loss in the Mark Cuban trial, it became only a matter of time before judges of the Southern District would begin to rebuke Bharara publicly while also overturning several of his convictions on appeal. By 2013, the tide of Bharara's aspirations had begun to turn.

In 2014, the appeals court not only reversed the conviction of two of Bharara's high-profile convictions, they scolded the "doctrinal novelty of Bharara's approach." In other words, they actually rebuked Bharara of making up his own rules as he was going along.[17] Many more of his convictions are currently on appeal. Soon thereafter, Judge Valerie Caproni of the Second Circuit chastised Bharara of orchestrating a "media blitz" around the prosecution of former New York State Assembly Speaker Sheldon Silver. "There is definitely a sense that Preet is a press hound," said a former SDNY prosecutor. "And there is something to it. There's declining patience on the bench and in the community."

The SEC began investigating Galleon in 2007 based on an alleged "anonymous" letter. They interviewed over twenty Galleon employees and found no evidence of any wrongdoing. Having come to a dead end, the FBI then went after two former Galleon employees: Roomy Khan (whom we had fired ten years prior) and Ali Far, both of whom were caught insider trading at their own firms. The FBI assured Khan and Far that if they were to testify against me, their sentences would be reduced. Ironically, these two cooperating witnesses who were the foundation of the prosecution's initial charge sheet against me proved to be too damaging to the prosecution, who chose not to use their testimony at my trial. Roomy Khan was caught in so many lies that prosecutors were worried about her credibility in front of a jury. Three months before my trial, Ali Far came clean and admitted that he had made it all up. (More details in Chapters 8 and 10, respectively.)

By 2016, Bharara found the shoe on the other foot as he and over a dozen other SDNY prosecutors and FBI agents were sued by David Ganek, a high-profile hedge fund manager at Level Global, a $4 billion hedge fund, for using false evidence and underhanded tactics in their overzealous pursuit of insider trading at Ganek's fund—where no insider trading had even occurred. Rather than dismissing the claims, as usually happens in cases involving prosecutorial misconduct, the judge ruled in favor of granting discovery, a decision that Bharara immediately appealed to the Second Circuit. Bharara ran roughshod over the truth in their war on Wall Street hedge funds. The National Association of Criminal Defense Lawyers wrote that the allegations described in the suit constituted "a serious case of misconduct." They went on to note, "In many respects, this case is extraordinary. It's not every day that the United States Attorney for the Southern District of New York is alleged to be so directly involved in the allegations underlying a civil rights lawsuit." This lawsuit stopped the self-proclaimed Sheriff of Wall Street in his tracks. He did not file a single insider trading lawsuit since. The scale tipped; unfortunately, the tipping came too late for Galleon, and for me.[18]

CHAPTER 8

ROOMY KHAN

In great mysteries and true crime movies, the pivotal, jaw-dropping moment takes place in pin-drop silence as the cold, hard reality of betrayal floods over the many expressions of the villain's face. He realizes he has been betrayed by one of his own co-conspirators. It is the "gotcha" moment. The jig is up. There is a nowhere-to-run moment. For me, there was no such moment.

After reading the government's formal written charges against me upon my arrest, I was baffled. Befuddled. The government, with all its resources, had based its sensational case on the apparent cooperation of Roomy Khan and Ali Far. Roomy Khan? Ali Far? They were inconsequential to any decision we would have made. Two former Galleon employees who had no authority or input into our investments. In fact, they were irrelevant to anything to do with Galleon. These two were the government's star witnesses in criminal and civil proceedings against me.

It became apparent to me that the allegations against me were effectively a Faustian bargain between the FBI and petty felons to ensnare me. Allegations that were made up by a felon whose jig was indeed up, and who traded in with the FBI her association with me in exchange for leniency for herself for her crimes, all of which were unrelated to me.

The foundation of the government's entire case, including the rationale for obtaining the wiretap authorization, was based on the tangential testimony of two people already compromised with the law. And in the days and months that followed, the government's star witnesses inevitably and definitively flickered out.

In the end, having set off a months-long avalanche of drama, neither was called to testify at my trial. The government was too wary of the reality of their respective and compromised histories. But by then the damage had been done. The great tidal wave had been set in motion.

From the very first moment of my arrest, the government trumpeted "evidence" provided by Khan and Far. The media gorged on every word fed by the prosecutors. They got whipped into a frenzy. They absorbed and regurgitated every word to the public. Never once did they stop to confirm accuracy or source.

The glorified and touted narrative: that Khan and Far each operated an extensive web of insider trading contacts at publicly traded companies and they kept me, sitting in the bull's-eyes of their respective webs, supplied with valuable, material, and confidential information.

Bharara delivered a Vanna White-like performance at his press conferences. The first took place within minutes of my arrest. He presented the intricate web of conspiracy to the public through highly stylized and effective diagrams. A picture is a thousand words. He had the picture; the media crafted the words. The intricate web with my face at the center launched a cascade of words. The web was crowded with names and faces of executives in publicly traded companies as well as other investors, all connected to me with arrows. Every arrow pointed straight to me. That image in flashing camera lights was my trial I was judged guilty by press conference, and an image created by U.S. attorney Preet Bharara.

In one fell swoop, Bharara decimated the cornerstone concept of our American system, "innocent until proven guilty." The media parroted every word. The web was woven and the story cast in stone. The press lapped up the drama, recreated its own graphics, and walked along the choreographed path carved out by Bharara's public statements and less public leaks. I was their golden meal ticket to fame and glory.

There was just one problem: none of it was true. And the government knew it.

Our legal team forged a different path. After the initial shock subsided, emotional disbelief and the fog of bewilderment gave way to realistic sobriety. I regained my footing and attacked the problem in the very same way that I approached investing: my legal team and I began to dig into the research and learn everything we could about the charges. I had many compelling reasons to do this, but two overarching reasons fueled the drive forward. First, digging and researching was the only way I knew to ferret out the facts, analyze the information, and understand what had happened. I had to defend myself. Second and importantly, I actually knew very little about Roomy Khan after her brief tenure at Galleon.

THE ROOMY KHAN I KNEW

MY FIRST CONTACT WITH ROOMY Khan was in January 1996. I was at Needham; she was at Intel. She cold called me wanting my input on the competitive dynamics of the microprocessor business—Intel's core business. Her request was not unusual. Sell-side analysts routinely got such calls. I gave her my point of view. Roomy would call every few months to talk about various semiconductor companies. As time went on, she began asking for my opinion on other stocks.

In January 1997, I launched Galleon. Roomy continued to contact me. Periodically, she would send me copies of *Microprocessor Report*, a technical journal that is still published by the Linley Group in Silicon Valley. I enjoyed reading these reports. Sometime late in 1997, Roomy told me she was unhappy at Intel and wanted to work for a Wall Street firm, ideally as a junior semiconductor analyst. She asked for my help with her résumé and in setting up interviews with several brokerage firms on the West Coast. I helped her much like I had helped countless other people in our industry.

By February 1998, Galleon was managing multiple billions in assets. We were expanding our research team. We opened a West Coast office in Santa Clara, the heart of Silicon Valley, with six technology analysts. We wanted our analysts to be physically close to the companies they followed. For me, this was a significant and necessary undertaking.

One may wonder fairly: given our significant investment in our own Galleon research team, why spend time listening to a range of market participants? Simple answer. At Galleon, we set up a core position supported by a long-term thesis about a company's performance. In the short term, we "traded around" those core positions. We based short-term decisions largely on market volatility. We had to understand how other market participants viewed short-term events and rumors. Why? To understand and trade around short-term price movements and to continuously pressure test our longer-term thesis. As investment professionals, our job was continuously to interpret a vast amount of information of varying degrees of reliability. The rumor mill was constant. It was our job to dissect every tendril of information and sort out the misinformation. Sift through volumes of Wall Street chatter. Toss the irrelevant and the speculation. Hold onto and vet the relevant for its actual relevance. Every day. This was our business. And to manage every investment thesis in the context of this cascade of incoming information for both the short and long term.

Roomy proactively reached out to me again. This time, she asked me to give her an opportunity to work at Galleon. Apparently, none of the other opportunities had panned out. On paper, she was a strong applicant—an engineering degree from Columbia University and an MBA from Berkeley. I was confident she would have no problem understanding the technology or the financials of a company. I was much less confident of her work ethic or analytical skill. Believing she was still employed at Intel, I did not call her management for reference. Instead, I asked her to send me a sample of work writing. I reviewed the documents quickly. Her work seemed professional.

In May 1998, we hired Roomy as a junior technology analyst in our West Coast office. At the onset, Roomy appeared to be competent. Within weeks, the professional facade began to fade. In fact, the facade began to crack. Roomy was unable to do the job she had signed up for. She was not process driven. Not disciplined. Not rigorous. She certainly could not conduct the fundamental analysis to any standard expected of our analysts.

She began quickly to fall far short of expectations. Short of an unlikely and significant course correction, it was apparent she would flail. Roomy was not the first person to struggle upon joining us. Others did as well—some rose to the challenge; others did not.

Capacity for rigorous analysis was not Roomy's only shortcoming. She had no capacity to maintain a stated rigorous ethical standard. We soon learned that Khan presented a far more serious concern. She had begun bragging to colleagues on the West Coast about the money she was making on her own behalf using Galleon research. She was actively trading her own brokerage account.

At Galleon, we adhered to a strict policy: staff were not allowed to trade in their own accounts. Ours was no different than most hedge funds and publicly traded companies. We were rigorous in adhering to this policy. Especially given that ours was a business based on trust, it was imperative to avoid real or apparent conflicts of interest with our investors. We encouraged employees to co-invest alongside investors in our funds. Roomy's conduct was a clear violation of our company's personal account trading policy. I should have fired her there and then. This was an error on my part, which is clear now.

On a business trip to the West Coast, I learned about Roomy's active personal trading. I confronted her. She admitted to breaking the policy. There appeared to be no remorse or understanding. Most egregiously, she boasted that by using Galleon's analyses and reports, she had made almost $30 million in her personal account. She seemed completely oblivious to the seriousness of the breach. My reaction was immediate. I fired her. No further questions were necessary. She was out.

But it did not end there. Galleon software analyst Zahra Maher-Skomra, also based at our West Coast office, called me. Zahra had run into Roomy at a technology conference in San Francisco and was surprised to see Roomy wearing a Galleon name tag. She had falsely registered as a Galleon employee. Identifying as Galleon allowed far greater access to management. We found out Roomy was identifying herself as a Galleon analyst at many technology conferences long after she left Galleon. I asked my administrative assistant to inform Roomy to stop misrepresenting her association at Galleon.

After that point, I had no contact with Roomy. In those years, Galleon grew to over 175 employees in five offices with over $5 billion assets under management. We had six distinct investment funds. I had never been busier investing and managing our operations.

In early July 2005, Roomy called me—again, out of the blue.

This time she had a sob story. Once again, she was looking for a job. She had lost all her money in the market. She had a $5 million mortgage on her house and desperately needed to go back to work. I was not surprised. Prior to starting her own company, she had only nine months of experience as a junior analyst at Galleon. My recollection was that she had done very little rigorous investment analysis, preferring instead to engage in idle chitchat.

She asked me for a job. I had no intention of hiring her again. But to get her off my back, I made chitchat about companies she knew and invested in—general questions I ask any investment professional. In the investment world, chitchat about companies is our version of small talk—no different from asking a tennis fan whether he thought Federer could win another Wimbledon or a movie buff for a recent film recommendation. Innocuous.

On July 5, 2005, she proactively sent me the following email:

> As per our [sic] discussion with you, the list of companies I have a decent edge at are INTC, CSCO, MAXIM, PLCM. If you recall from my stay with you, I am hardworking. And I am obsessed with making money. If you give me a break again, I don't think you will be disappointed. I will cover whatever names you would like me to cover. As you know I am obsessed with the business, right now the scale is against me. Want to go and visit more companies/develop better relations which I believe I will be able to do if I am part of Galleon.

The prosecution would allege, via leaks to the press, that Roomy's use of the word "edge" was indeed a call for "inside information." However, those in the investment industry understand "edge" as jargon, a widely used term to describe the rigorous and incisive work done by analysts in the course of their jobs. "Edge" was the equivalent of swimming in a firehose of information, and asking, "Where is the hook?" When analysts presented their stock recommendations at the morning meeting, our leading question was always "what's your edge?" This was to gauge how much work the analyst had done and their level of conviction. And Roomy spoke our language—in this email, which was her audition for a job, she wanted me to know that she, like other finance professionals, had an investment thesis that would add value.

What the prosecution did not tell the public was that on at least two occasions—August 21, 2006, and October 12, 2006—while still looking for a job, Roomy sent emails to two investment firms asserting she had a fairly good "edge" on various companies. She used exactly the same word to others that she used with me. Cleverly, after touting the word "edge" in the press, the government never used that word at my trial. The government's choreographed narrative was set into motion.

This job audition, however, fell flat. I did not hire her. I had no intention to hire her. Now or ever. Full stop.

But Roomy was persistent. Over the next four years, she made and sent phone calls, emails, and instant messages. The further away from contact I went, the harder she tried to stay close. From my perspective, she was desperately trying to keep in touch, whether it was for a job opportunity or to get access to the work of our analysts. The persistence became intense around earnings season. To me, it seemed that her business model was either trading in Wall Street gossip or foraging off other people's work. Even my administrative staff knew her name and knew to keep her away from me.

Here is an example of an IM chain between two Galleon administrative staff:

Admin 1: is raj by u

Admin 2: he's in his brother's office

Admin 1: can u let him know I have roomy on the phone and she needs to speak to him. Let me know if he can take it

Admin 2: ok he said to tell her he is in a mtg. well actually **he said to tell her he's dead** [emphasis added] but I prefer the mtg line"[19]

Much later, I learned that Roomy admitted to the FBI that she would sometimes use *67 to disguise her phone number to try to get through to me. Occasionally, she would get through.

As an investment professional, I regularly spoke to between fifty and one hundred fellow professionals a week—sell-side analysts, salespeople, other portfolio managers, and so forth. Some of these people I talked to daily. Roomy was not one of them.

On any given day, between five hundred and a thousand emails would hit my inbox. Most were on the companies we followed, both internal Galleon analyses and those conducted by other sell-side professionals. It was a figurative blizzard of information daily. Our Galleon team worked together to identify the sound amid the incessant noise. Add to that the drumbeat of IMs and one gets a picture of the intensity of the workday. Khan's persistent emails and IMs were irrelevant to our actual investing decisions.

I have described Khan to have been largely irrelevant to my work at Galleon. She was actually more of a nuisance. Little did I realize exactly how much of a nuisance she would prove to be.

THE ROOMY KHAN I NEVER KNEW: KHAN'S IMPLAUSIBLE TALES

As MY LAWYERS AND I immersed ourselves in the charges against me, I was surprised to find that the government focused its attention on three different companies for which Khan claimed to have provided material, nonpublic information that I utilized in certain trades. I did not specifically remember any of these trades. They were wholly insignificant given the vast number of trades that I initiated and the relatively minor amount at value in these trades. And I certainly had no reason to remember Khan's outreaches to me—simply put, I would never base my trade on information from Khan, especially given the slew of better researched and thought-out analysis available to me.

But the government had identified these three companies and Roomy's description of her outreach to me as proof of illegal trading. The government had no evidence—written, IMs, or recorded calls—to support these allegations. And our job—mine and my legal team's—was to go back, focus on data and evidence rather than simplistic allegations and determine what really mattered. We established that every one of my trades in these stocks was supported by Galleon research and investment plans. In law, they say that documents do not have a character test. Our documents proved my innocence of these charges.

Polycom

The first company in the charging documents on which the government focused was Polycom. Polycom, trading under the symbol PLCM, is a leading video conferencing equipment manufacturer. By year-end 2005, Galleon owned over 1.3 million shares of Polycom, worth over $20 million.[20] The rationale for our position in PLCM was well-documented and our position, significant.

In early January 2006, Roomy called to wish me a happy New Year and segued to ask about my best stock idea. I told her my favorite pick at the time was Intersil (ISIL). In turn, she volunteered hers: Polycom.

Our records further show that on January 9 and 10, 2005, Galleon technology analysts and I attended the Needham Annual Technology Conference. The Needham tech conference remained an excellent forum to get to get the latest updates from companies just before they announced their fourth-quarter results. The Galleon team had scheduled private meetings with the senior management of ninety-five technology companies at the conference. This was reflective of the type of rigorous work we routinely did.

During the second day of the conference, January 10, from 11 to 11:30 a.m., Galleon communications analyst Nat Cohen met one-on-one with Dan Floyd, CFO of Polycom. As our practice, soon afterward, at 11:42 a.m. Nat sent an email to the tech and trading groups with an update on the meeting: "My analysis suggests: Tone on trends in both VoIP and video constructive and don't see similar issues that Tandberg saw this quarter." Nat was articulating his conviction that the trends for Polycom looked positive and that they were not experiencing the soft demand that one of the competitors (Tandberg) had discussed earlier.

Two days later, on January 12, 2006, Thomas Weisel Partners (TWP), a brokerage firm that Galleon did business with, issued its earnings preview on Polycom. Ian Horowitz, my trader, forwarded the preview to me via IM well ahead of that day's market opening:

> TWP reiterates strong buy and $21 target—channel checks indicate key video product shipping earlier and more aggressively than anticipated. Bodes well for Q4 results. Street est. 0.18 and ours is 0.22.

TWP's note was consistent with Nat's written analysis. Based on this information and analysis, I made the decision to increase gradually our position in Polycom going into their earnings release on January 25. If we were correct in our assessment, the company would report stronger results than generally anticipated.

I instructed Ian via IM:

"Buy 60K PLCM"

The records show that on that day, Galleon bought an additional sixty thousand shares of Polycom at $16.65 through TWP.

On January 25, after the market close, Polycom announced results that beat Wall Street's consensus expectations. The stock that had closed at $16.98 per share opened up the next day at $18.98, up 8 percent. We sold some of the additional shares, purchased recently, and locked in profits for our investors.

None of this information—all of which was available to the government—was included in any of the government's charging materials. Instead, they focused exclusively and nonsensically on a string of unsolicited and unanswered IMs:

> 01/09/06 02:47 p.m. Roomy81: do not buy plcm till I het [sic] guidance. Want to make sure guidance ok

01/09/06 05:47 p.m. Roomy81: Hi…

01/10/06 09:58 a.m. Roomy81: hi U there?

01/12/06 10:30 a.m. Roomy81: hi u there?

01/13/06 12:43 p.m. Roomy81: hi mchp [Microchip] what you read

01/17/06 04:16 p.m. Roomy81: raj u the best on intc [Intel]

01/18/06 01:53 p.m. Roomy81: hi

01/19/06 01:30 p.m. Roomy81: Hi call u?

01/19/06 02:21 p.m. Roomy81: Hi anything on SIRF [SIRF Technologies] has come in a lot and acts bad

01/19/06 05:57 p.m. Roomy81: u there?

01/20/06 11:26 a.m. Roomy81: Hi

01/23/06 10:30 a.m. Roomy81: good morning

01/23/06 11:42 a.m. Roomy81: u there

01/23/06 12:58 p.m. Roomy81: roomy@digitalage-llcs.myemailroomy@digitalage-llcs.com

01/24/06 02:09 p.m. Roomy81: hi isil [Intersil]

01/25/06 11:35 p.m. Roomy81: hi[21]

This was a typical example of Roomy persistently pumping me for my thoughts on Intersil, Microchip, and SIRF during earnings season. I ignored all of them. The government was fully aware of this IM. Instead, the government jumped immediately to the next IM that Roomy sent to me, the first and only one to which I actually bothered to reply in this chain:

01/25/06 Roomy81: great call isil

The next day, I responded:

01/26/06 Raj at Galleon: hey thanks for the plcm idea

You cannot change the facts; you can only ignore them. The records make clear that I had a large Polycom position before Khan mentioned it to me as her "best idea." The Galleon records make clear that the additional shares I bought in January were based on Galleon's rigorous research and analysis.

Instead, the government elevated this exchange to form the basis for their allegation that Khan and I conspired to trade illegally in Polycom.

Hilton

The second company the government alleged to be part of an implausible conspiracy between Khan and me was the well-known hotel chain, Hilton Hotels. As with Polycom, there was pivotal background that fully explains the basis for our trading, none of which involved Khan.

Review the Galleon records. The statements alone confirm the facts.

Going into the summer of 2007, speculation of Hilton Hotels (HLT) had already begun. The company was rumored to be a buyout candidate by a private equity group. As early as May 24, 2007, at 8:29 a.m., Citibank sent an email to Galleon and others on Wall Street stating that while "we have no specific knowledge of a deal, we point out: 1. Private market demand for real estate is robust; 2. HLT's valuation is significantly below peers and recent deals in the sector."

Galleon's analyst, Gregg Moskowitz, who followed the company closely, believed that Hilton would be acquired. We began to buy HTL.

By June 30, 2007, Galleon funds owned four hundred seventy-five thousand shares of Hilton for a total value of $15.7 million.[22]

On July 2, 2007, the call options volume for Hilton stock started exploding. Call options are complex, highly levered securities that allow investors to buy a large position for a low investment with the goal of a big payout. A significant increase in options activity indicates that someone out there knows something and that something is expected to happen quickly. On the morning of July 2, a number of brokerage firms made public recommendations for Hilton as a "buy"—including Merrill Lynch, Bear Stearns, Citibank, UBS, and Jefferies. Spurred by both Galleon's research over the past several months and that morning's volume of buy recommendations from leading firms, four of our portfolio managers bought more shares of Hilton.

On the morning of July 3, the day of the buyout announcement, the wires were exploding with Hilton announcements. At 7:23 a.m. Citibank sent an alert: "HTL is at the top of our top 10 largest implied vol 1-day move up." At 8:14 a.m., TheStreet.com (a website that aggregates news) blasted an email: "Jefferies names Hilton Hotel as their top pick of the week. The firm notes recent private equity activity in the group and says the company should command a higher valuation."

During that day's morning meeting, we had a rigorous discussion on Hilton: all aspects of the takeout rumors; the significant increase in call option volume; and a review of all research available to us thus far, including the Street's and Galleon's. By the time the meeting ended that morning, we were all convinced. Our conclusion was simple and straightforward: a buyout was a distinct possibility. The risk/reward ratio for Hilton was attractive. We decided to increase our position in Hilton.

After the meeting, eight of our portfolio managers, including me, bought Hilton shares. By midday, word of an impending private equity takeout of Hilton was catching fire. At 1:04 p.m. Bloomberg News reported that "Hilton's options volume and volatility are elevated as HLT rallies 6 percent." For the day, the options volume on HLT was roughly seven times the average.

At 4:01 p.m., one minute after the market closed, Hilton announced it was being acquired by the Blackstone group for $47.50 per share, at a premium of approximately eleven dollars. I sold the fund's share, making profits for our investors. At 10:18 p.m. that evening, analyst Gregg Moscowitz sent all the portfolio managers the following email: "Awesome, we got lucky."

Of course, it wasn't luck. We had months of analysis supporting our investment thesis. All of it was initiated and backed up by our research team. We had hours of discussion and volumes of documented research supporting our rationale to buy Hilton. The collective depth of Galleon's analysis was remarkable and accurate, and not one shred of this was included in the government's allegations against me.

Instead, the prosecutors took the word of one lonely person, sitting on the periphery of our business and in the isolation of her home, as the basis for Galleon's trading on behalf of our investors.

As it turns out, based solely on what she offered to the government as her recollection, Roomy called before Galleon's July 3 morning meeting to state what was, by that time, the obvious: Roomy was also "hearing rumors of a takeout" at Hilton. Months and volumes of Galleon research and online snippets later, Roomy's message was not "news" by any definition. It was a quick call. I remember speaking to her. But I had no time to humor her that morning. She was stating the obvious and I had a lot to get done that morning. In fact, I did not recall this communication until I read about it in the government allegations. The call was simply not memorable.

Yet again, the prosecutors ignored the facts. They ignored the fact of volumes of already existing research that formed the basis of our thinking on Hilton. They ignored the hours of time spent on HTL during morning meetings. Instead, they substituted an expedient and single data point: a quick, unrecorded call documented in the telephone bill and presented as "irrefutable" evidence. They leaked the call to the press who, in turn, reported unsubstantiated facts in articles, which allowed the public to arrive at their own conclusions. There was no recording of the call. There was no further correspondence between Khan and me. And it would not have mattered if they did have a recording of the call. Our trades were based on hard work and documented analysis by Galleon analysts. The government manipulated the facts to secure their goals.

Google

The third leg of the government's empty allegations involved Google. At that time, Google was the largest and fastest-growing internet company. Galleon internet analyst, Steve Granoff, built his own detailed financial model and projections and did extensive work on the company. He met regularly with

Google management at investor conferences and kept close tabs on the company's business trends.

Galleon's history with Google is well documented and widely available. Galleon invested in Google when it went public in August 2004, and never looked back. Google remained unwaveringly a core position for the firm. We always owned a significant number of shares, and traded around that core position almost every quarterly earnings release. As a large and liquid stock, our strategy was to hold onto that core position for the long term.

At the same time, our Galleon research team noted that Google's share prices moved an average of 5 percent up or down the day after it reported earnings. A consistent 5 percent move up or down was a strategic opportunity to trade around a core position and lock in gains for our investors. In fact, over the prior twelve months, we had traded almost a billion dollars' worth of Google stock ($979.6 million, to be exact). In the second half of 2007, we began preparing for Google's second-quarter earnings report on July 17.

As of June 30, 2007, Galleon owned one hundred twenty-five thousand shares of Google (a $70 million position). The stock was at $525.

On July 11, at 7:11 a.m., Steve Granoff sent the following internal IM:

"My near-term target is 550 and would buy the stock if it pulls back to the $500 level."

$550 per share would have been Google's all-time high. On July 13, 2007, when the stock price approached my price target, I sent an IM to my trader, Ian Horowitz:

"Sell all the Google when it hits our price target of $550."

Ian sold all one hundred twenty-five thousand shares at $551.25 per share. Since Granoff had indicated that he would buy the stock if it were to pull back to the $500 level, we shorted the stock at around $550 with the goal of buying back at $500 per share.

A few days later, on July 15, 2007, at 7:35 a.m., Granoff put out his usual quarterly earnings preview on Google: The "near term risk/reward unfavorable (thinking $15 up/$40 down). Unwilling to take the speculative long into print. Prefer add close to $505-520."

Translation: Granoff believed it was unwise to own shares prior to the earnings announcement ("long into the print") but thought it would be a good buy if share price were to decline to between $505 and $520. I agreed with his thinking. I shorted more.

On July 19, 2007 Google reported after market close. Earnings fell short of Wall Street's expectations. The stock began to drop. I covered my short position between $510 and $528 and bought shares long at $507, following exactly the game plan outlined by Steve Granoff.

In its allegations, the government did not mention a word of our months-long strategy for our trades in Google. They ignored our rationale around core positions and trading around core positions. We provided them with all the access to these records. As with the other stocks, they did nothing. They did not interview any of the Galleon employees immediately involved in the analyses supporting our investing. And they certainly did not appear to understand the volume of research which substantiated the bulk of our investment theses. Our research was the lifeblood of our work and the prosecution chose to ignore almost the entirety of it. Instead, what did they do? They marched ahead with their charges based solely on Roomy's (desperate) allegations.

The government relied solely on an allegation from Khan that she had called me on July 17, 2007, to inform me she was hearing from Google investor relations that they were having a tough quarter. Again, I had no recollection of any such call and there was no recording. I had no idea whom her investor relations contact was. And in any event, these people are trained to provide lawful information to investors and analysts. Even if I had spoken to Khan, none of it would have influenced my trading—I relied on the hard work of my Galleon team. But yet, with no evidence other than Roomy's word, the prosecutors charged me with insider trading on Google.

In every instance, including Google, of the government's allegations about my "conspiracy" to commit insider trading with Roomy Khan, the pattern was clear: the government ignored the fact of our intensive research and plowed ahead with theirs. So why did the government land where it did and follow this implausible theory? To understand that, one has to understand—as I learned after my arrest—about the government's love of the cooperating witness. Roomy was the government's first cooperating witness against me. They say that Helen of Troy was the face that launched a thousand ships. Well, Roomy Khan's "cooperation" are the lies that launched a thousand careers. And, as we would soon learn, she was a very special cooperator, unlike any other.

SOMETIMES, YOU CAN ALSO SHOOT THE MESSENGER

HAD THE GOVERNMENT DEMONSTRATED DILIGENCE, it was not only the emptiness of Roomy Khan's "message" to the government that would have crumbled under scrutiny. As we uncovered almost immediately after my arrest, Khan was a deeply flawed "cooperator" with an unsavory history. This is not the usual name-calling in the criminal process to which government witnesses are often subjected; the government violated virtually every standard it applies to crediting a witness testimony in choosing to prioritize her word over the Galleon research. Dowd, who like all of us was astonished by what was uncovered about Khan, liked to refer to her as a "human crime wave." On this one count, he was not far off.

First, a word about the cooperation process and what it means to be a cooperator in the Southern District of New York. The government divides its witnesses into two broad categories: pure fact witnesses and cooperating witnesses. Pure fact witnesses are just that: individuals who have firsthand knowledge about events and/or conversations relevant to the government's prosecution. They are not believed to have any criminal exposure or role in the alleged crime themselves.

A cooperator is also in fact a witness who claims to have firsthand knowledge about information relevant to the government's prosecution. However, a cooperator is a fact witness whom the government also believes was involved in the commission of the alleged crime and therefore could be a criminal defendant themselves if not for their willingness to help the government prosecute others.

The government builds the overwhelming majority of its cases on the backs of such cooperating witnesses. The time-honored strategy of prosecutors is to utilize small fish to take down the big fish. In this regard, the government followed in its mind its playbook in cultivating Khan's cooperation against me. I was the big fish. In other words, the prosecution of me was a media headline; any prosecution of Khan, the smaller fish, would not burnish anyone's reputation.

What does the government require of a cooperator? Although the precise standards differ from DOJ office to office around the country, the Southern District standards are well-known and self-proclaimed to be nonnegotiable. In order to be accepted as a "cooperator," a witness with exposure must volunteer to the government all of his or her wrongdoing from the beginning of time. Witnesses "proffering," a legal term for auditioning to be a cooperator, are required to share any and all incriminating information about themselves and then if believed, to share any and all incriminating information in their possession about others. They are required to provide all hard evidence—recordings, cell phones, computers, documents—that are even possibly relevant. They are not allowed to be selective when providing evidence to protect friends or family from government scrutiny and even prosecution. And they are required at all times going forward to be completely honest and candid.

If the government accepts that the individual is being honest, fully forthcoming, and has valuable information that may lead to the arrest of others, the government will offer him or her a cooperation agreement. Under this arrangement, the government typically requires the witness to plead guilty to certain counts to record their admitted wrongdoing. The witness must then be available at the government's beck and call to prepare with the government and, if called upon, provide testimony at trial against others. If the witness fulfils his or her obligations, the government agrees to provide to the court at sentencing a letter describing the witness's bad acts but also the assistance that has been provided to the government. As a practical matter, these letters are worth their weight in gold. The judges in the Southern District, most of whom are former prosecutors, understand that the justice system relies on securing cooperation from witnesses and rarely sentence cooperating witnesses, especially in white-collar cases, to any jail time.

The stakes for a cooperator to be honest are high. As the government routinely represents to judges and juries, cooperators are held to the very highest standard. Any intentional untruth and failure to conduct themselves beyond reproach, no matter how small, results in a ripping up of the cooperator agreement by the government. That means no letter to the sentencing judge and therefore likely no reduction in sentence. No ability to withdraw the guilty plea. And no second chances. The government idealizes cooperation as the complete and total turning of the page, leaving any criminality or dishonesty behind. It is precisely this high standard imposed by the Southern District that makes their cooperating witnesses bulletproof—incredibly hard for a defendant's lawyers to impeach at trial.

It was this high standard that the government certified about Khan when electing to enter into a cooperation agreement with her and immediately deploy information to bring charges against and arrest me.

The government could not have been more wrong about Roomy Khan. As just a little bit of digging by our lawyers and investigators showed, Khan violated every standard that the Southern District proudly claimed. And she did it with panache.

In our post-arrest research, I spent more time reading about Roomy than I could ever have imagined. We learned through our hard work, publicly available information, and FBI interviews that Roomy started Digital Age, her own hedge fund managing her own money, which was based out of her house in Atherton, California. When money was good, Roomy lived well, sustaining a voracious taste for the high life. Public records show that Roomy bought a house in Atherton for $10 million and a Ferrari that cost over $200,000. She also collected art and bought expensive jewelry.

We also learned that Khan had an arrogant mean streak. At Digital Age she had just one employee—a relative named Rohit Malik. After a quarrel with him, moved by a nasty bit of spite, Roomy reported Malik to the immigration authorities, exposing him for having overstayed his visa.

Roomy, however, ran afoul of securities laws before joining Galleon. We learned from court filings in California that her prior employer Intel had brought in the FBI to address suspicions about Roomy's illegal conduct while she was still employed at Intel. The FBI investigated her covertly. In the fall of 2000, almost two years after Roomy had left Intel, the FBI confronted Roomy about her illegal trades in Intel stock.

Roomy first vigorously denied then acquiesced to the accusations of insider trading while still at Intel. Fearful of going to jail, she agreed to cooperate with the FBI. For Roomy with the California prosecutors, cooperation involved implicating others in her quest for leniency. I became her target. Roomy told the investigators she had passed Intel information on to me, and to Choo-Beng Lee, who was then a sell-side semiconductor analyst at John Hancock. Covertly, the FBI did a thorough investigation of me and my firm's trading of Intel stock. After an exhaustive analysis using trading data from our prime brokers, the FBI found no wrongdoing by me or Galleon. They dropped their investigation. Roomy's first effort to entrap me failed. This was all to my amazement; I had no idea of any of this.

The government did enter into a cooperation agreement between the California U.S. Attorney's Office and Khan. As part of that agreement, Khan pled guilty to trading on confidential Intel internal information for her own benefit. The government, crediting her cooperation and believing that she had turned over a new leaf of lawfulness, wrote a letter on her behalf at sentencing. Khan avoided any prison time, as is the norm for cooperators. Instead, she was fined $120,000 and given six months of house arrest and a three-year probation.

The prosecutors in California kept this whole investigation and the subsequent conviction under seal from the public (although not from their fellow prosecutors in the Southern District).

As part of our discovery process in 2010, we sought an order from the California court to get the records from 2001 unsealed. We found that in those sentencing documents, the government stated that "Based on the information obtained to date, Rajaratnam cannot be tied to illegal insider trading connected to the Intel information."[23]

Roomy's lies were exposed. But only to the prosecutor.

The court documents also stated that Roomy's plea agreement in 2001 included her assertion that "I will not reveal my cooperation or any information related to anyone without the prior consent of the government; I will participate in undercover activities under supervision of law enforcement agents or the U.S. Attorney's Office." She also agreed "not to commit or attempt to commit any crimes…"[24]

And also, for inexplicable reasons, the file was sealed under a name misspelled as K-A-H-N, not K-H-A-N. For what purpose?

I had no idea that I was even in a position to be exonerated or named in a file that was kept hidden under a misspelled name and sealed for possible use at a later, undefined time.

Far from walking the straight and narrow, Khan once again reverted to engaging in criminal conduct related to trading in her personal account. As we would later learn, Khan developed a network of contacts in Silicon Valley, where she lived and worked. And in the absence of any capacity for conducting rigorous research, this network constituted her lifeline to profitmaking and kept her hooked, like a drug, on inside information—both nonpublic and material. Roomy used this information to trade for her own accounts and to maintain her exorbitant, lavish lifestyle. Less than ten years earlier, before she discovered Wall Street, she was making less than $100,000 per year as a midlevel analyst at Intel.

In August 2007, while doing a routine review of possible suspicious trading in the aftermath of the Hilton buyout, Roomy Khan's name stood out. The SEC and FBI were familiar with Roomy Khan and began yet another investigation. This time, they followed the money trail. They determined that soon after the Hilton transaction, Roomy Khan had wire transferred $15,000 to Deep Shah, an analyst following the hotel sector at Moody's Investor Service. Deep Shah was actively involved in the Hilton transaction. Roomy's outsized trading in Hilton and the coincidental transfer of money alerted the prosecutors.

On November 20, 2007, two FBI agents—BJ Kang and Kathleen Queally—approached Roomy Khan at her house in Atherton. Khan's response followed the same blueprint as before: first, she denied receiving any inside information on Hilton. As she comically said, she bought Hilton because Paris Hilton was arrested and the resulting publicity would benefit Hilton's stock! When presented with the facts of her contact with Moody's and irrefutable evidence of telephone records with and payment to Deep Shah, Roomy quickly reversed course. She offered to cooperate. She agreed to help them ensnare others, including me. FBI records show that Roomy identified her inside sources and pointed fingers at several portfolio managers at other funds. Once again, I was the highest profile target in her orbit.

Here, responsible prosecutors who followed their own standards would have immediately rejected this overture. In the language of prosecutors, Khan fit the mold of a classic "ailed cooperator—one who had received the benefit of prior cooperation in return for her promise to live lawfully and had reneged on that promise. The government never provides a failed cooperator with a second bite at the cooperation apple. To do so would be anathema to the integrity of the cooperation process.

Unless you offer up Raj Rajaratnam and Galleon. Which Khan did.

As part of her second and wildly illegitimate round of secret plea bargaining, Roomy agreed to make "consensual calls" to try to entrap me once again with some type of inside information exchange. A consensual call is one in which one party (in this case, Roomy) gives consent for the FBI to listen and record the call; meanwhile, the other party (me) has no idea anyone else is in on the conversation. The FBI's ultimate goal was to wiretap my phone. But for them to get authorization to do so, they needed to demonstrate both probable cause and necessity, as the next chapter will discuss. The goal of the consensual calls was to demonstrate probable cause.

On three different recorded consensual phone calls made between January and March 2008, Roomy tried to get me to talk about Intel, Xilinx, and Broadcom. While I do not know exactly what coaching FBI Agent Kang gave Roomy for those particular calls, as testimony from my trial would later reveal, he had given instructions to other cooperative witnesses to "use any tactic" necessary, including lying to entrap me.[25] How could I have engaged in insider trading with no investment position in any of these stocks and also, I did not trade these stocks subsequently? Kang was fully aware I had no investment position and chose to ignore this fact in order to forge ahead with the case. He purposefully omitted this fact in his wiretap appeal. (See Chapter 9: Wiretaps and "Reckless Disregard for the Truth.")

Kang personally led the posse of agents who came to arrest me on October 16, 2009. The potential of ensuing fame and certainty of career enhancement was too alluring to pass up. While many FBI agents are hard-working, honest, and principled professionals, Kang was part of a corrupt strand of the FBI.

Having played the government in California and still been afforded a second chance to cooperate, Khan demonstrated no restraint. While committing to being fully transparent and honest (again) with the government to pursue cooperation, Khan again charted her own deceitful course. While she was working as an informant for the FBI and professing her honesty and complete candor, Roomy secretly bought a cell phone in the name of her gardener. She did so for a very specific purpose, again toxic to cooperation efforts. Aware that the government might be tracking her normal phone about which they knew, Khan used the secret cell phone to warn some others that they were under investigation.

Deep Shah fled to his native India after being tipped off by Khan. Shah, charged criminally and sued by the SEC, remains a fugitive to this day. Roomy also deleted incriminating emails from her boss at Trivium Capital, where she was a consultant. Both of these actions violate every standard insisted upon typically by the government. Under any normal circumstance, such misconduct would have further disqualified her from being signed up by the government as a cooperating witness. Moreover, tipping off others about an ongoing investigation is grounds for a separate prosecution for obstruction of justice.

Roomy was equally dishonest and deceptive in her personal affairs. After being sued by her former housekeeper for unpaid overtime, Roomy fabricated an employment contract and forged the housekeeper's signature.

When deposed under oath, under the penalty of perjury, Roomy repeatedly lied about the forged document. Caught lying by the court, Roomy settled with her housekeeper out of court.

Yet the government turned a blind eye to each and every one of these otherwise disqualifying actions by Khan. Apparently, the promise of being able to secure a wiretap based on her distorted information—the first of its kind to be sought in a white-collar securities context—was too alluring. And the ability to charge me with all the pomp, circumstance, and headlines was also too much to forego for the sake of principles.

The government was confident we would not uncover what we did. When we did, it merely pivoted and built its case without calling Khan to the witness stand to protect its case from being tarnished with her lies and its cooperation process from being cheapened by their untenable compromises.

REFLECTIONS

The FBI was well aware of Roomy Khan's serial criminal history. Multiple counts of insider trading. False accusations and lies. Forgeries. And obstruction of justice. Yet, over several years and on multiple occasions, they continued to use the same tainted source to initiate surveillance and full-blown investigations targeting me. Having mined the source and consistently coming up empty, intoxicating the public with their insinuations and innuendoes, they marched ahead, undeterred.

The Polycom accusation was especially frustrating. It was the pivot point SEC attorney Andrew Michaelson used to turn the case from a routine regulatory investigation into a full-scale criminal case. Roomy's IM (1/9/06 2:47p.m.) telling me not to buy the stock until she got guidance became the smoking gun to launch a full-fledged criminal investigation against me based entirely on the testimony of a twice-failed cooperating witness and completely ignoring the extensive research conducted on these companies, which both the SEC and FBI had in their files. The used information trumpeted as "evidence" to implicate me. Never mind that I did not reply to the message. And never mind that I saw it well after the Needham conference.

And most importantly, Michaelson ignored the fact that I did the exact opposite of what Roomy said to do on her IM—I bought additional shares of Polycom on 1/12, 1/17, 1/19, and 1/24.

During his closing arguments at my trial, John Dowd would forcefully make this point: "What is missing is any call between Roomy Khan and Raj after she spoke with Sunil Bhalla [then senior vice president and general manager at Polycom]. There is no call between Khan and Raj. All you see is one-way instant messages that say "hi are you there?" That is the entire content of the instant message. No inside information and no response from Raj and no phone call. Absolutely no evidence that Raj and Khan spoke. None."

Characteristically, the press chose to go along with the prosecution's narrative, parroting their line: "Investigators found that Rajaratnam and Khan had called each other frequently after the IM exchange and begun trading heavily in Polycom stock."[26]

I often wondered why John Dowd did not call Roomy to the stand to expose her character. It would have demonstrated the kind of person the government used to bring charges against me. Despite my numerous suggestions, John never did call Roomy as a hostile witness.

As for her own charges, while Roomy's sentencing guidelines called for eight to ten years, the judge sentenced Roomy to a simple one year in prison. Even though she had provided the prosecutors with assistance, the judge said that her actions, particularly lying to federal investigators, were serious enough to warrant at least some jail time. Roomy's last words in court were: "I've lost all my money, and my education is rendered useless. I have been ostracized by most of my family and friends and I lead my life as a pariah in isolation."

In retrospect, I wonder why I ever responded to Roomy when she contacted me five years after I had fired her from Galleon. Time had passed and she was going through hardship. I had no intention of hiring her again, but if she called, I had no issue with chatting with her sporadically. When other former employees of Galleon called, I would chat with them. Had I known she was a convicted felon, I would never have chatted with her. I was blind to the extent of her total disregard for the law on the decisions she made either professionally or personally.

This was the Roomy Khan I did not know.

I sat squarely at the intersection of a triad made up of

1. A serial criminal who made repeated false allegations to save her skin. Roomy Khan craved the high life like a drug, entirely unsupported by a mediocre analytical skill set. Her craving was insatiable and she knew it. She relied on the only means and sources for her temporary "fixes:" pumping corporate insiders and other investors for information.

2. A corrupt strand of the FBI—BJ Kang—who made repeated false allegations in his sworn affidavit to obtain wiretap authorizations and willfully chose to ignore the facts. Like Roomy, he wanted the glory and without the facts to support him. The judge called his sworn affidavit "full of reckless disregard for the truth." When law enforcement is allowed to lie in sworn affidavits with impunity, it speaks volumes about how the Justice Department operates.

3. An ambitious rooky U.S. attorney, Preet Bharara, blinded by the potential fame and resulting adulation of his first high-profile case. Bharara sensationalized fiction into facts and underhandedly leaked to the press information taken completely out of context. Later on, in a moment of rare reflection, Bharara would say on reflection "the insider trading cases did nothing change our lives but enhanced our reputations."

Hubris or repentance?

Whatever the case, the collateral damage from this "perfect storm" of characters was enormous.

Roomy Khan and her lies constituted the launch pad of the Galleon take-down. The launch pad was a house of cards that brought down the lives of eighty-one other people, ruining careers and livelihoods. Yet again, another eerie reminder of the infamous words of the most influential of Stalin's KGB chiefs, Lavrentiy Pavlovich Beria, who said, "Show me the man and I will show you the crime."

Although the public has only recently become acutely aware of "fake news" and the Deep State, it was alive and well and in covert operation during the Galleon case.

TIMELINE

August 1995—Roomy Khan joins Intel

January 1996—Khan cold calls Raj at Needham

January 1997—Raj starts Galleon

Late 1997—Khan expresses dissatisfaction at Intel and asks for help finding a job on Wall Street

April 1998—Khan fired from Intel for illegally trading on Intel stock

May 1998—Khan joins Galleon's West Coast office as a junior technology analyst. Galleon unaware of Roomy Khan's firing from Intel

February 1999—Khan fired from Galleon for violating firm trading policy

June 1999—Khan launches Digital Age with her own funds

2000—FBI approaches Khan about her trading of Intel stock while employed at Intel. Roomy pleads guilty and targets Galleon. Roomy is sentenced to six months house arrest, fine of $120,000, and three years of probation

2001—After thorough investigation using prime brokerage data, Galleon investigation is dropped

November 2007—FBI approaches Khan about insider trading in several technology stocks. Khan agrees to cooperate again in exchange for leniency. She points directly to Galleon and other portfolio managers. Roomy Khan trades with the FBI on the basis of her acquaintance with Raj in exchange for leniency for herself

January 2008—Roomy makes consensual calls to Raj to attempt to entrap him again

August 2008—FBI agent files false affidavit to obtain wiretaps authorization on Raj's cell phone

CHAPTER 9

WIRETAPS AND "RECKLESS DISREGARD FOR THE TRUTH"

My criminal prosecution achieved a number of firsts. It was the first prosecution in which the government packaged a series of wholly unrelated trades in different companies as part of its case. It was the first prosecution in which the government alleged that an entire financial institution was somehow corrupt without ever engaging with its counsel prior to bringing charges. And, most painfully, it was the first insider trading prosecution in which a defendant was sentenced to eleven years of prison, ordered to pay a forfeiture of $53 million, and forced to pay SEC treble damages of over $90 million.

But first among these and other firsts in my case was the use by the government of telephonic wiretaps in order to build their insider trading case. Intended for use against the mafia and other violent and secretive organized crime entities, Title III had never before been deployed in pursuit of a white-collar case involving a financial institution. I would be the federal government's guinea pig as it sought to break new ground with use of this investigative tool in a purely commercial case. And it was the issue that dominated my prosecution and my subsequent appeals. It was, to say the very least, the wildest of wild rides.

A BRIEF HISTORY OF WIRETAPS

As a matter of critical background, there is no dispute that wiretapping—the act of the government surreptitiously listening in on and recording phone calls between private parties—strikes against the very core American principle of respect for individual privacy and liberty. It also is inherently a departure from the concept of limited government as it marks the government's unfettered intrusion into the lives of its citizens.

For this very reason, Congress struggled mightily when debating whether or not to grant the federal government authority to wiretap its own citizens for law enforcement purposes. And the context in which Congress took up this issue and ultimately granted limited permission to the government was a far cry from the context around my prosecution.

By 1967, organized crime had evolved into a pervasive and violent feature in American life, led by the now-legendary efforts of the Italian mafia, or La Cosa Nostra. These gangs, ruthless and notoriously vicious, extended their reach and their criminal enterprises by imposing a culture of secrecy, fear, and silence among their members. They were an "organization" unlike traditional commercial enterprises, maintaining few if any paper records and consistently trying to avoid any surveillance by the government. This organization threatened its members and associates with violence if they spoke of the gang activities to anyone or even acknowledged its existence or their involvement.

The inherently violent and criminal nature of these organized groups often stymied traditional law enforcement efforts and tools. As has been widely described in news accounts and depicted in television and film, these crime organizations took great pains to insulate themselves from any disclosures of their illicit activities. They established ostensibly legal businesses to disguise their criminality, engaged in wholly unrelated commerce to serve as a front. Simultaneously, organized crime leadership proudly defied any overtures by law enforcement, issuing blanket denials and refusing any requests for information. On a parallel track, these organized crime entities brutally enforced an edict of resistance with law enforcement efforts, leading with murder and brutal physical assault of any perceived cooperators to any future cooperation.

This code and rigid discipline stymied law enforcement. The largely unimpeded criminality of these organizations spread throughout the '30s, '40s, and '50s, hollowing out civil society in many areas. The increasingly public acts of violence grew impossible to ignore and Congress was forced to fashion a solution to break the code of silence and opaqueness of these criminal organizations.

In the late 1960s, the government proposed a solution. In response to this very specific problem of organized crime, the DOJ asked Congress to grant it the authority to conduct electronic surveillance of mobsters by secretly listening to their telephone calls. Wiretapping, in the popular vernacular. The DOJ had determined that working with the American telephone companies, it could access, listen to, and record conversations between telephone customers unbeknownst to the customers. This would be a powerful and fail-safe way around the barriers that organized crime had erected to avoid detection of their criminality.

There was just one problem. Wiretapping would mark a virtually unprecedented intrusion into the basic American principle and right of privacy. And in the throes of the social upheaval of the '60s, this move for greater government intervention in public life was even more controversial. As the Supreme Court had warned as late as 1967, "few threats to liberty exist which are greater than that posed by the use of eavesdropping devices."[27]

After a lengthy and vigorous debate, Congress fashioned a compromise, one that balanced the government's desperate need to combat the violence of organized crime against the privacy interests of the public. Congress passed the Omnibus Crime Control and Safe Streets Act of 1968. In Title II of the Act, Congress granted law enforcement the authority to utilize wiretaps as an investigative tool. But only under very narrow circumstances.

Congress through the Act made clear that wiretaps were to be available to the government only as a last resort, rather than a first choice, in fighting crime. To do so, Congress required by statute stringent conditions to be met prior to their use. Unlike a normal search warrant, Title III requires the government to provide 1) a "full and complete" statement of the facts and circumstances relied upon by the applicant "to establish probable cause," and 2) a "full and complete statement as to whether or not other investigative procedures have been tried and failed or why they reasonably appear unlikely to succeed if tried or to be too dangerous."[28] This representation by the government was required by Congress to be presented to a sitting District Court judge for review, consideration and if appropriate, approval. The consequences of failing to heed this admonition are severe: *Evidence resulting from an improperly obtained wiretap is prohibited from use at trial.*

Congress enacted Title III and its tightly circumscribed conditions for approval in direct response to the government's stated purpose of combatting highly secretive and often violent criminal organizations. In particular, Congress insisted on the requirement that the government demonstrate a "full and complete statement as to whether or not other investigative procedures have been tried and failed or why they reasonably appear unlikely to succeed if tried to be too dangerous." This stringent requirement honored the political and public policy concerns surrounding Title III's enactment. Namely, the necessity requirement, as this provision has since been named, obligated the government to represent that traditional, less intrusive investigative techniques had been tried and had failed, thereby showing an authorizing judge that there were no other investigative approaches available to the government. In other words, the government had to represent faithfully that the wiretap was a last resort, reflecting the failure of traditional investigative methods.

Moreover, the DOJ established a check to ensure that wiretaps were sought only in cases that met Title III's exacting requirements. No DOJ branch office was permitted to seek authorization for a wiretap independently. Instead, a DOJ branch office was required as a matter of internal policy to first seek approval from Main Justice (another reference for DOJ Headquarters in Washington, D.C.) even to submit a request for authorization from a district court. Such an application was required to include a draft sworn affidavit from a federal law enforcement agent that laid out probable cause to show that the phone in question was believed to be used in criminal conduct and representations that a wiretap was necessary because other investigative techniques had been tried and failed or were obviously futile.

In in the Southern District of New York in particular, the government had developed a clear checklist for seeking wiretap authorization that tracked the necessity requirements and a boilerplate application that reflected this checklist. For the necessity section of an application, the government represented that it had failed in its efforts to secure evidence through specific traditional law enforcement techniques: subpoenas for relevant documents, routine surveillance, and/or interviews of their targets or other relevant people.

In the four decades since the passage of Title III, the government routinely asked District Court judges for such authority in organized crime cases and other narcotics investigations and others involving violence with near complete success. Partially, the policy allowed for Main Justice to pre-vet applications for probable success as well as to weed out weak applications. Partially, the policy also served as a check to District Court judges who were known rarely to deny applications. The policy most importantly allowed Main Justice to advise prosecutors of fatal weaknesses in their applications and encouraged prosecutors to withdraw and strengthen applications that were deficient.

And for the overwhelming lion's share of organized crime and narcotics cases for which wiretap authorization was sought, the necessity requirement was the most minor of speedbumps—if that—in the process. Of the more than nineteen thousand wiretap applications submitted from 2005 to 2012 (almost all for organized crime and drug trafficking cases), all but six were approved. This makes sense. The government can always represent that it would be fruitless to serve a document subpoena on a mafia family or a narcotics organization. Such records are not maintained by organizations that were engaged in fundamentally criminal enterprise. Similarly, it was challenging, if not impossible, to conduct meaningful surveillance of such organizations because of the danger implicit in trying to do so. And finally, the government had little difficulty in explaining why interviewing a suspect involved in an organized crime or narcotics investigation was fruitless. No one would admit to the conduct being investigated because it is inherently illegal—be it narcotics or violence. And seeking to interview a suspect would almost certainly lead him or her to share this information with others in their inherently illegal ventures to warn them of the government's awareness of their illicit ventures.

THE WIRETAP APPLICATION AGAINST ME

FAST FORWARD TO MY ARREST on October 16, 2009. Bharara's press strategy celebrated the fact that this was the very first of its kind, in which wiretaps were used to prosecute a white-collar insider trading case. The criminal complaint—and of course Bharara's press conference and press leaks—highlighted snippets of recorded conversations from the wiretap that on first glance seemed damning without any context or completeness. But such was the power of wiretaps.

Left unsaid in Bharara's self-congratulatory press junket is that there is a very good reason *why* wiretap authorization had never before been approved in a circumstance such as this. One can say many things about me and one can say many things about Galleon—but I was not a Mafia don (although my friends tease me about looking like a Tamil film villain) and Galleon was not an organized crime operation. Galleon was not a "front" for unlawful business—we were, as advertised, a fully operational hedge fund, pursuing numerous legal investment strategies on behalf of our numerous institutional and individual investors.

Unlike the cloak of secrecy and violence shrouding the organized crime families for whom the wiretaps were intended, Galleon was registered with the SEC and heavily regulated. The SEC conducted numerous audits and inquiries into our operations and we were always a proverbial open book, answering all questions and providing all requested materials. Moreover, we took the unusual step of allowing our investors open access to our standing 8:30 a.m. team meetings at which we discussed our best trading ideas and strategies. My philosophy was that our investors were our partners and since they entrusted us with investing their hard-earned funds, we had an obligation of transparency to them.

We were protective of our trading strategies and positions when it came to the outside world. We considered these ideas our proprietary information—the product of painstaking analysis, expensive outside research and data services, and hours of mental sweat equity. Although I and my colleagues talked often with a wide range of market participants to hear other ideas and to pressure test our premises, we were always guarded about the magnitude of our positions and our prospective trading. Given the size of the positions we took based on our assets under management, we had to be mindful of our strategies getting out into the market and undercutting our intended trading. As a result, we all spoke carefully to outsiders when we spoke about stocks and ideas, often reminding them to keep our discussions confidential.

But the threat of violence against potential witnesses, whistleblowers or other market participants? Please. We at Galleon considered ourselves lovers, not fighters. Well, at least traders, analysts, and quants, not fighters. To be more serious, after the most intrusive investigation into our business practices by the government, there was never once a suggestion of any threats or force. Nor could there have been.

So while Bharara and the government celebrated their use of wiretaps against us, my lawyers were baffled as to how the government had secured such authorization. My lawyers pressed and were able to accelerate the government's production of the 2008 wiretap application to the District Court, which had been made over a year prior to my arrest. The application had been submitted to the court for review and approval under seal and ex parte. The court, as it does in every case, relies on the government's obligation to make only truthful and complete representations to it.

But when we reviewed the application—including Agent Kang's affidavit—as to both probable cause and necessity, we were stunned. The application was severely flawed. Actually, that is an understatement. Agent Kang, with the assistance of the federal prosecutors in charge, intentionally misrepresented to the reviewing District Court judge crucial facts omitted others regarding both probable cause and necessity, the two prerequisites for the grant of wiretap authority. These were not minor details that may have been honest misunderstandings or misinterpretations—the falsity of the application was pervasive.

PROBABLE CAUSE

THE FIRST SECTION OF THE application contained the government's representations as to probable cause. For a wiretap application, the government was required to show that it was more likely than not that the specific phone being targeted had been used in recent times for communications in furtherance of a federal crime. In this instance, the government relied on the proactive cooperation of Roomy Khan to show probably cause. As we learned, the government had instructed Khan to make consensually recorded calls to me on my cell phone, which the government then recorded. Khan had apparently told the government that the recorded call cited was a part of a scheme between Khan and I to engage in insider trading by sharing MNPI.

Now, the government is not required to prove its case beyond a reasonable doubt in order to secure wiretap authorization. It must only show enough to convince a judge that the recorded call was more likely than not in furtherance of a crime. A low standard indeed, especially in a one-sided presentation, but a normal part of this process.

However, the government under no circumstance is permitted to mislead the court, either through false statements or material omissions. And the government in its wiretap application against me did just that. It crafted its application with blatant falsehoods and crucial omissions to demonstrate probable cause for its wiretap authorization.

The government's misrepresentations took two primary forms. First, their application would rise or fall on the word of Roomy Khan and her efforts, working on the government's behalf, to entrap me. So the government had to give the court confidence that Khan could be trusted.

Of course, given what we were now learning about her criminal past, this was no small task for the government. And it chose not to explain Khan's misdeeds. Instead, it simply whitewashed those details in the application to the court. The government represented to the authorizing court that Roomy was totally trustworthy.

This was false and materially incomplete. In reality, Khan had previously pled guilty to fraud and insider trading. She had previously tried to implicate me in wrongdoing and failed. And after being given leniency for her previous efforts as a cooperating witness, she had nonetheless recidivated. In fact, the government hid completely Khan's prior crimes and cooperation efforts, instead suggesting that her work with the government had commenced in 2007, a statement that was patently false.

The government also had to strategize around weaknesses in the substantive information that Khan provided. One of the challenges for the government to securing wiretap authorization was to demonstrate that the target phone—in this instance, my personal cell phone—was being utilized to commit crimes. In other words, the government needed to get a recent dirty call to present to the court as proof of ongoing criminality using the phone in question.

Khan, under the coaching of the government, had secretly recorded a phone call with me in which we had a brief conversation about three companies: Broadcom, Intel, and Xilinx. These were three companies in our Galleon technology portfolio that we were studying closely, but we had not taken any position in them.

At first blush, the government's description of the surreptitiously recorded call could be interpreted as suspicious. As the government narrated to the Court, Khan asked Rajaratnam whether he was "getting anything on Intel" and Rajaratnam proceeded to tell (Khan) that Intel would be "up 9 percent to 10 percent and then guide down 8 percent and that margins would be good." The standard for probable cause is fairly low and perhaps such a statement may have been sufficient.

That is, it may have been sufficient had it been accurate. My lawyers also received in discovery the actual recording of the recorded call. And to our astonishment, the government had not faithfully reported its contents to the court, instead strategically omitting parts of the call that were *exculpatory* to me. In reality, the recording actually memorialized that I had qualified my predictions with '*I think.*' The government strategically omitted this from its presentation to the court. I also said on the full recording that I expressed some doubt and stated that I thought margins the next quarter will be lower because the volumes are down based on our Galleon research. The government omitted this too and instead falsely opined that, "Rajaratnam seems certain about the Intel numbers without giving any reason why."

With respect to Xilinx, the government engaged in similar subterfuge. The government's sworn submission asserted that Rajaratnam "said he expected Xilinx to be below street," prompting Khan to ask "whether he got it from someone at the company and Raj Rajaratnam said yes, someone who knows." The recording belied the government's representation again. Rather than confirming that I based my expectation from someone at the company, I in fact interrupted Khan on the recording to say that I knew from "somebody who knows their stuff." While I have no recollection of this conversation, given how trivial it was, I describe many financial professionals as those who "know their stuff"—our Galleon investment analysts, other third-party analysts, and other financial professionals. Yet again, the government misrepresented information to the court in its quest to gain wiretap authorization.

NECESSITY SECTION

THE GOVERNMENT FAILED IN ITS obligation of truthfulness in its effort to demonstrate probable cause of insider trading. The government's abject misrepresentations on the application's necessity section were equally astonishing.

Prior to seeing the governments wiretap applications, my lawyers were befuddled as to how the government could have secured authorization. Congress, in enacting Title III in 1968, had required that the government would be granted permission to wiretap only as a last resort after showing that other traditional investigative techniques had failed. Those techniques included methods used routinely with success in securities cases such as this:

subpoenas for company records, interviews of individuals with information and traditional surveillance and other conventional techniques.

These investigative tools were very difficult, if not impossible, to implement in investigating an organized crime syndicate. The mob doesn't keep records of its activities, let alone comply with government issued subpoenas. Organized crime members do not sit for law enforcement interviews or even admit their affiliation with their bosses or confederates. And these criminal enterprises were difficult to watch, given their deep suspicion of outsiders and the omnipresent threat of violence.

After my arrest, I sat in a conference room with my attorneys and they educated me as to the government's need to show that these traditional techniques could not be used, therefore making a wiretap grant necessary. Their heads nearly exploded when I described the extensive cooperation that Galleon had shown the government. As it turns out, the SEC had conducted an investigation into my younger brother Rengan's hedge fund Sedna, in which I personally had invested funds as had Galleon, for suspicion of securities violations including front-running and preferential trading.

When the SEC approach us in our capacity as investors, I told my attorneys, we complied fully. We produced voluminous documents from the Galleon database including trading records, analyst work, and compliance materials. We withheld nothing. And the SEC had access to anything else that the government wanted—after all, we were an SEC-registered entity and fully subjected ourselves to their regulations.

The cherry on the sundae for my attorneys came when they asked whether I had met with the SEC personally. I told them that the SEC had asked to take my sworn testimony and deposition in connection with the Sedna matter and that I had sat for several hours in a deposition. I did not appreciate the significance of this at the moment—after all, I had nothing to hide; why would I not comply? But my attorneys were dumbfounded. We quickly retrieved the transcript of the deposition and it was clear, knowing what we now knew from my arrest, that the SEC had used the Sedna deposition to investigate me. And I had answered each and every question to the best of my ability.

Sensing that this information had seemingly had a profound impact on my counsel, I asked why this all mattered. One of my lawyers said simply, "If you sat for an interview and answered their questions and produced documents in response to a subpoena, how did the government convince the court in seeking wiretap authorization that traditional law enforcement techniques hadn't worked? How could they have proven necessity?"

When we received and reviewed their application to the court, the answer was plain to see. The government had lied to the court. Over and over and over again.

○ The government had told the court in its application that interviewing Rajaratnam and other targets is an "investigative route" that is "too risky at the present time." This was an outright lie. *I had already been interviewed twice and sat for a day-long recorded deposition under oath. And I answered every question. Twenty other Galleon employees had cooperated fully with the government and also answered every question.*

○ The government further claimed to the court that "the conventional use of search warrants is not appropriate at this stage of the investigation as the locations where records related to the scheme have not been full identified at all." Again, this was flatly false. To the contrary, the government had already accumulated or had access to four million Galleon documents obtained through either the SEC or grand jury subpoenas and had built a compelling circumstantial case of insider trading in several securities. To add injury to insult, we learned that the government had not had the time to review all of the documents.

○ The government represented to the court that it could not issue subpoenas for Galleon trading records. To do so, it claimed, "would jeopardize the investigation because clearing firms sometimes alert traders to the requests." *In reality*, the SEC had already issued over two hundred subpoenas for, inter alia, trading records, and the grand jury had issued such subpoenas as well.[29]

It was glaringly obvious from our review of the wiretap application that this was far from normal. The government had misled the court through affirmative misrepresentations and material omissions in numerous places, both with respect to probable cause and necessity, throughout its application prepared and submitted by the prosecutors and the accompanying sworn affidavit from Special Agent Kang. This was not a matter of finding a thread of dispute—the application was a virtually a wholesale fabrication. It crossed ethical norms for the prosecutors and agent but most immediately, it raised the specter that the wiretap recordings that formed the backbone of the government's prosecution had been obtained fraudulently.

Our legal team quickly prepared a motion to suppress, which it filed with the trial court. In it, my lawyers pointed to these grave misrepresentations and omissions. It emphasized that the authorizing court was required to have found that probable cause existed and that traditional law enforcement investigative techniques either had been tried unsuccessfully or were not practical to even attempt. We pointed out that the authorizing court could not have made a proper finding in this regard, given that the government had lied to it on the very substance on which it relied. The remedy, my lawyers posited, would be for the court to "suppress" the wiretap recordings—in other words, to disallow their use in my prosecution because they had been unlawfully obtained. The government responded in true Nixonian speak that mistakes were made, but they asked the court for a reprieve and to be permitted to keep their precious wiretap evidence.

To me, as a layperson, it seemed fairly simple. The government had lied. It had misled the court. We had caught them and there was no putting the genie back in the bottle. Believing in our justice system, I was confident that the court would hold the government accountable. Dowd was exuberant—he promised victory and told everyone in the legal community and public who would listen that the wiretaps would be suppressed. But others on my legal team were more cautious. They warned that courts were very reluctant to suppress evidence against the government, let alone in a high-profile matter such as this. While agreeing that the government abuse here was wildly egregious and warranted suppression, they were concerned.

On August 16, 2010, the court made a preliminary ruling that caught the legal world by surprise. Judge Holwell ordered that a *Franks* hearing—a public proceeding in which the government would have to defend its wiretap application—would be held. The court allowed us to call government witnesses and explore the raft of falsehoods and omissions that had riddled the application. I was elated. Contrary to the naysayers, I believed that this was a crucial step toward justice prevailing.

The showdown had been calendared. The *Franks* hearing—the very first of its kind in the Southern District since the passing of Title III—would be must-see viewing and threatened to upend the government's most celebrated prosecution. I believed in my heart that the *Franks* hearing was the first step to my vindication.

CHAPTER 10

THE *FRANKS* HEARING AND RULING

Why would Agent Kang have needed to lie? Even now, this question remains puzzling. After all, 99.9 percent of wiretap applications are granted.

From the initial indictment, we had already seen that the prosecution would take snippets of phone calls and recast them in a way which was not just inaccurate, but also seemingly sinister. Although we had not found any transmission of "inside information" on the wiretap transcripts, we worried that these bits of conversation would be used to mislead a jury, especially one with little understanding of how investment professionals operate and communicate. A sentence taken out of context (or even just one key word being omitted) would allow an unethical prosecutor to transform it into something substantially different than originally intended.

Furthermore, the FBI had tapped only my cell phone, and not my office phone, selectively ignoring the great majority of business conversations I had. The government disregarded (intentionally, in my opinion) many, if not most, of the phone calls I regularly had with fifty to sixty analysts from various other firms. These calls would not only have emphasized that the data points and assumptions we discussed were based on publicly available information, but also would have allowed a jury to get a much fuller and more accurate picture of the information on which we had based our decisions.

Based on the false statements and material omissions in Agent Kang's affidavit, we made a motion to suppress the wiretaps. Judge Holwell was troubled enough to order an evidentiary hearing, known as a *Franks* hearing. The hearing lasted for four days, from October 20th to 24th, 2010. During the hearing, Judge Holwell learned that the Galleon investigation had begun as an offshoot from an investigation in 2007 of Sedna Capital, a hedge fund run by my younger brother Rengan. UBS, Sedna's prime broker, had alerted the SEC about possible account irregularities at Sedna.

At the *Franks* hearing, the government said that "the investigation came to a standstill and did not meet our objectives." One might believe, or at least hope, that the authorities would close the file and move on. Unfortunately, there is a strong and persistent bias in the Justice Department against high-profile individuals in finance.

Agent Kang had been so determined to find something on me that he resorted to using Roomy Khan to make consensual calls to me about three particular stocks (Xilinx, Intel, and Broadcom) right around their respective earnings announcements, between March and December of 2008. I had innocently shared Galleon's own internal research and our thoughts on these companies, but did not provide any inside information *because I had none.*

Incredibly, Agent Kang would twist what was said on these calls into a basis for probable cause in his application for permission to wiretap me. Even some basic investigative work would have shown that I had no positions in these three stocks at the time of the calls. How can you accuse someone of insider trading when they did not even trade the stocks in question? Agent Kang neglected to inform the judge who would review and authorize the wiretap application of this. He also blatantly lied and intentionally left out key words that I used on the calls like "I think," which illustrated my opinion versus a piece of information from an inside tip.

After the evidentiary hearing, Judge Holwell found that "false and misleading statements and omissions pervaded the affidavit so extensively that it was impossible for the authorizing judge to have made the constitutionally and statutory required determination for the issuance of the wiretaps." Judge Holwell then went to on highlight several discrepancies between the sworn affidavit of Agent Kang and the facts uncovered during the *Franks* hearing in both the probable cause and necessity sections below.

Judge Holwell also stated that rather than provide a "full and complete statement" as required by the law, the wiretap affidavit made a "full and a complete omission"[30] and that FBI Agent Kang included "literally false" information in his affidavit.[31] He went on further to state that the wiretap application was made with "reckless disregard for the truth with respect to both probable cause and necessity."

Despite these condemnations, Judge Holwell inexplicably denied the suppression of the wiretaps. We were stunned.

The Supreme Court has held that Title III requires suppression whenever "there is failure to satisfy any of those statutory requirements that directly and substantially implement the Congressional intention to limit the use of intercept procedures to those situations clearly calling for this investigative device." (Giordano, 416 U.S., at 527.)

To this day, my defense team and I remain baffled by Judge Holwell's decision. We can only assume that the public media and back-channel political pressure on him was so great that he succumbed. He certainly understood that wiretaps could easily be misused.

Eighteen months after my trial, at an all-day legal conference at Columbia University on November 16, 2012, Judge Holwell said, "It's difficult to overstate how damaging wiretap evidence can be to a jury. Playing a recording in front of a jury of you calling your mother to ask what you're going to have for Sunday dinner sounds criminal."[32]

More than a year later, Holwell gave an interview to *Frontline* on January 7, 2014. He was asked how tough the wiretapping decision had been for him. He answered, "It is difficult; I think any judge who says otherwise [is] probably fibbing. It is hard when you're in the fishbowl of a highly publicized trial to make some decisions and you have to reinforce yourself. You have a case that's on the cover of the *New York Post* every day."[33]

Not only did Bharara's media strategy impact the public opinions, his manipulation most likely affected judicial decisions. We will never know to what extent the manipulation influenced the jury.

Many distinguished legal scholars and former federal judges found Judge Holwell's decision to allow the wiretaps into evidence disturbing. A coalition of retired federal judges (active federal judges are prevented from doing so) filed an amicus brief on my behalf. According to these amici, "the government's omission of a full and complete statement *always requires that the proceeds be suppressed, without regard for the materiality of the omissions.*" Without a full and complete statement, judges cannot fulfill the mandate of Title III—to prevent unwarranted intrusions on privacy—unless the government is completely forthright during the wiretap applications process.

Professor Robert Blakely, a foremost authority on wiretaps and Title III (indeed, in 1968, he was one of its original draftsmen) also filed an amicus brief on my behalf. He wrote,

> More than 40 years ago, Congress and its leaders foresaw the dangers of law enforcement initiatives that compromise personal privacy in single-minded pursuit of crime. Congress passed Title III as a comprehensive statutory scheme to define narrowly the preconditions law enforcement agents must satisfy to monitor legally and constitutionally a person's phone calls or related communications. Anyone—public or private—who taps a phone without satisfying these preconditions when possible, commits a crime, forfeits any benefits gained by his other transgression and must civilly make whole the damage inflicted on the victim. That has been the law since 1968 and ought not to change now through the judiciary.[34]

Legal expert Josh Cohen characterized Judge Holwell's decision as follows: "The Second Circuit has turned Title III upside down. A statute that requires a 'full and complete statement' about traditional investigative techniques as a prerequisite to wiretapping a wire has been interpreted in such a way that the element is never required at all...The real injury inflicted by the case goes much deeper. By emasculating the necessity requirement, Rajaratnam strikes at the very heart of Title III. Worse, there is no practical way to contain the damage."[35]

REFLECTIONS

THE GOVERNMENT'S FAILURE TO PROVIDE a "full and complete statement" of both probable cause and necessity violated the core conditions for a lawful wiretap under Title III and should have rendered the resulting wiretaps illegal and inadmissible at trial. Later, Judge Holwell stated, "the case turned in many important respects on the wiretap decision."[36]

Although it may seem like a technicality, the problem with wiretaps is far worse than most people realize. Phrases, words, or even tone of voice can be easily taken out of context and misunderstood. If judges allow the FBI to lie in sworn affidavits with no repercussions, then any person can be wiretapped or charged at the government's whim.

I was learning firsthand that there is one set of rules for the average citizen and another for the government. Like most average citizens, *I was an outsider looking in at an insider's game.* Clearly, I was facing a battle that extended well beyond the courtroom. I was about to take on the most powerful institution in the world: the U.S. Government.

CHAPTER 11

ALI FAR:
"I Made It All Up"

The role of Ali Far in the Galleon case is a classic example of how prosecutors intimidate and manipulate weak and vulnerable defendants in their effort to implicate higher profile targets.

When I first met Ali Far in early 1999, he was a sell-side semiconductor analyst for Prudential Securities. The Prudential institutional salesperson who was assigned to cover Galleon brought Ali to meet me and my team and present his thoughts on the semiconductor industry.

From what Ali later told me, his father had been an officer in the Iranian Army, and after the overthrow of the Shah, like many of the Shah's loyalists, he and his family left Iran. They moved to California in the late 1970s. Ali obtained an undergraduate engineering degree as well a joint master's degree in law and business. He then worked at several technology companies in the semiconductor industry.

After that, he moved to Wall Street, joining Prudential Securities as a semiconductor analyst. It was a natural transition for people who wanted to leverage their industry knowledge into Wall Street careers. His prior industry experience was definitely an *edge* in doing research in the industry and picking stocks. These picks were marketed by Prudential salespeople to their clients, including Galleon. If we determined that the ideas were good, we would typically trade through Prudential. Prudential's incentive would be earning the commission on the trade. This is basic to how the securities industry business works and was the reason why Ali presented at Galleon.

Soon after the presentation, Ali Far approached me about working as a semiconductor analyst for Galleon on the West Coast. He said he did not enjoy writing research reports and marketing to institutional clients, wanting instead to work on the buy side. In June 1999, we hired Ali Far as a semiconductor analyst in our West Coast office. Ironically, Roomy Khan was also working there at the same time. Ali did a good job as semiconductor analyst.

Three or four years later, he expressed a desire to be a portfolio manager. I encouraged him to move to the East Coast, which he did. He lived in the adjacent building to mine, and often we would walk the fifteen minutes home together. We became friends.

However, Ali was not thriving as a portfolio manager. A good analyst is not necessarily a good portfolio manager. A good portfolio manager has to have the courage to take risks; know when to reduce exposure and when to increase it; have a point of view on the market direction; react quickly to breaking news; and constantly assimilate and process all the variables that might move stocks. In addition, unlike analysts, portfolio managers' overall compensation is directly proportional to a manager's investment returns. In 2004 and 2005, Ali's portfolio was basically flat. Ali was not a risk taker. He often over analyzed certain facts and trends.

In 2006, I made the decision to reassign Ali. Most portfolio managers go through some rough patches, but two years was too long. Although Ali managed only a portion of our technology fund, it was my fiduciary duty to maximize returns to our investors. I offered Ali the job of acting as a mentor to the junior technology analysts, which I believed to be a better fit for him. He graciously accepted the offer, but I knew he was not happy.

Predictably, at the end of 2006, Ali informed me that he wanted to go back to California to start his own hedge fund. I wished him well and invested some of my personal funds with him as I had done with other ex-Galleon analysts who had moved on to start their own funds. I invested my money with them to support their new businesses. The prosecutors would disingenuously insinuate that I invested with Ali to gain inside information.

Ali launched Spherix in mid-2007. Spherix did well in 2007 and really stood out in 2008 when they made 10 percent in a year when most long short equity hedge funds posted losses due to the market meltdown. To provide context, the average equity hedge fund lost 18 percent in 2008. In retrospect, it appears that Ali was actively nurturing a wide range of fellow Iranian technology executives to obtain MNPI.

Although insider trading rules are murky at times, there are two classic instances in which it is indisputable that a trade is an illegal insider trade.

1. If someone obtains granular revenue and/or earnings numbers from an officer or senior executive of a company who has access to confidential information

2. If someone obtains a tip on a merger or acquisition transaction that is about to occur from someone who knows confidential information

In December 2008, Ali Hariri, a vice president of marketing for Atheros, called Ali Far after an executive committee meeting and told him (in Farsi) that Atheros's revenues were coming in well below Wall Street's estimates and the company's guidance. Ali Far immediately shorted the stock. That afternoon after the market closed, Atheros preannounced the shortfall in revenues. The stock fell about 25 percent. Ali Far made money by then covering his short. This is a classic example of a trade on MNPI (inside information). Fortunately, I had no investment position on Atheros at that time. Neither Ali nor the prosecutors could claim that Ali had given me insider trading on Atheros.

Ali was caught red-handed because the FBI recorded this call. Around April 2009, the FBI quietly contacted Ali Far and showed him the evidence they had about his trading in Atheros and other stocks. There was none of the fanfare and media attention that typically went with this type of arrest. They kept it very quiet. They were attempting to use Ali to go after a bigger fish: me.

Faced with indisputable evidence of insider trading, Ali Far not only pleaded guilty, but went one step further and entered into a plea-bargaining agreement with the prosecutors. This is a critical point and cannot be overemphasized: cooperation in a plea bargain often means providing evidence against a target, sometimes with little regard for the truth. The greater the evidence provided, the lesser the sentence, giving the cooperators a tremendous incentive to make things up. Ali Far fabricated stories about his business interactions with me in an effort to avoid being prosecuted for his own insider trading offenses. He told the prosecutors that he had kept me supplied with inside information from Iranian technology specialists, people I have never met nor known about.

Ali Far went further. He provided the prosecutors a list of more than twenty companies along with details of his contacts at these companies, claiming they were regularly providing him with inside information that he passed on to me. Because of this, I would be charged in the superseding indictment with many of the stocks Ali identified. This was based solely on Ali Far's accusations. Ali was a friend. I was in a state of shock. I was stunned to learn that Ali Far was prepared to testify against me at trial, under oath, as a part of his plea bargain. His cowardice disappointed me.

We now had to expand the defense team and thoroughly analyze our trading around these companies, which led to millions of dollars in additional legal fees.

Ali Far's reckless claims of identifying as his inside sources caused many senior Iranian executives to be suspended or lose their jobs. The collateral damage outside Galleon was widespread. All of this was irrelevant to the prosecutors, who made no effort to leak the information to the press.

In May 2009, one month after his arrest and with the coaching of the FBI, his new masters, Ali Far called and informed me that due to health problems, he was shutting down his fund. This was a recorded call. Ali attempted to talk about stocks. My responses were entirely focused on the health and well-being of my friend.

With the help of the FBI, Ali Far remained persistent in his attempts to entrap me. He made seven consensual calls to me over the next several weeks. He asked if we could stay in touch so he could get my thoughts on stocks for trading in his personal account. He made these calls with the FBI listening and recording him. Unfortunately for Ali and the FBI, there was nothing in these seven calls that was the least bit incriminating. In retrospect, Agent Kang's fingerprints were evident: the consensual calls from Ali were eerily similar to the ones from Roomy Khan. He played on my sympathies just as she had.

In all, Ali Far made 244 recorded calls on behalf of the FBI, attempting to entrap various investment professionals. Many of these calls were to his friends and ex-colleagues at Galleon, including Nat Cohen (networking analyst), Nadeem Janmohamed (semiconductor analyst), and Joe Liu (Taiwanese analyst)—all in an effort to try to get them to incriminate themselves. The FBI's strategy was to accuse and threaten these Galleon employees in order to get them to testify against me. Again, the FBI came up empty, as there was nothing incriminating in these calls, either. They got nothing because there was nothing to get.

After my arrest in October 2009, the FBI had no incentive to maintain its silence on Ali Far. They informed the media of Ali Far's arrest. They had every incentive to publicize Ali's arrest and continue on their strategy to mislead the press about the extent of my "inside network."

The next month, November 2009, the FBI arrested Ali Hariri of Atheros. Although he had no connection whatsoever with me or with Galleon, the prosecution used a complicit media to generate a level of coverage that transformed this into a sinister and far-reaching case. They did not need Hariri's cooperation, so they did not offer him a plea bargain deal. In January 2011, Ali Hariri pled guilty and was sentenced to eighteen months in federal prison. In court, Hariri told the judge, "I had a big mouth and was absolutely wrong. I'm not blaming Ali (Far). It was my own mistake. When you're in Silicon Valley and when you're a techie working on a product, the furthest thing from your mind is insider trading," Hariri said. "You say something. You don't think about it."[37]

Once again, erroneously and possibly complicitly, the press headlines screamed "Galleon defendant Hariri sentenced to prison"—even though

Hariri had nothing to do with Galleon, and I had never conducted any business with him. This was another premeditated gambit to tie Galleon to insider trading rings. Another attempt to mislead the public about the size and the scope of the Galleon case. I cannot remember even one person in the press questioning how Hariri could be legitimately tied to me or to Galleon. Bharara was proving to be the master puppeteer behind the scenes.

On many occasions, Bharara unveiled a chart of insider trading rings with me at the center. The chart was gleefully posted all over the national networks. The immediate impact was clear—I was portrayed as the master central brain orchestrating this huge network of operatives. What Bharara was radio silent about was that his allegations of extensive insider trading constituted less than 0.01 percent of all my trades between 2005 and 2009.

Fortunately, around February 2011, about two months before my trial, *Ali Far made the stunning confession that he had fabricated all the allegations against me.*[38] The charges stemming from Ali Far's false allegations were dropped. The prosecutors were radio silent. No mention of Ali Far or his shenanigans at any point during the trial. Not one word from the prosecution or the media. Nothing about the collateral damage of Ali Far's allegations.

As a reward for his cooperation, Ali did not spend a day in prison. Without his cooperation, Ali faced up to four years and nine months in prison according to federal sentencing guidelines. He was sentenced to a year of probation, one hundred days of community service, and ordered to pay $100,000 fine.

As his lawyer accurately reflected, Ali's "cooperation was all in." The message was clear—whether lying or not, if you play nicely with the government, it will take good care of you.

The government had a huge problem. Both Ali Far and Roomy Khan who were used by the government to jumpstart the criminal case against me and make consensual calls were not credible to testify at my trial. Never mind that their words were deemed credible to arrest me.

Rather than drop the case and get egg all over their face, they now had to troll for new cooperating witnesses to achieve an effective prosecution of me.

CHAPTER 12

DANIELLE CHIESI:
Stocks, Sports, And Sex

The hedge fund business is gladiatorial. Every day, you did not just walk in to work; you walked in to war. It was a sink-or-swim environment. Life jackets were not easily found when you were drowning. Hedge funds are dominated by alpha male energy. Dominant personalities. Dominant egos.

I first met Danielle Chiesi sometime in early 2006 through Nadeem Janmohamed, a Galleon analyst. Within twenty minutes of my meeting her, she let it be known that her three most favorite things in life began with the letter *s*: stocks, sports, and sex. "Not necessarily in that order," she purred. Never having met someone quite like her, I was amused. She liked to present herself as a fighter whose armor was her bold swagger. Early in any conversation, she would disarm others with her blunt, often crude, and forthright language—blunt, sometimes to the point of coarseness—cutting through any formality to establish herself as a person to be noticed.

A few months later, I ran into Dani again at one of the technology conferences. We overlapped at a few of the company meetings. Dani would call me periodically to discuss the market and various stocks. Over time, I learned that Dani spoke to many portfolio managers including me. Dani was a bit of a chatterbox. While I was open with my thoughts, I was careful not to divulge any of our stock positions. I also learned that Dani had been in the business for over fifteen years, had worked both as an analyst and a portfolio manager at New Castle. She indicated that she worked from home because she got distracted by the noise and chatter of the trading desk at New Castle.

In early 2008, the FBI began secretly recorded Dani's conversations. These included conversations with me. They eventually alleged that Dani gave me inside information on Akamai and Advanced Micro Devices (AMD).

AKAMAI

AKAMAI WAS A COMPANY THAT Galleon knew well. The company had developed technology that helped internet traffic move faster. Galleon's internet analyst Jessica Kourakos followed Akamai closely. In March 2008, Jessica recommended a short position on the company, saying that emerging competitive pressure in their market was negatively impacting its business.

Based on Jessica's analysis, I initiated a short position in March 2008. So did several other Galleon portfolio managers. Jessica's weekly internal reports from March through July 2008 continued to reinforce Akamai as her top short idea.

Some of the leading analysts on the Street had also determined that Akamai was going to have a mediocre quarter. In fact, on May 22, 2008, Goldman Sachs put Akamai on its "conviction sell list," a strong indicator that they expected the stock to decline. I shorted more Akamai on that very day.

Akamai's quarterly earnings were due on July 30, 2008. My strategy was to increase incrementally our existing short position into the earnings event. I shorted more Akamai on July 2, July 3, July 10, and July 17. By July 24, 2008, six days before the earnings announcement, I had accumulated a short position in Akamai of three hundred thousand shares. Other Galleon managers did the same, independently and based on Jessica's analysis. On July 24, Galleon's overall short position on Akamai was over one million five hundred seventy thousand shares, or approximately $49 million.

That evening (July 24), while I was relaxing at home with my family, I received a call from Dani at 9:11 pm. Calling me at home was unusual. In her usual dramatic fashion, referring to Akamai, she said, "They're going to guide down; I just got a call from my guy. I played him like a finely tuned piano." I responded that I was already short the stock. I quickly realized I made a mistake by divulging our stock position. I told her to "maintain radio silence."

Usually, portfolio managers and traders don't share their short positions with other portfolio managers. The trade could become crowded and impact a fund's ability to make money for their investors.

Dani was saying nothing we did not already know. We were already short Akamai and planned to short more into the earnings.

As it turns out, the prosecutors were secretly recording Dani's outgoing calls and asserted that the phone call from Dani on July 24, 2008, at 9:11 p.m. was evidence of us exchanging MNPI. Despite having full access to Galleon's research reports and the fact that I had been short Akamai before the conversation, they disingenuously made that claim. In so doing, they disregarded the depth of Galleon's research—all of which they had access to—and ignored the fact that I had been short on Akamai *before* that conversation.

I continued to follow Jessica's recommendation of increasing the short position into the earnings. Between July 24 and July 30, I shorted an additional seventy-five thousand shares. When Akamai reported on July 30, 2008, their quarterly results were even worse than we had anticipated. Jessica's analysis was spot-on.

It was during the discovery process while preparing for the Galleon case that our defense team found out that Dani's "my guy" was Kieran Taylor, a midlevel marketing person at Akamai. I had never heard of him until that point. When I refer to "my guy," the reference was always to our in-house Galleon analysts. I did not think much about the call.

What is unusual—in fact, absurd—is that neither the prosecutors nor the FBI ever interviewed Kieran Taylor to determine the truth. Why? The rationale is Machiavellian: if Kieran Taylor were to have denied having provided Dani with inside information, the prosecution would have had to drop the Akamai charge against Dani and me.

Ironically, Kieran Taylor, through his lawyer, categorically denied he gave any inside information to Danielle. As a midlevel marketing manager, he did not have access to such information. The prosecutors chose not to charge him, the alleged tippee. Nor did they ask him to testify against Dani. Winning was more important than the truth, a recurring theme in the Galleon case.

In their eagerness to put together a case, the prosecutors viewed any recorded conversation about stocks as evidence of an insider trading tip, eyeing any innocuous conversation through their own sinister lens. They went to great pains to highlight the phrase "radio silent," effectively whipping the press into a frenzy around two words. The press was more intent on chasing the tail of "radio silence" than on sifting through the facts. There was no mention that months before the alleged tip, our Galleon analyst had recommended a short position on Akamai. There was no inquiry by the media digging into the factual substance of the prosecutor's assertions. The press did no fact-checking; the prosecutors had all the facts but chose a false narrative to feed the press.

ADVANCED MICRO DEVICES (AMD)

THE PROSECUTION WOULD ALSO CHARGE Dani with providing me with MNPI on AMD based on a recorded call on September 2, 2008.

Dani had a habit of dropping names of CEOs and high-ranking executives she claimed to know. I soon realized this was all a facade. She was playing the player, attempting to be a player with her colorful talk. For example, she would talk as if she knew something really proprietary, that she had some type of scoop, but in reality, it was usually common gossip, with a sports or sex metaphor thrown in.

On that recorded call on September 2, 2008, she told me that if the AMD stock goes up too much on the expected announcement of its asset-lite program, a new initiative AMD was instituting, people will be looking at her, presumably because she was talking about AMD to everyone and because she was "a chick."

I responded, "Don't hide behind that bullshit! Do I ever hide behind being a Sri Lankan?" Dani continued, "I have AMD stamped on my forehead and it's almost impossible to prove that I really know anything, but a man doesn't want to be beaten by a blonde, big-titted chick." In a moment of seriousness, she added she did "*not know anything for real.*" This was just one of many locker-room comments Dani used to prove she belonged in the male-dominated hedge fund business.

Throughout 2008, AMD had been talking about its asset-lite strategy. Galleon had a large position in AMD in anticipation of the program rolling out. This had nothing to do with Dani's colorful commentary. In discovery, we learned that Dani chatted about AMD to many, many others. It's almost as if she made up her analysis as she went along, name-dropping along the way to suit her purpose at that moment.

For example, on August 27, 2008, at 11:09 a.m., Dani called Rich Grodin, a hedge fund manager, to talk about AMD's ability to pull off the asset-lite strategy and almost ordered him to buy AMD. She says "I am dead if this leaks. My career is over. I'll be like Martha fucking Stewart…I suggest you don't ask any more questions and just trade it. Buy Intel. Think about this: *So, Raj is buying it for different reasons.* Raj thinks they are running ahead of plan…It's not why I'm buying it. If you were not Danielle, if you didn't talk to Danielle, would you ever believe AMD could pull anything like this? Never! I'd be short the fucking thing or at least I wouldn't be involved. I would say it goes to Babe Ruth." In this call, Dani definitively asserts that I am buying AMD for different reasons and not on any information she is providing. The prosecutors would once again ignore this.

That same afternoon, Dani also called her doorman on her cell phone to say that she needed to fix the static on her internal building phone. She then went on to say, "Do you want a stock tip? I never do this…I shouldn't even do this…but you can't tell anyone. I didn't tell my mother. AMD, like my cat's name, Amadea. If it were me, I'd quit my job and buy that stock 110 percent. I know this is a tough time in this depression. I have to be careful because I want to be legal, but AMD, I think it's trading at 6.24, could go to 30. You never heard this from me."

The prosecution would later point to these recorded calls as being "suspicious" exchanges and classified the information as being inside information. In reality, Dani owned AMD stock herself, loved the company, and wore her heart on her sleeve. She couldn't help telling anyone and everyone (even her doorman) how great they were.

Dani was arrested on the same day I was—October 16, 2009—together with her boss Mark Kurland, the head of New Castle Partners, and Robert Moffat, a senior vice president at IBM. Preet Bharara alleged that Moffat passed along information on IBM, Sun Microsystems, and Advanced Micro Devices to Dani and that, in turn, she passed along the information to Mark and the two traded on the news. In addition, the U.S. attorney charged that Dani traded on inside information on Akamai. The three were referred to in the press as the New Castle ring.

The government linked the New Castle ring with a supposed "Galleon ring." I did not know Mark Kurland or Bob Moffat. Once again, Preet Bharara misled the public. He insinuated I was the central figure in several large, concurrent, and sinister insider trading rings.

Initially, Dani, Mark Kurland, and Bob Moffat all pleaded not guilty and were given bail. Soon thereafter, both Mark Kurland and Bob Moffat pled guilty to cut their losses. They were sentenced to prison for twenty-seven and six months, respectively. They appeared to have succumbed to the prosecutors' threats and intimidation. Bob Moffat was rumored to be at that time a leading candidate to be the next CEO of IBM. He lost his job and a reported $50 million in pension benefits. New Castle, a billion-dollar hedge fund, had to close. Several employees were laid off. The collateral damage of Preet Bharara's campaign to promote himself and willfully misinterpret insider trading laws was enormous.

Dani fought the charges for over a year until her funds ran out. On January 11, 2011, just two months before her trial, Dani had no option but to succumb. The night before she threw in the towel, Dani called me in tears to inform me of her decision. I could empathize with the excruciating pain I heard in her voice. She said that she had no choice but to take the less risky option and plead guilty. She felt her colorful language on the recorded wiretaps would prejudice the jury against her. She said by pleading guilty, she was "taking the risk out of the trade," hoping she would get a lesser sentence. I was deeply disturbed that she had to give in to Bharara's bullying tactics.

In her guilty plea, she acknowledged her insider trading of Sun Microsystems, IBM, and Lenovo—none of which were part of the charges against me. Nonetheless, the prosecutors provided the media with misleading information, connecting me with Dani's trades on those stocks. The press, apparently in cahoots with the prosecution, questioned nothing. In fact, they were radio silent.

Dani was sentenced to a total of thirty months in prison. I have a great deal of respect for Dani—she refused to turn into an informant or falsely try to entrap others. She fought for her innocence as long as she could. Further demonstrating her character, even after pleading guilty, when my attorneys contacted her, Dani offered to write an affidavit attesting that I knew nothing of Kieran Taylor or that she had provided me with inside information.

Astonishingly, Kieran Taylor was not charged criminally, but the SEC filed a civil lawsuit instead. Rather than wage a costly legal battle, Taylor settled with the SEC, paying a $145,000 fine without admitting guilt. The stark contrast with the eighteen months of imprisonment imposed on Ali Hariri (Ali Far's tipper from Atheros per Chapter 10) is a textbook illustration of how arbitrarily enforced insider trading laws can be.

CHAPTER 13

RAJIV GOEL

The government had created the foundation of its case against me through the cooperation of Roomy Khan and Ali Far. The proactive cooperation by Khan had enabled the government to secure its wiretap and Far's information allowed the government to develop further the charges that it would bring in spectacular fashion against me and my codefendants. However, it took very little pressure testing by my counsel to lay bare serious structural flaws in the government's "foundation," between Khan's prior criminal conduct and dishonesty and Far's outright fabrications. But one thing that I have learned over the course of this experience is what prosecutors may lack in diligence and substantive financial knowledge, they compensate for in brute power and cunning.

Faced with the collapse of Khan and Far as witnesses, the government turned quickly to my codefendants. First on their radar was Rajiv Goel. Goel, a Wharton classmate and, at that time, a midlevel manager at Intel Capital, was arrested on the same day that I was: October 19, 2009. The government charged Goel with insider trading, specifically alleging that he provided me with MNPI with respect to Intel's investment in Clearwire.

Rajiv, like me, was startled by the government's false allegations. But after the initial shock subsided, Rajiv pleaded not guilty. And he did so because he was just that—not guilty. After the immediate flurry of post-arrest excitement—much of it prompted by Bharara's indictment "road show" with the media—Rajiv's lawyer and others joined with my counsel to begin educating the government of their mistakes as part of a joint defense. Our lawyers worked together to share the information that provided full context to the government's misguided allegations. Neither one of us had any doubt that we would resolve this charge successfully.

This was the fall of 2008, after our arrests. By the time my trial commenced in 2010, Rajiv Goel no longer stood shoulder to shoulder with me to rebut the government's allegation. Instead, he had flipped, or determined it was instead in his interests to cooperate with the government and testify against me to limit his own risk. It was a strategic choice by Rajiv, not one anchored in any way to the truth. And while I genuinely believed that I knew Rajiv, who unlike Khan or Far was a dear friend, it turned out that there were weaknesses in Rajiv's personal life that I did not know. And the government seized on those weaknesses to resuscitate their prosecution.

THE BEGINNING

I MET RAJIV AT WHARTON in 1981. We remained casual acquaintances through business school, sharing like many people do the bonds of being classmates. In addition, we were a part of the immigrant community at Wharton, sharing the experience with many of our other fellow students from around the world of being separated from our families and our familiar cultures and immersed in Americana. Rajiv graduated in 1983 and took a job at Metropolitan Life in New York. After a few years, he left New York to work in his native India. In January 2000, Rajiv returned to the United States, taking a position in California with Intel Capital, the private equity arm of the Intel corporation. We reconnected.

We now had several more meaningful points of friendship. In addition to familiarity based on our time together at Wharton and our cultural backgrounds, our families were very similar. We each had two daughters and one son, all around the same ages, and were as a result sharing the experience of raising children in this new world so distinct from our own upbringings. Our families became close, vacationing together during the summers, once in Italy, another time in France. We got to know each other and over time, we became friends.

Our family friendship dovetailed with our personal friendship. Because we both worked in the technology sector, we would often discuss trends in the technology industry, companies, their strategies, new developments— the types of things that one would discuss with any family friend with similar interests or work experiences. I enjoyed speaking with Rajiv about the technology sector. Rajiv and I approached the valuation of technology companies from opposing perspectives: he from a private equity viewpoint and I from a public investment viewpoint. These different vantage points provided for lively and often spirited discussions about the value of various technology companies and industry trends, much like two friends who also happened to share a knowledge of professional basketball or some other common interest.

As our family and personal relationship deepened, Rajiv sought my guidance on several personal issues as is common among friends. At a professional level, Rajiv's career was stagnating. Again, there was nothing unusual about this. After a successful run, Rajiv was plateauing in his role at Intel. On several occasions, he asked for my help in getting a new job. He wanted to return to India and I encouraged him to do so.

As we all do for our friends, I tried to leverage my professional networks to help him find a good fit for the next phase of his career. I arranged for an interview with a private equity fund that invested in India. I advised him on a presentation he made to the Tata Group, one of India's largest conglomerates, which was planning to launch another private equity fund. He asked for my opinion on whether to join a small technology company or remain at Intel. I recommended that he leave Intel if he were unhappy. Despite a lot of thinking, talking, and support from me to move on from Intel Capital, Rajiv stayed put. He was hesitant to take a risk.

This was not unusual. Galleon's growing financial strength gave me access to considerable corridors of power that I never imagined possible. Highly positioned executives at privately and publicly traded companies sought Galleon's investment to buoy their stock prices. The sell side of the market was constantly cultivating a relationship with us in hopes of commercial gain. And the financial elite in the United States and abroad took note of our growth. I say this not to boast, but to explain that I quickly was in a position to help friends seeking new professional opportunities. And I did so for Rajiv. I had no interest in his continuing in a dead-end position at Intel. My only interest was to help my friend find his own professional and financial happiness.

Rajiv also confided in me some of his financial pressures. Whether this was a function of our friendship, my increasing success at Galleon, or a combination, I will never know. But it was not uncommon, as word of my financial good fortune spread, for friends and strangers alike to approach me for investments, loans, or even outright gifts. I often helped friends and family when needed, discreetly and in my discretion. I never asked for a security, merely telling them to pay me back when they could. These friends were from various walks of life but in all cases, it was the bond of friendship which inspired my help when they needed it. Rajiv was no different.

In the summer of 2005, he was looking to buy a house, and asked me for a loan of $100,000 toward the down payment. I lent him the money and he gave me a promissory note in August on which he wrote "Once again, thanks for the help. Will plan to repay the loan as soon as I can." A year later, in 2006, he called me in a panic from a hospital in India. He told me that his father was in the emergency room. He was worried that his father might end up losing the family apartment in Bombay. He said that he needed to borrow some money urgently and asked me for another loan, this time for $500,000. This hit home for me, as my own elderly parents lived with me in New York, and I had seen firsthand their struggles with aging. I sent him the money on the same day, with the understanding that he would pay it back over time.

As time went on, Rajiv would also periodically ask me for my best stock ideas. I encouraged him to invest with Galleon, but Rajiv's personal brokerage account at Schwab was not large enough to meet Galleon's account minimums, so I would give him input on what stocks he could choose to buy or sell. I did not share with him or any of my other friends or even professional relationships the specifics of Galleon's positions in various companies—that would betray the interests of my investors, which was my paramount concern. But in the spirit of conversation and intellectual engagement, I was open with Rajiv and many others about companies that I liked and my reaction to news and trends that I believed might influence the market. And I welcomed their thoughts in the same vein, as part of the healthy dialogue that makes investing so enjoyable for me.

At the time of our arrest in the fall of 2009, the government knew none of this. They had not interviewed me. They had not interviewed Rajiv. Instead, armed with certain select wiretap recordings of friendly conversations between myself and Rajiv, the government assumed the worst and brought their criminal charges against us. And after Rajiv pled not guilty and began to prepare to fight for his innocence alongside me, they applied the full force of the government to Rajiv and hoped that he would crack. And sadly, he did.

CLEARWIRE

I SHOULD PREFACE THE FOLLOWING discussion with the following mea culpa. I do not have a perfect recall of the conversations between myself and Rajiv that were recorded on the wiretaps. In fact, I will make this admission that is more sweeping. I do not have a perfect recall of any of those conversations. If this is startling, it shouldn't be. None of these calls were moments of high criminal drama or intrigue, windows into some stunning illegality that would stick in my "guilty" conscience or memory. No, these were all normal, run-of-the-mill conversations in the course of my life. While the government highlighted a handful of calls out of context, they disregarded the thousands upon thousands of calls in which I discussed the financial industry with friends and colleagues and the thousands of calls in which I talked about family, life, friends, and the daily filler of life.

But the government's out-of-context interpretation of wiretap calls between myself and Rajiv led them first to a company called Clearwire.

Back in 2008, Clearwire owned a technology called WiMAX (4G) that newer cell phones and other wireless devices could use. Clearwire had authority over half the country's spectrum, or footprint; Sprint had the other half. Clearwire and Sprint formed a joint venture giving the combined entity a nationwide footprint. In December 2005, Intel invested $620 million in Clearwire, making it the company's largest investor. All this information was available to the public, already having been disclosed by the respective companies.

Given this history, speculation of the joint venture had been in play for months. On January 29, 2008, MarketWatch publicly reported, "[t]he two companies, whose original deal collapsed in November, are looking for 'non-traditional' partners—such as Intel, Google, and Best Buy—to help finance their proposed venture, the *Wall Street Journal* reported Tuesday on its website. An earlier negotiation between the two companies fell apart after the ouster of Gary Forsee as Sprint Nextel's CEO the previous October 2007." Forsee had been a staunch supporter of WiMAX. According to the *Journal*, Sprint Nextel floated a plan under which it would spin off its WiMAX operations and merge them with Clearwire, a young firm that went public in 2007. Kirkland, Wash.-based Clearwire is funded by wealthy cellular pioneer Craig McCaw. Investors have been waiting to see whether his successor, Dan Hesse, would continue Sprint Nextel's WiMAX strategy or pursue a different course.

Our technology group of traders and analysts at Galleon, as was their mandate, was keenly aware of these developments. On January 20, 2008, the *Wall Street Journal* reported that Clearwire was in talks with Sprint regarding the WiMAX joint venture from Google, Intel, and others. The market reacted to this news and the Clearwire stock was up 25 percent on that day alone. The professional investor's knowledge of this joint venture was in the public domain—it was public information.

On February 15, 2008, Naph Joseph, the Galleon telecom analyst, sent an email to Galleon portfolio managers citing an article on TheStreet.com, a popular investment website, highlighting the view that, "[t]he deal... could be announced in the next few days... through a joint venture with Clearwire and a big investment from Intel." Clearwire stock rose 5 percent that day.

In addition, the CEOs of Sprint and Clearwire discussed the joint venture openly. In its earnings conference call on March 3, 2008, the topic came up and Clearwire management talked about it. As was par for the course for Galleon in pursuit of its investors' interests, Naph Joseph was on this call. After the conference call, TheStreet.com reported that "Clearwire says that it continues active and regular discussions with Sprint. Hopes to announce deal soon." Joseph reported this back to Galleon through our normal and required channels of communication internally.

On March 5 and 6, 2008, Intel hosted its annual investor meeting that was attended by over one hundred analysts. Again, as per the Galleon protocols for our investors, Naph Joseph joined the call, listening carefully for all information explicit and implicit that we could use for our investors' benefit. Intel executives gave a detailed presentation on WiMax. A sell-side analyst from Stanford Research who also attended the meeting wrote on March 7 that he spoke to Intel execs from the WiMAX group, and it supported "their expectations of a WiMAX partnership between Sprint and Clearwire and Intel."

Clearwire was on the Galleon radar screen at this moment in time. Although it did not stand out among the countless companies and industries that Galleon tracked, even the basic review of records refreshed my memory once I—unlike the government—understood the broader context. And it is with this fuller picture of all the work that Galleon had put into Clearwire, that my conversation with Rajiv on March 20, 2008, which unbeknownst to either of us was being recorded by the government, must be understood.

Our discussion did not involve any secret passing of information from Rajiv to me. Rajiv was not working on the Clearwire deal. He therefore had no specific material nonpublic information.

But the absence of any covert passing of MNPI should have been obvious from the recording itself. The recording, if anything, exculpated me. On March 20 and 21, 2008, Rajiv and I discussed, as part of our broader social conversations, questions around valuation. Such a discussion, like countless between Rajiv and I before and after this, focused on how would I as a public investor might value the company, as opposed to how would he, as a private equity investor, might. The salient point was that the information was already public.

Rajiv confirmed the innocuousness of this discussion between us subsequently in court when he was cross-examined by one of my attorneys, Terry Lynam.

Q: So the spectrum will be worth several billion dollars, right? You said that, right?

Goel: That is correct sir, that was from my perspective.

Q: And you said that because Sprint will be transferring its spectrum to the new entity, right?

Goel: Sir, you have to understand I'm talking from the long-term perspective in my views. I look at spectrum. I look at who is on the board of directors, etc. That is my perspective, sir.

Q: I'm just asking you about spectrum. Your view was you have to value this company based from this nationwide spectrum. Is that right?

Goel: This is my view.

Q: I understand that. That's what I am asking. Mr. Rajaratnam had a different view.

Goel: He was mathematical.

Q: So this is a hypothetical discussion of two people who have different points of view on how to value a company. Right?

Goel: Sir, my view is different from Mr. Rajaratnam's view. Mr. Rajaratnam looks at perspective from the public markets. My view is that I invest in small $10 million investments, $2 million investments. We have a different perspective is what I'm trying to say, sir.

The import of this examination by Terry was profound. To digress for a moment, Terry, unlike most of the lawyers involved in the litigation from either the government or my defense team, was sophisticated with respect to the financial industry. He drew out of Rajiv on cross-examination a crucial point—not in the *Perry Mason* gotcha style of Hollywood lore, but as a matter of carefully building a factual record. Terry elicited sworn testimony from Rajiv that he and I, over the course of these recorded conversations, disagreed as to the appropriate way to value Clearwire. If in fact Rajiv was providing me with MNPI, there would be no room for disagreement—Rajiv would have been providing me with information that I did not already have through publicly available information.

My conversations with Rajiv over March 20 and 21 had no impact on me or on Galleon's trading decisions. They were typical of the more academic discussions we shared as friends. Because ultimately, my foundation for trading was the incredible independent research from my Galleon team. I trained my colleagues and expected them to scour every piece of publicly available information and they did just that. With respect to Clearwire, we expected the deal to be announced at the beginning of April at the upcoming cable show in Las Vegas, an event Naph Joseph, would be attending. Adopting our long-standing event-based trading strategy, one week before the event, on March 24, I started buying a small "placeholder" position (about $3 million) with a plan to increase it to around $20 million (less than 2 percent of the technology portfolio) by April 1. To a mom-and-pop fund or the day trader upon whom the government typically focuses for its insider prosecutions, these may have been big positions, suspicious on their face. For a vibrant hedge fund like Galleon with assets of over $6 or $7 billion under management (AUM) at the time, this was a placeholder bet and for a sophisticated financial observer, nothing terribly special.

Following our initial investment on the very next day, on March 25, two Galleon analysts, Naph Joseph and my brother Rengan, travelled to

Washington, D.C. to meet with the CEO of LCCI International, a wireless company, as well as with an industry consultant who was in the business of buying and selling spectrum. Galleon was focused on Clearwire and our analysts wanted to understand how to value the nationwide spectrum of the joint venture. The purpose of these meetings, all of which were appropriate and never questioned, were part of our intense diligence.

Understand that Galleon was not the only hedge fund or investor circling this idea. We had, based on our research, our view of its outcome and believed that we were early in reaching that investment conclusion. We believed we were ahead of the investment curve. However, that evening, the *Wall Street Journal*, which had also been following the Sprint/Clearwire deal closely, published an article in its online edition asserting that a consortium of companies, including Intel, were paying $3.2 billion into the joint venture to help fund the build out of the network. This news in the *Journal* made public Galleon's thesis on Clearwire, which we had developed over time, and undercut our hard work.

My younger brother, Rengan, called me from D.C. at 8:11 that evening frustrated by the *Wall Street Journal's* having broken the news. As captured on the wiretap recording, unbeknownst to us, Rengan said, "We're fucked man. It just hit the *Wall Street Journal*." I asked him what they were referring to, and Rengan responded, "The Clearwire stuff. It's all over the *Wall Street Journal*." I asked, "What price did they say?" and Rengan replied, "They are short on details but they kinda say, you know, they're looking to raise as much as $3 billion, but they don't have any of the equity splits. But they have named Comcast, they named Time Warner, Clearwire and Sprint." I said, "Okay. Shit," frustrated that we had not completed our work and built a full position. Rengan ended the call with, "I don't know how much we got in today."

Rengan was clearly frustrated that as we were completing our analysis and starting to accumulate a position, the WSJ was ahead of us—and probably other professional investors who had been following the story for months. Perhaps understandably, Rengan was equally frustrated as his entire day of travel to and from Washington, D.C. had lost its utility in light of the

Journal report while on his way back. It did not take a genius to figure out that the article would prompt countless investors to follow the reporting and invest accordingly. And, as a result, the stock was going to open higher, and Galleon's costs for pursuing our longer-standing investment strategy would be higher. That same night at 8:32 p.m., Naph Joseph sent me an email about the D.C. visit, stating "too little too late—literally was about to send it out before the WSJ scooped me."

INTEL

HAVING BROKEN RAJIV, THE PROSECUTORS coached him to further build their case. Clearwire was not enough. They pressed him to come up with another accusation of insider trading. Under pressure, he came up with the story that "once" in his nine years at Intel, he gave me inside information about Intel's earning results. In his first interview with the FBI, which was recorded on FBI Form 302, the official record of the interview, Rajiv claimed it was for Intel's second quarter 2007, reported in July 2007. When a review of my trading pattern undermined his story, the FBI and Rajiv shifted the timeframe to the first quarter, in April 2007.

At trial, Rajiv's testimony contradicted his own interviews with the FBI prior to trial. When he was shown the written notes of the FBI interview by my defense lawyer, Rajiv dismissed them out of hand, stating that the FBI had it wrong.

Rajiv and I had talked often about Intel. We had also talked extensively about Galleon. This was far from an exchange of illegal information. Instead, this was the normal back-and-forth between two friends whose families socialized and talked about their work. No more, no less. I would never have asked Rajiv to violate his obligations, but he could not have done so anyway. As a midlevel executive at one of its subsidiaries, Rajiv had no access to Intel's financials—whether first, second, or any quarter of 2007, as Rajiv admitted to the FBI. Galleon's estimates of Intel's results were often closer than his! This was because we had a full-time analyst at Galleon who following the semiconductor industry and Intel very closely, meeting with company management, building their own financial projections, following earnings conference calls, and tracking Intel's main competitor, AMD. We also had access to over thirty sell-side analysts at other Wall Street brokerage firms who also followed Intel and published reports.

Despite the extensive wiretaps of my phone, there is not a single instance of a wiretap in which Rajiv and I discuss Intel's quarterly results. Rajiv himself does not remember what he told me about Intel's results that one time. He told the jury that he got "some information" about Intel's financial results from Alex Lemke, one of Intel's investor relations managers, which he then conveyed to me. However, when questioned by both the prosecution and the defense lawyers, he could not remember anything about the information.

> **Prosecution**: Don't you recall exactly what you spoke to Mr. Lemke about on each of this [sic] conversation?

> **Goel**: I do not.

When my defense lawyers cross-examined him, he said the same thing:

> **Q**: Do you recall what you spoke to Mr. Lemke about in each of these conversations?

> **Goel**: No, sir. I do not.

> **Q**: You don't know whether it was good or bad information.

> **Goel**: I do not remember whether it was good or bad.

> **Q**: *Your testimony is that one time after seven years you told him some information that you can't specifically remember? Is that your testimony?*

> **Goel**: *Yes, sir.*

The government's allegations of Goel supplying me with information on Intel were just another example of the prosecution manufacturing a charge. To try to fill this hole in their case, one of the prosecutors, Reed

Brodsky, in his final summation, deliberately misled both the court and the jury. Brodsky said, "Lemke got some good news," and that Mr. Goel told Mr. Rajaratnam, "Things aren't so bad, I told you it was bad before, but things are getting a little bit better."

But this summation was directly contrary to Rajiv's testimony. Rajiv said he didn't remember what Mr. Lemke had told him. If the defense counsel had simply made things up in front of the jury and the court, they could have been disbarred. Brodsky did just that with no consequences whatsoever.

How can one be charged with a crime when there is absolutely no evidence, written or otherwise, and the only witness can't remember anything, and admits as much under oath? And how can one be convicted of the crime when the prosecution turns the testimony on its head by stating exactly the opposite of what the person under oath said? The prosecution acted with impunity.

My defense lawyer, John Dowd, in his summation pointed this out to the jury, "Why do you think Mr. Brodsky mischaracterized Goel's testimony in this way? Because he needs to. It's a hole in the government's case—a huge hole. The government hasn't offered any evidence of what Mr. Goel actually said to Mr. Rajaratnam."

He continued, "If anything, and ladies and gentlemen, you cannot convict Raj on the basis of material and nonpublic information because the government has not proven what the information was. How are you supposed to assess whether it was material? How are you supposed to assess whether it was nonpublic? You can't! That's why you have to acquit. That's why Mr. Brodsky mischaracterized Mr. Goel's testimony."[39]

There was simply too much information for the jury to track. The truth boiled down to small and very essential details. This was information overload. The prosecutors orchestrated a data dump onto a jury already overloaded and unable to track the chronology or the facts. They created an alternate reality during their closing comments, a fabrication to fit their summation narrative. The government's lawyers said anything they wished. Judge Holwell stayed silent.

I have often wondered whether Holwell was just as confused and said nothing in order to hide his own confusion.

RAJIV'S CAPITULATION

Nothing Rajiv and I had discussed was inside information.

I had assumed that he shared this view and as a result, it was no surprise that he initially plead not guilty. I also assumed that his lawyers' willingness to enter into a joint defense agreement with my lawyers, share documents, and move to educate the government as to what had actually happened was par for the course with the pursuit of justice.

However, about a month after our arrests, we got the startling news— Rajiv had flipped and was now working with the prosecution. Under the conventions of a joint defense agreement, Rajiv and his counsel could no longer work with us, having chosen instead to implicate me. I was confused—what would have caused my friend to suddenly reverse course and presumably provide false testimony to the government all for the purposes of turning against me?

LOANS VERSUS GIFTS

The answer, as it turns out, would have nothing to do with insider trading. Instead, the government twisted the fact of my loans to Rajiv of $600,000 against him to bring him to his proverbial knees.

The government felt as though it had made a breakthrough when it discovered these transfers from me to him. This was there moment—proof that I had paid Rajiv for MNPI based on his employment at Intel. It confronted Rajiv, who had a larger but related problem. Rajiv, as it turns out, had never disclosed these loans as a part of his tax filings. Moreover, and further unbeknownst to me, Rajiv had not used these funds for the family reasons for which he had requested them. Instead, he had used them for a series of personal and luxury expenses. And, worse yet, he had deposited them in foreign bank accounts, including inexplicable Swiss accounts that he had opened.

For the government, this was prosecutorial gold: payments from one defendant to another that were ultimately deposited in Swiss bank accounts. The relevant facts and context did not matter—the optics were horrific for me and great for the government. They then paired this with Rajiv's exposure for his tax failings to pressure him to cooperate. The choice was simple—paint a narrative that connects these unrelated dots against me and in return, cooperation would likely result for Rajiv in no jail time and a significant diminution of his mounting legal fees. For anyone in this position other than a person of principle, there was just one choice: cooperate.

When I learned of this, I was shocked. For me, the real betrayal by Rajiv was his misuse of my loans and his willingness to lie to the government. I had no intention of "gifting" Goel a total of $600,000. I had the loan document to prove the fact of a loan to Goel. And nor were these funds payment to Goel for irrelevant "insider" information. The prosecutors found ways to manipulate clear-cut facts into sinister plot twists. They continued to insist the payments were "gifts." For the prosecutors and their case against me, the distinction was a crucial one—they needed the payments to be acknowledged by Goel and understood by the jury as being "gifts"—this was the only way to justify their existence as being payments for inside information.

During the discovery phase of my case, my attorneys and I had found the promissory note for the $100,000, which neutralized the first part of this argument. At my trial, Rajiv continued to maintain that the $500,000 loan was a gift. However, upon cross-examination by my defense, even while being evasive, he finally had to admit that there was no connection between the $500,000 loan and any supposed inside information, much to the chagrin of the prosecutors.

Q: Well at some point you told him that you were over in India taking care of your father, right, and he was sick, right?

Goel: I remember that conversation. I was at the hospital at that time. I do not remember whether it was 2005, 2006, or 2007, but I spoke to him once. I remember I was in the hospital.

Q: You also expressed concern to Mr. Rajaratnam about whether you could keep his apartment in the family if he passed away?

Goel: That's correct.

Q: You again asked Mr. Rajaratnam for help?

Goel: Sir, I don't recall whether I asked him or he offered.

Q: And it was 2006, a full year before you claim that you gave information about earnings in the beginning of April 2007, right, this was a full year earlier?

Goel: Why are you bringing earnings into the picture? I am not seeing the nexus.

Q: The attorney was supposed to buy your father's apartment in India, right?

Goel: That was the original intent, sir, that is why he gifted the money.

Q: But you used the money to repair your house in California, didn't you?

Goel: We had some urgent repairs that cropped up.

Q: So you actually misled Mr. Rajaratnam about what the money was for?

Goel: No sir, I did not.[40]

The government's strategy of trying to connect my loan to Rajiv as payment for inside information fell flat on its face when Rajiv admitted inadvertently, much to the chagrin of the prosecutors, "Why are you bringing earnings into the picture? I am not seeing the nexus." He did not get it.

My defense counsel, Terry Lynam, elicited Goel's acknowledgement that he had called me for financial assistance from his father's hospital bed in

India. Lynam went much further: he elicited the astonishing admission that he had not used the funds to help his father but to help himself refurbish his own home in California. The layers of deception continued. He deceived me using his father's failing health as a rationale. Subsequently, I found out the depth of the deception: With the funds I sent him for his father, Goel had also purchased a brand-new BMW 7 series in 2007, traveling to Germany to pick it up directly from the factory floor!

In cross-examination, Rajiv's penchant for offshore accounts was also fully exposed:

Q: You didn't report your Swiss bank account on your tax reports?

Goel: I did not report it.

Q: You also had accounts in Singapore and India that you did not report?

Goel: Yes, sir.

Q: And I believe you also testified that you thought there was a mystique to having a Swiss bank account. Is that right?

Goel: Yes, at that time, yes, sir.

Q: And you knowingly failed to report that on your returns, right?

Goel: Yes, sir.[41]

"Mystique?" About a Swiss bank account? An ultimate cliché.

AN ODD PLOT TWIST

Even after Rajiv's implausible testimony under oath that contributed to my conviction, there was an even more bizarre coda to this story. Years after my conviction, the government charged my brother Rengan with insider trading for, among other things, his trading in Clearwire with me. The government, as in my case, alleged that Rengan traded at Galleon based on MNPI received from Rajiv.

However, while my federal grand jury convicted me of these allegations raised as part of the fuller panoply of its allegations against, a separate federal grand jury was presented with these allegations against Rengan in a much narrower context. The press circus had subsided. Rengan's trial was largely an afterthought. And the government had only a more limited set of charges against him.

The federal grand jury heard the very same information regarding our trading in Clearwire against Rengan that a separate grand jury years earlier had heard against me. I know because I paid for my lawyers to provide Rengan's counsel with all of the information that we had developed, which Rengan's lawyer presented to this federal jury.

Rengan was acquitted at trial. Including for the allegations that he and I had committed insider trading with respect to Clearwire based on Rajiv's alleged information. Same information, opposite result.

REFLECTIONS

THE PROSECUTORS WERE FLAT-OUT WRONG to charge Rajiv and me with sharing inside information both about the Clearwire joint venture and Intel's quarterly earnings. No inside information was ever given or received.

Rajiv's real crimes were twofold: the first was tax evasion—conducted over many years through a series of offshore accounts. The second was obstruction of justice with the destruction of his laptop after his arrest in an attempt to hide these accounts. Upon his arrest, he had been fired from Intel and lacked the resources for a sustained legal fight. He made the decision to plead guilty, cooperate with the prosecutors, and testify against me to avoid jail time. In the end, Rajiv avoided prison altogether and got away with only two years of probation!

There were several gaps in the prosecutor's charges.

If Rajiv and I were actually "conspirators," how could our conspiracy percolate to the surface only once in seven or eight years? How could that one time be "something" he told me about Intel and which he could not remember as being "good or bad?" Based on vague details, how could a jury determine whether it was material nonpublic information or not? The information about the Clearwire/Sprint joint venture was clearly in the public domain.

Another hurdle for the prosecutors was the fact that I had encouraged Rajiv to pursue career paths beyond Intel. If Rajiv really had been such a valuable informant, it would not make sense for me to help him leave Intel—I would have wanted him to stay there and continue to provide inside information. Once again, Rajiv would have to bob and weave on the witness stand when confronted with the facts. Even after admitting that I had indeed set up a job interview for him with a private equity fund and had given him input on leaving, he insisted that he had not been "actively looking" to leave Intel. Yet, completely contrary to his testimony, the March 20, 2008, a Clearwire call recorded Rajiv imploring me to "get me a job with one of your powerful friends, man; I am tired of this company."

In late September or early October 2009, about two weeks before our arrests, Rajiv took his then high school senior daughter to visit the University of Pennsylvania. There he met a mutual former Wharton classman, Tushar Mody, who lived in Philadelphia at the time. Much after the trial, Tushar told me that Rajiv had told him, "I'm trying to get into Raj's inner circle." This perhaps more than anything speaks volumes about Rajiv's agenda and lack of character. I was totally blindsided by someone I had considered a friend.

For his cooperation against me, Rajiv Goel received a two-year probation and no prison time for tax evasion or obstruction of justice. Rajiv's gamble, with the truth as his currency that he was willing to spend, had paid off.

CHAPTER 14

ADAM SMITH:
You Won't See Your Sons for Twenty Years

From the initial press conference upon my arrest to November 2010, the government trumpeted Galleon as a criminal organization, one built upon and rife with insider trading and illegal conduct that permeated the firm. However, they had one glaring problem: they could not find a single Galleon employee who would affirm their wild allegations against the firm.

The fact that the government found themselves in this hole, just six months away from trial, was extraordinary. As I learned, normally when the government has concerns of potential improper activity at a major financial institution, they have a standard playbook. The government contacts the firm, typically through its legal department or outside counsel. And so begins a very orderly process, almost entirely out of the public eye, where the government and the firm through its counsel negotiate in the shadows. The purpose of such deliberate and careful investigation without rushing to bring public charges was to allow the institution to continue its good work while the government narrowly explored for any misconduct. Executives and employees are all afforded their own independent lawyers and the government discreetly conducts extensive employee interviews with relevant documents to determine if any wrongdoing has occurred.

In my case, the government took precisely the opposite approach. I was arrested, paraded through the proverbial town square, and proclaimed guilty in the press. In a flash, Galleon was destroyed and branded a den of financial iniquity. But a strange thing happened as the government followed up with now former Galleon employees, who had every reason to be angry and point fingers. Not one of them did. Instead, a parade of Galleon portfolio managers, analysts, and employees—all represented by independent counsel—met with the government and often with my attorneys and, one by one, disputed any allegations of insider trading at Galleon, let alone the pervasive culture of impropriety that Bharara and the government had rolled out to the world.

As trial approached, the government was facing a mixed bag of witnesses to support their overheated rhetoric against me. No company insiders cooperated or agreed to disclosing MNPI. Roomy Khan's severe credibility problems and criminal history had metastasized. Ali Far had recanted. And the government's remaining witnesses, my friends Rajiv Goel and Anil Kumar, had no connection to Galleon.

The government was missing a key weapon in their arsenal against me: a Galleon insider willing to validate and authenticate their false narrative. They had combed through all of Galleon's records, all of Galleon's trades, and interviewed several key Galleon employees who had something to do on the investment side. This happened with many employees multiple times. *All stated unequivocally that they had never been a part of or witnessed anything remotely like insider trading at Galleon.*

For the government, this was a roadblock of astronomical proportions. Unlike in most prior insider trading prosecutions, the government had elected here not to accuse me of being some day trader who engaged in a stray and improbably successful stock trade. No, the government contended that my core business was corrupt. They told the public that the research, analysis, conferences, third-party sell-side data—all of the *hard work* that we constructed as the foundation of Galleon's extensive trading—was all suspect.

And yet, not a credible Galleon or former Galleon employee would confirm this. Having pored over Galleon's extensive trading records, the government could conjure up only allegations that composed less than 0.01 percent of the totality of my trades over the previous five-year period. And no one that was on the ground and in our offices to validate their false charges.

The danger to the government was palpable. If they were unable to produce a Galleon employee with an insider's view, the jury would be left with a very different impression. Namely, that strong investment returns were possible with good, old-fashioned, in-depth research in sharp contrast to the allegations of inside information that formed the crux of Bharara's and Kang's submission to the courts and to the public. The humorist Jonathan Swift said in 1710, "falsehood flies and the truth comes limping after it." Well, with trial approach, the truth in the form of resolute and proud Galleon employees was gaining ground.

Ironically, the government needed to corrupt someone on the inside in order to profit from their public allegations. The government began looking for someone with just the right kind of vulnerabilities. They settled on Adam Smith, the former portfolio manager of the Galleon Communications Fund.

ADAM SMITH AT GALLEON

ADAM SMITH JOINED GALLEON AS a technology analyst in 2002. Previously he worked as a banker at Morgan Stanley in their Silicon Valley offices, dealing with a variety of technology companies. Eager to move to the investment side of the business, he contacted me through a mutual business associate and joined Galleon in 2002.

At Galleon, he started as a junior analyst in the technology sector. The career path for a junior analyst is to become a senior analyst and then eventually a portfolio manager. Adam Smith followed just this path. In the seven years he had worked at Galleon, Adam moved up the ladder to portfolio manager. His performance as a portfolio manager between 2006 and 2009 was quite good.

By 2006, we realized the growing importance of Taiwan in the technology manufacturing ecosystem, and we opened a Taiwanese office with four technology analysts. As part of his research, Adam would travel to Taiwan every two or three months to meet with electronic companies. Many cell phones and motherboards (the guts of a PC) were assembled in Taiwan. Adam was meeting with Taiwanese electronics companies to do channel checks. Often, up to 30 percent of his portfolio was invested in Taiwanese companies. As was Galleon policy, during these trips, he would write a report about what he had learned each day and circulate it to the other analysts and portfolio managers of the technology group. This was precisely the type of painstaking research and analysis that we at Galleon demanded to get ahead: good old-fashioned investments of capital, time, and personal sacrifice. This is how we built Galleon and established standards of excellence.

Over time, I realized for all of Adam's significant strengths, he was far from perfect for Galleon. When Adam was promoted to portfolio manager, I asked him to mentor some of our newer analysts, much as I had mentored him in his early days at Galleon. He did it half-heartedly for a couple of months and then dropped the ball, saying that "There's nothing in it for me." I had initially believed that Adam had the ethos to become a member of the senior team at Galleon. But after this and other similar self-focused incidents, I regarded him more as a hired gun than as a team player. It was clear that Adam Smith looked out for only Adam Smith.

Immediately after my arrest, Adam was visibly angered and upset. As with all Galleon employees at the time, we arranged for Adam to consult with and be represented by fully independent counsel, drawing from the best reputations in the New York legal market (and at the highest price points). These lawyers were required, both by design and legal ethics, to represent their client and their client only, irrespective of whether their testimony would help or hurt me or Galleon.

Each of the Galleon employees had the option not to participate in interviews with my attorneys. In the normal situation where the government takes pains not to disrupt an ongoing business, employees are under intrinsic pressure—they have to worry that refusal to cooperate with company counsel could result in negative consequences at work or, worse yet, termination. Here, however, the government had destroyed Galleon before even attempting to prove their allegations. As such, our former employees were in a sense liberated—they could speak their minds freely without fearing any repercussions from Galleon. We went one step further. I was asked by my attorneys not to participate in these meetings, specifically to avoid any undue pressure on Adam (or any of the other witnesses). I fully agreed with this approach—I was comfortable with the truth and I wanted my Galleon employees to feel at ease sharing information with my lawyers outside of my presence.

Adam, like every other Galleon employee, voluntarily offered to help me in any way he could. Together with his lawyer, he voluntarily met with my defense lawyers from Akin Gump (John Dowd, Terry Lynam, Rob Hotz, and Samidh Guha) as well with the Galleon corporate lawyers from Shearman & Sterling (Adam Hakki and John Nathanson). They met on two occasions: February 2010 and July 2010. At this first meeting, Adam indicated that he was unaware of any insider trading at Galleon at any time and that he never engaged in insider trading. My lawyers understood that the government had focused on trading in two companies—AMD and ATYT. At the follow-up meeting in July 2010, Adam was asked about AMD's acquisition of ATYT. He said that like everyone in the technology sector, he was aware of constant chatter in the marketplace regarding the potential acquisition of ATYT by AMD or Intel. He reiterated that he viewed these rumors as "distractions as they brought speculative money into the market and distorted the ATYT stock."

My lawyers took copious notes and wrote their customary memos to the case files. Adam came across as knowledgeable, candid, and completely firm in his view that no wrongdoing had occurred at Galleon.

ADAM SMITH'S POST-GALLEON TURN

AFTER GALLEON SHUT DOWN, ADAM decided to start his own fund, Rose Lane Capital. John Pernell, founding member of the investment management firm, Polaris Investments, provided Rose Lane Capital with $25 million in seed capital. John Pernell had been one of my early investors at Needham and later at Galleon. He called me for my recommendation regarding investing with Adam. I provided my strong recommendation.

Rose Lane Capital launched in January 2010. The road, however, was not smooth. Without the kind of a disciplined research team he had at his fingertips at Galleon, Adam floundered. On his own, he was essentially a one-man shop with a skeletal research team. And equally crucially, without the formal oversight and structure of the Galleon risk-management group, Adam took on a lot more risk than we would have tolerated at any of Galleon's funds. He leveraged his portfolio to levels well beyond any of the triggers we had at Galleon. In fact, on a few occasions, John Pernell called me, concerned about Adam's risk control approach. Adam made no money for his investors. His performance was flat in 2010.

Adam Smith's struggles at Rose Lane Capital were Agent Kang's opportunity. Time was running out for the government to somehow secure testimony from a Galleon employee. Although I question Kang's honesty, I have to admire his guile. Somehow, Smith had made it to Kang's radar. We learned later that Kang approached an FBI informant named Tom Lin, an acquaintance of Adam, to get to Adam. Tom Lin never worked for Galleon. Lin was part of a roster of FBI informants who were at Kang's beck and call. At Kang's instruction, Lin strapped on a wire and made consensual calls to Adam that were secretly recorded.

Approaching Adam at this time was strategically very wise. Smith—like Roomy Khan and Ali Far before him and obviously in sharp contrast to my own circumstances—was in financial peril. Without the Galleon architecture, research, and resources, he did not have the tools to do the analysis that I and my colleagues did at Galleon. The financial strain on him, like that felt by Khan and Far earlier, took its toll. Coached by Kang, Tom discussed stocks with Adam, teased Adam with stock information that was clearly improper, and Adam seized the opportunity. And it was all on tape.

A few days later, Kang approached Adam Smith and replayed the calls to Adam. The threats of criminal charges and catastrophe to Smith were immediate. He was witnessing the pressure of the government on me now turning on him—but unlike me, Adam was guilty in his post-Galleon life of cheating to reclaim his Galleon success.

Kang pounced. Using the very same words with Adam that he used with me, Kang threatened Adam with twenty years in prison. Kang jeered at Adam, explicit in his stark description of a probable reality: Adam would not see his two young boys for a very long time.

Adam immediately called John Pernell. He asked to speak to Polaris's outside counsel at Seward & Kissel. John Pernell arranged for a one-hour conference call with Adam and the attorneys from Seward and Kissel. The lawyers shed as much light as they could on the vague contours of insider trading laws. Adam was certain he had done nothing wrong. But he was uncertain about navigating law that had been intentionally left obscure. Adam realized the enormity of his situation. He, like most defendants, had three choices: 1) Plead guilty and take his medicine, 2) fight for his innocence, or 3) cooperate with the government to minimize the damage to himself.

As it would turn out, my assessment of Adam Smith was spot-on. Adam Smith looked out only for Adam Smith. Normally, when the government "auditions" or proffers a potential cooperator, they listen first to what the would-be cooperator knows and determine if the witness is truthful and if his or her information would be useful. Here, there was no need for this dance or courtship. With my trial looming, Adam knew exactly what information would be useful and the government knew exactly what information they needed. The question of truthfulness went immediately by the wayside.

Adam agreed to testify against me. The FBI got what they badly wanted and needed: a Galleon insider whom they could force feed the narrative they had spun to the public over a year ago.

On January 28, 2011, Adam signed a plea agreement with the prosecutors. Implicating me was just the beginning. Once he cleared the emotional hurdle of becoming a turncoat, he became almost eager to entrap several others, including even his own trader, Ian Horowitz.

Soon after my arrest, I sent a memo to all employees to preserve all documents and to return all company laptops. We also removed all shredders from the office. Adam Smith was the only one who did not return his laptop, claiming it was lost. At that time, I did not think it was unusual for someone to lose their laptop. During the discovery process, Adam Smith changed his story. He told the prosecutors that on the day of my arrest, he drove to his country house in upstate New York and destroyed his laptop. The contradiction is stark and clear. Galleon and I had nothing to hide. Adam Smith had something to hide. It begs the question: What? What did Adam Smith have to hide?

My attorneys and I later found out through Adam's interviews with the FBI that during his quarterly trips to Taiwan to conduct channel checks, he was obtaining inside information from executives of several local Taiwanese technology companies. Often, up to 30 percent of his portfolio was invested in these Taiwanese companies. I had no idea that Adam's investing decisions were based on inside information. Portfolio managers at Galleon made their own buy/sell decisions. I did not invest in any of these local Taiwanese technology companies. In retrospect, I have no doubt that if I had, it would have opened up yet another avenue of attack for Bharara and Kang.

ADAM SMITH'S SECOND THOUGHTS

ON FEBRUARY 4, 2011, JUST five days after signing his plea deal, Adam had breakfast with John Pernell at the Cornell Club in New York City. He was distraught and spoke freely. Adam confided to John Pernell that the FBI had intimidated him into pleading guilty.

John Pernell called me immediately after the breakfast. He spoke with urgency. He asked me to have lunch with him. Over lunch, he summarized what he had heard from Adam. I asked John if he would send a memo recapping his meeting with Adam to my lead lawyer, John Dowd. John Pernell agreed to do so. Here is that memo in relevant portion:

February 4th 2011

To: John Dowd

Breakfast with Adam Smith

Cornell Club, Wednesday, February 2, 2011 8:00 A.M.

Breakfast meeting lasted approx. 1 hour, 40 minutes. I mostly listened and asked a few questions. It began with him apologizing for what he put me through and the partners of the two funds. Adam stated that he was told that if he did not plead guilty and cooperate, he would not see his children until they had reached age 20. His two sons are 3 & 5. He further stated that the 5 or so trades he is being charged with are not necessarily correct as being based on executed with inside info.

He named 3 or so companies and stated that he told the DA that he had not traded on these based on nonpublic, inside information. He stated that the DA's response was "it did not matter, if it wasn't these, there would be others they could charge him with." *He told me he thinks they want to link the MS [Morgan Stanley] banker with him and they wanted him to wear a wire.*

I asked Adam if he knew this guy well. He said that he met him some years ago and he was not that smart. The DA has agreed to immunization on any other potential findings through 2010, which his counsel insisted on. They would not agree to anything else until after the trial concludes. He said this was *procedural so if he's cross examined, he can state that he has not received any preferential treatment.* [emphasis added] Adam said they were very callous and did not care about anything relative to him or his family situation, etc. It was a good cop, bad cop experience.

Adam was extremely open and truthful with John Pernell. At that time, little did Adam know that John Pernell would testify at my trial about his breakfast conversation with Adam.

ADAM SMITH AS GOVERNMENT PUPPET

THE GOVERNMENT WAS REQUIRED, ESPECIALLY with trial approaching, to disclose to me and my counsel that Adam was cooperating. This set off a scramble on my legal team; we had interviewed Adam twice and he had denied any wrongdoing at Galleon, by me or anyone else for that matter. He had been represented by highly qualified lawyers at that time who would not have brought him to our meeting to lie to us. We were at a loss as to what he was now saying to the government.

As we would soon learn, Adam Smith regurgitated exactly what the FBI had force-fed him. He identified Kamal Ahmed, a former coworker from Adam's Morgan Stanley days, and proposed that Ahmed was a source of inside information for him and others at Galleon. Following Kang's instructions, Adam Smith alleged that in July 2006, Ahmed provided him with inside information about 1) Integrated Devices' (IDTI's) acquisition of Integrated Circuit Systems (ICST) in June 2005, and 2) AMD's acquisition of ATI Technologies (ATYT) in July 2006. All of this was a complete reversal of his statements to our lawyers previously.

Predictably, the FBI's force-fed narrative was false. Ahmed, like so many of the other "insiders" implicated by the government in connection with other cooperators, insisted that he *never* gave any MNPI to Adam. In a December 2, 2010, letter to the prosecution, Doug Tween, Ahmed's lawyer, informed the prosecutors that it was Adam who asked the invasive questions regarding Ahmed's work. Adam's probing had made Ahmed increasingly uncomfortable. By early 2009, Ahmed stopped talking to Adam.

Kamal Ahmed was never charged with any wrongdoing. Nothing. One would think, logically, that the easiest way to test Adam's newly minted claims was the obvious: ask Ahmed himself. Remarkably, despite the outpouring of taxpayer dollars and investigative resources expended, neither the prosecutors nor the FBI spoke to Ahmed. They could not. Because if they had interviewed Ahmed, every word would have to be disclosed to my team as exculpatory information. And it would have subjected Adam and other witnesses to cross-examination. The decision by the government not to interview Ahmed but to press Adam's untested allegations anyway was a calculated decision, one designed to support their false narrative.

I did not know Kamal Ahmed before or after my case. Ahmed via his lawyers stated that he may have met me once at a Morgan Stanley technology conference over the years. There are typically over one thousand investors at these conferences. I do have a recollection of saying hello. Kamal Ahmed, a rising star and a managing director in Morgan Stanley's technology group, was initially suspended and then fired in October 2011 after my trial. This was just more collateral damage of prosecutorial misconduct in the Galleon case.

Well before the time of Adam's alleged tips, Galleon had positions in both ISCT and ATYT. These stocks were rated single best ideas by Galleon analysts, Eric Rothdeutsch (ICST) and Nadeem Janmohamed (ATYT), based on their research. Each analyst was required to have a single best idea to emphasize their conviction levels.

Galleon trading records and weekly reports do not support any of Adam's allegations.

Witnesses at trial are trained to tell the government's story on direct examination. Led in a largely scripted and carefully rehearsed manner, the government lawyers elicit testimony from the witness to build the government's case and often to hide its weaknesses. There are moments of feigned disappointment by the government as it "draws the sting" of the witness's prior bad acts—in other words, the government sternly asks the witness about his wrongdoing and the witness in turn summons up his most remorseful expression. With cooperating witnesses, the government makes a big show before the jury of the fact that the witness has pled guilty to crimes and does not know what sentence he will receive later in time.

Cooperators—especially white-collar cooperators—are well aware that the government's seal of approval virtually ensures that the court will not sentence them to any jail time. Given that the judges on the bench are overwhelmingly former prosecutors from the Southern District themselves, the game is well-known to all the participants: the judges, the prosecutors, the defense lawyers, and the cooperating witnesses. In my case, not a single witness who cooperated and testified—no matter what the extent of their wrongdoing—was sentenced to a single moment in jail.

Adam Smith knew the score. He may have been many things, but he was no dummy. And he had no integrity when it came to protecting his own interests. So Adam proceeded at trial to walk through a choreographed set of fictions regarding two stocks—ICST and ATYT—designed with care to avoid any paper trail that would expose his lies.

ICST

ADAM MAINTAINED FOR THE FIRST time that Ahmed had given him a tip about an ICST acquisition that allowed me to trade profitably. There were no IMs, wiretaps, or emails to support Adam's word. Knowing this, Adam disingenuously said that he had received the tip from Ahmed in person in March 2005 at the Morgan Stanley technology conference.

Well before the Morgan Stanley conference in early March 2005, Galleon owned 1,244,985 shares of ICST based on our own internal analysis.

As early as January 2005, Galleon analyst Eric Rothdeutsch was picking up rumors that ICST was looking to sell itself.

On January 21, 2005, Eric sent an email on ICST saying "checks show that the company is *shopping* itself." [emphasis added]

Then on February 10, 2005, with the stock now trading at close to its fifty-two-week low, Eric sent another email saying, "I like ICST as a long right here...I think that there is a compelling trade to the low 20s." After discussing ICST in that day's morning meeting, several Galleon portfolio managers started building long positions on ICST.

Between recommending ICST in February 2005 and its acquisition by IDTI on June 15, Eric consistently maintained ICST as his top long in his weekly analyst reports.

When ICST was acquired by IDTI on June 15, 2005, we owned 1,272,314 shares, *essentially the same amount as before the alleged tip*. This makes no sense because if Adam had tipped us and we traded on it, we would have significantly increased our ownership of ICST between early March and June 15.

ATYT

ADAM'S SECOND TAKEOVER-RELATED ALLEGATION WAS that in March 2006 at the Morgan Stanley technology conference, Ahmed tipped Adam about the acquisition of ATYT by AMD. With no recorded conversations with Ahmed or any evidence of interactions between them, Adam cleverly and duplicitously once again identified the Morgan Stanley technology conferences in March 2005 and March 2006 as the locations for Ahmed's surreptitious communications to him.

This was, once again, wholly inconsistent with what Adam told my defense team on February 18, 2010. At that time, he told us that followed ATYT in his role as a portfolio manager, that he always traded this stock around earnings events, and that his trades were always based on the stock's fundamentals. Adam also told my team that he was aware of the chatter in the marketplace regarding ATYT's potential acquisition by AMD or Intel. He said that he ignored these rumors and typically viewed them as a distraction, as they brought speculative money into the market and distorted ATYT's short-term stock price movement.

Numerous emails Adam sent to others at Galleon confirm that he was truthful to my lawyers and lying to the prosecutors and to the jury. In fact, on May 31, 2006, after a sell-side analyst made a big call that ATYT and AMD would merge, Adam sent an IM to his trader, Ian, that he "would be shocked if an ATYT/AMD tie was true."

This was well *after* he claimed that Ahmed tipped him about AMD buying ATYT in March 2006.

The closest professional relationship a portfolio manager has is with his own trader. They work as a team, with the trader functioning as the eyes and ears on the market for the portfolio manager. The trader alerts the portfolio manager to any breaking news items and is given the leeway to add to or trim positions if the portfolio manager is travelling or otherwise unavailable.

Typically, a portfolio manager would never mislead their own trader. This instant message to Ian (months after Adam claimed that Ahmed tipped him on ATYT) totally undermines Adam's claim of trading on inside information. Adam would have had difficulty explaining this IM to the jury, but to my surprise and dismay, my defense lawyers did not bring it up at trial. With so much information and details occurring in real time at the trial, the defense lawyers were constantly stretched.

FABRICATING EMAILS

HOWEVER, THE MOST DAMAGING AND false accusation Adam made on the witness stand caught me completely off guard. Adam alleged I had asked him to fabricate an email on June 29, 2006, to "cover" for buying more shares of ATYT. I was flabbergasted—the next trade I did on ATYT was to sell, not buy more.

That morning, ATYT reported its quarterly earnings and held a conference call to discuss the results with investors and analysts, as is typical of public companies. Adam sent an email saying "Adam on ATYT cc (conference call) and not in morning meeting." I stopped by Adam's office after the morning meeting, and asked him to send me an email *as to what he had learned from the call*. This was standard operating procedure at Galleon. Adam sent me an email summarizing the conference call.

Adam's allegations were false on two fronts: 1) Instead of the email *covering* for buying more shares of ATYT, I actually *sold* shares of ATYT. I actually sold not bought. 2) If I wanted to buy more shares of ATYT, I did not need "a cover." It was the top long idea of our analyst Nadeem Janmohamed.

When cross-examined by the prosecution, Adam forcefully asserted that this email was fabricated on my instructions as a cover-up to buy more ATYT shares. However, under some tough cross-examination by my defense lawyers, Adam softened and said that it was just his "belief" that I wanted a cover-up. He never asserted that I had asked him to fabricate any emails. However, the damage was done.

The prosecutors were now able to claim, and the media did their part in repeatedly reporting, that I frequently instructed Galleon analysts to write "fake" emails as a cover-up furthering the narrative that Galleon was a criminal enterprise headed by me.

Q: And you also testified that on the morning this announcement came out you didn't go to the morning meeting at Galleon because you were on the call that ATI had to discuss their earnings, right?

Smith: That's correct.

Q: Now the call that they had is typically after the earnings are released, the company has a call where the analysts can participate in the conference call and ask questions about this report, right?

Smith: Yes.

Q: So you missed the morning meeting that morning?

Smith: I did.

Q: Now you testified that—let me ask you. After that morning meeting Mr. Rajaratnam stopped by your office to ask you what happened on the earnings call that you had just participated in, isn't that right?

Smith: He stopped by my office and asked me to send him an email saying what to do with ATI stock.

Q: So he wanted to know from you, he wanted you to justify your position for continuing to buy ATI, right? That's why he asked you to tell you to tell him what he should do, right?

Smith: My *belief* was that he wanted me to give him reasons that we'd already covered, fundamental reasons to cover up any

purchases he would make that day because he knew that the company was going to be bought.

Q: Well, you testified that the only thing he said to you was after you missed the meeting, that the only thing he said to you was tell me why we should buy ATI, right?

Smith: That's all he said. [emphasis added]

Q: What to do on ATI, right, words to that effect?

Smith: Correct.

Q: Now in June 2006, you had only been a portfolio manager for about six months, right?

Smith: Correct.

Q: Mr. Rajaratnam was trying to train you to be better, wasn't he?

Smith: Always.

Q: He wanted you to have discipline; he wanted you to justify your position to why you wanted to buy stock, right?

Smith: That's true, yes.

Additionally, to please his new masters, the prosecutors and the FBI, Adam also tried to entrap his partner and trader, Ian Horowitz. Fortunately, even though Ian had no idea he was been taped, he did not fall for the trap. He told the truth. Adam tried to get him to say that there was widespread insider trading at Galleon, Horowitz replied, "I don't know what you are talking about."

Q: Now you were asked about the call that you made to Mr. Horowitz at the request of the FBI, right, when you were cooperating?

Smith: Yes.

Q: You got instructions from the FBI about how to proceed, right?

Smith: Correct.

Q: And they told you should lie if you were asked if you were recording the call. Right?

Smith: Yes.

Q: But you did not testify that they told you you should lie if Horowitz said he had no inside information, you didn't testify that they told you to lie about that, did you?

Smith: *Well, what they told me is that I could say anything I could think up or use any tactic I could try to get Mr. Horowitz to say what they wanted him to say.* [emphasis added]

So, Adam himself testified in court under oath that FBI Agent Kang told him that he could use any tactic he could to get Ian to say what they wanted him to say. I believe Agent Kang gave Roomy Khan the same instructions in a wiretapped call attempting to entrap me in January 2008: say anything you can think of to help us convict Raj, including lying. Kang undoubtedly was a corrupt strand of the FBI. He consistently threatened, lied, and cheated his way to achieving his goals, regardless of the facts.

Adam then made a feeble attempt to claim that he regularly gave me inside information about the earnings of a technology company called Intersil. He said that he received the information from an Intersil employee in Taiwan. Another lie. When the defense showed the jury that on many occasions, my trading on Intersil was opposite to Adam's (he was long and I was short or vice versa), the prosecutors quietly dropped the charges around Intersil. This Intersil example highlights two important aspects about my case:

1. The prosecutors had not done their homework before bringing the charges. Or, perhaps they were willful in misleading the public and the jury. Had they been prepared or truthful, they would have seen the discrepancy between my Intersil trading and that of Adam's in our respective portfolios. The prosecutors simply

tried to throw as much mud as possible against the wall, hoping much or at least some of it would stick.

2. My trading was consistent with the written recommendation of our internal Galleon analyst, Nadeem Janmohamed. This was powerful proof that regardless of whatever Adam Smith supposedly told me about Intersil, I traded in line with and on the basis of my analyst's recommendations.

ADAM SMITH SKATES ON CROSS-EXAMINATION

The cross-examination of Adam was handled by Akin Gump partner Terry Lynam. Terry is a wonderful persona and an even better attorney. He had a very effective way of cross-examining a witness, avoiding the high-volume theatrics of some defense lawyers but instead persistently chipping away at the truth with a comprehensive knowledge of the documents and an eye for internal consistencies.

But there is only so much a cross-examination can achieve when the witness is primed to lie, the prosecutors are willing to enable, and the court elects not to intervene.

At my trial, Adam testified that could not remember any details of his highly damaging conversation with John Pernell in February 2011, in which Adam wavered in a moment of honesty about the pressure the government had brought to bear and their suggestion that he fabricate the events of which he had just testified. Adam and the government obviously knew of this glaring weakness. So, suddenly, the same Adam Smith who testified at the government's urging with great clarity alleged conversations with Ahmed in 2005 and 2006 suddenly could not remember a single detail from his meeting with Pernell just two months before trial. Short-term amnesia? Or coached by his new masters, the FBI?

Our legal team anticipated Adam's chicanery. And we had two witnesses to counter him. First, we called John Pernell to the witness stand. Pernell had no incentive to testify or to perjure himself other than an interest in the truth. As such, he was a potentially powerful witness. The government took their first shot at preemptively stopping Pernell's testimony. A couple of nights before John Pernell took the witness stand at my trial, one of the prosecutors, Reed Brodsky, called him. Brodsky tried to intimidate John Pernell. This would have been a clear case of witness tampering. Not so at my trial. John Pernell testified truthfully about his February 2011 breakfast conversation with Adam.

Then, inexplicably, Judge Holwell intervened. Now, the court is supposed to be a neutral referee at a trial, favoring no side and protecting the sanctity of the proceeding by ensuring that the jury received a full and fair recitation of the facts. And Judge Holwell had largely allowed the testimony to proceed throughout trial without interference. However, when it came to Adam Smith, Judge Holwell refused to allow John Pernell's memo that had memorialized in real time Adam's admissions to be shown to the jury as evidence. Holwell also restricted John Pernell's statements about Adam committing perjury or having been pressured by Agent Kang. For the jury, these were critical details.

Our second witness promised to be an unimpeachable counter to Adam. My defense lawyers questioned Adam about those two meetings with my lawyers prior to his decision to cooperate. In particular, they pressed him on the fact that at those meetings he had asserted he was *"unaware of any insider trading by anyone at Galleon at any time."* Even though these meetings were less than a year before the trial, Adam once again went into "I don't recall" mode. However, Rob Hotz, one of the Akin Gump lawyers who was present at both meetings, testified as to the content of Adam's statements to the group at those meetings in February and July 2010. Hotz, like Pernell, had no incentive to stretch the truth one iota. And anyone who knows Hotz, himself a decorated former SDNY prosecutor, will attest to his unflinching honesty.

As the trial continued, Judge Holwell increasingly inserted himself into the proceedings. He suppressed important details. I had to remind myself that this was the same judge who had also ruled to allow the wiretaps as evidence in the first place, despite the dubious nature of the warrant request, which he himself characterized as "a blatant disregard for the truth." As I would later learn, Judge Holwell had an independent reason to see this high-profile trial completed quickly and without any chance for a lengthy retrial if the jury was unable to reach a decision. Just months after my conviction and sentencing, Judge Holwell left the bench to start his own white-collar boutique law firm. This was extremely rare: he had served on the bench for only a short time relative to his lifetime appointment. And starting a law firm from scratch is, as I understand it, a project that requires lead time and planning. Judge Holwell, like so many others in this case, sought to cash in on my trial. He spent his first several months in private practice commenting publicly on the lecture circuit, television, and panels about my case and his impressions—all while my appeals and his rulings were still being appealed. I had a favorable impression of Judge Holwell during trial—but the lure of capitalizing on this circus was apparently too much for even him.

REFLECTIONS

THROUGHOUT THE CASE, THE PROSECUTORS unscrupulously pressured the cooperators to come up with unsubstantiated accusations. There was no fact-checking. Even more, they were well aware that we live in a fast-moving media world and simply the suggestion of impropriety is enough to nudge the jury or the public to believe the worst.

These tactics were standard operating procedure for the reckless prosecution and Justice Department that acted with no accountability and no responsibility.

Yet again, Judge Holwell remained silent.

In the end, Adam Smith revealed himself to be a self-centered person who was easily intimidated and manipulated by Kang. When he was caught insider trading at his own firm, he proved to be a most cooperative witness. He lied with impunity to implicate others. On the stand, Adam not only suffered from "selective amnesia," but went even further with his blatant distortion about my asking him to fabricate an email implying Galleon was a crooked company. His gnarled and twisted narrative became enormously damaging. His force-fed falsehoods made it seem that I ran a crooked company where analysts were instructed to fabricate emails to cover up illicit activities. The prosecution used this to further their false narratives against me, both in front of the jury and with the most compliant media. When I've spoken with many former Galleon employees in the years since the trial, they expressed their outrage with Adam's deception and duplicity as he besmirched not only myself but our entire organization.

The fearful deserve our sympathy, but in this instance, I would not know how to justify that stance. Adam Smith lied to save his own skin. And in the process, he took down the reputations of many good people at the firm. In keeping with the Justice Department's policy of leniency toward and rewarding cooperating witnesses, Adam Smith received a two-year probation and no jail time.

The larger issue here is the specific machinations of the U.S. justice system. Convicting defendants on the testimony of compromised government witnesses desperate for leniency or a reward, is unique to the U.S. justice system.

Federal obstruction of justice and witness bribery statutes clearly criminalize bribing or offering anything "of value" to witnesses. There is no doubt about illegality in the language of the statutes on exerting undue pressure to obtain favorable testimony. Exerting pressure is an offense. It is illegal. If defense lawyers were to engage in such practice, they would be indicted.

However, as it turns out, the U.S. justice system is a clubby world. The courts—where most of the judges are themselves ex-prosecutors—have acted as if prosecutors are exempt from strictures against obstruction of justice or witness tampering. Such sweeping exemptions are insidious. Too often, a cooperating witness, already charged with a crime, is sentenced only after the obligation required by his or her prosecutorial master is fulfilled in court. In other words, the cooperating witness is judged by the success of his or her "singing." Sentencing is based on the successful "extent of the cooperation"—a significant incentive for false testimony. Not just singing, but composing as well.

CHAPTER 15

ANIL KUMAR

Anil Kumar was arrested in New York at the same time I was, on the morning of October 16, 2009. I was led out of my building in hand-cuffs. Anil was rolled away on a hospital gurney. He fainted into the arms of the FBI agents arriving at his apartment to arrest him. The image perfectly illustrates this man's ever-enduring weak nature. In this pivotal moment, he was unable to stand up for himself—indeed, he was unable to stand up at all.

In subsequent months, Anil became the government's star witness, the source of most of the false information and insinuation in the case against me. In this capacity, Anil was given a free pass to say anything he conjured up because the FBI promised his words would never be used against him. He used that free pass with wild abandon. Galleon trading records showed a very different story from the fabricated reality woven by Anil Kumar.

Anil's overriding narrative was that he had led an exemplary life. In essence, he claimed there was never a time when he deviated from following both the letter of the law as well as its guiding principles, as a citizen and as a partner at McKinsey & Company. He testified under oath that this was the case...until he and I made contact in 2002, he seeking me, a classmate at Wharton. At trial and in his sentencing memorandum in which he begged for leniency, he accused me of being the root cause of his subterfuge, corruption, and fraud. It was I and I alone who made him do it all.

Anil carried this insane false narrative all the way to the end, even stating in his plea-bargaining brief that he was so disturbed about being manipulated by me that he saw a psychiatrist to understand how he could be so susceptible. Comical. His words would be actually comical if their consequences had not been so drastic. In fact, he was controlled by the demons of his own unbridled greed and ambition long before we resumed contact in 2002.

On June 27, 2009 after spending a day with me at the Wimbledon tennis tournament, Anil sent me the following email:

"Yesterday was a true highlight and will always be a fond memory. Perfect in so many ways. I hope we can continue to laugh and play forever. Thanks Raj—I feel so good about the choices you are making on so many fronts, most importantly your relationships. Best, Anil."

Less than six months later, as a government cooperator, he alleged that I had, in fact, begun his corruption in 2002 when we resumed contact. What changed? Why did he so completely reverse what he had written in black and white? This changed: Anil got caught for tax evasion and setting up secret consulting companies in order to deceive his partners at McKinsey. He needed fall guys. I was the first. Anil first turned on me. And then he turned on his friend and mentor, Rajat Gupta, his boss at McKinsey. All in a calculated and ruthless effort to make us the scapegoats for his crimes.

My defense counsel, John Dowd, a seasoned lawyer with over forty years of experience and several high-profile cases, personally cross-examined Anil Kumar. Over the previous fifteen months, he and his team had reviewed thousands of emails, documents, and tax filings—all related to Anil Kumar. John Dowd had developed an intimate familiarity with the basic corruption of Anil Kumar's past actions. In his summation, John could not avoid hiding his disgust and disdain for Anil Kumar's lies under oath. He opined, "one of the greediest and most corrupt people you have ever met in your life, a man who made millions of dollars a year but squirreled away millions more in offshore accounts to avoid paying taxes, a man who giggled his way through testimony about all the times he lied and cheated his friends and his business partners and the IRS." He continued, "Kumar's testimony is worthless. He is the worst liar to take the stand in any courtroom in this building...but when the government came knocking, Kumar played dumb. He blamed it all on Raj."[42] In fact, he fainted right into the arms of the government.

At the time of his arrest, Anil Kumar was a partner at McKinsey & Company, a large consulting firm. Anil and I met at Wharton in 1981, after both of us had completed our undergraduate degrees in engineering, he in India and I in England.

At Wharton, we were not close, although we had a few mutual friends. As I look back on those two years, I remember Anil as a bland personality. He was someone who needed others around to infuse any energy into a conversation or to lead it to a higher level. I have no memory of Anil spending any time with anyone who did not appear to be obviously successful, where his criteria of success were a combination of family wealth, ambition, or grades. I also remember his being inordinately curious about the grades of fellow South Asian students. It was his way keeping score.

As it turned out, he would spend his entire adult life keeping score, tracking the failure and successes of others, and using any means available to get ahead. People who were not obviously successful as defined in his rigid, material way were deemed unworthy of his time.

While at Wharton, Anil's dream job was to work at McKinsey. Anil did not get his much-desired job offer. Instead, he joined Hewlett-Packard in Silicon Valley. Disappointed but not daunted, he remained focused on McKinsey, and a few years later, he succeeded in getting a job in McKinsey's Silicon Valley office.

In 1993, Anil relocated to McKinsey's office in India. In Delhi, he became an expert in business process outsourcing (BPO), one of the fastest growing sectors in India, which had and has an abundance of highly educated but relatively cheap software engineers. For American companies faced with relentless pressure to improve profit margins, India's educated human capital became an integral part of their business model. They began to outsource virtually all their computer services and back-office support needs to India, which in turn helped transform India's corporate landscape. With its

English-speaking, relatively well-educated middle class, India essentially cornered the market in BPO, and in the process it helped spawn a tremendous number of new and successful companies.

In 2002, more than five years after I had founded Galleon, Anil contacted me. By this time, Galleon had achieved considerable success, managing several billion dollars. It had been years since Anil and I had spoken. Soon, he introduced me to Rajat Gupta, the managing partner of McKinsey. Rajat aspired to establish a world-class business school in Hyderabad, India, to be called the Indian School of Business (ISB). Their agreed-upon intent was to solicit a donation, and I agreed to give them $1 million anonymously. I thought the school was a great idea, but consistent with most of my charitable donations, I preferred the low-key approach and wanted no plaques or fanfare.

After this introduction, Anil made a concerted effort to stay in touch with me. When he was in New York, he would often call. I was on his approved list now. Over time, I learned that Anil had not kept in touch with any of our other Wharton West Coast classmates. None of them made the grade. The prevailing impression about Anil was that he was a relentless social climber. One Wharton classmate, Rajiv Goel (Chapter 12), went so far as to tell me "Anil is so arrogant that if you aren't a mover or a shaker, he won't even say hello to you." Rajiv was a midlevel executive at Intel who was not one of those who made Anil's grade.

By 2002, Anil was a partner at McKinsey earning over $2 million a year. Yet he would often complain that he was being short-changed. Perhaps it was galling to be living in Silicon Valley during the dot-com boom, surrounded by instant mega-millionaires. Stories about early employees of Yahoo, eBay, and others catapulting into what seemed like instant wealth filled Anil with deep dissatisfaction. His tendency to keep count had not abated with time.

LIE #1: MINDSPIRIT: MOONLIGHTING 2001

TWO YEARS BEFORE ANIL INTRODUCED me to Rajat, both men—one a senior executive at McKinsey and the other the corporate head of McKinsey globally, both at the pinnacle of their professional lives—*were secretly moonlighting, securing pay for consulting work done outside McKinsey's official purview.*

In 2001, Anil and Rajat established Mindspirit LLC as a consulting company registered in Nevada in the names of their wives, Anita and Mala, who functioned as managers. Mala was a manager of Mindspirit LLC. The other manager was Anita Gupta through a family partnership called Rosewood Partners. Both wives were homemakers, one living in Connecticut and the other in California. Neither was involved in the business world in any capacity. Mindspirit engaged in consulting efforts that were in direct competition with McKinsey's, and all work was conducted by Anil and Rajat. The income generated was funneled through Mindspirit, through the wives, to both men.

One of their assignments was a consulting agreement with a public company, InfoUSA, a database company whose CEO was of Indian origin. The consulting contract stated,

"This is to confirm that Mindspirit will provide advice and guidance to the CEO of the company on the strategic issues associated with the growth and sustainability of the company. Mindspirit will be reimbursed for out-of-pocket expenses associated with such advice." According to public documents, on April 18, 2001, they received two hundred thousand options to be vested over four years at the strike price of seven dollars per share, netting almost $2 million.

The language of Mindspirit's contract with InfoUSA was startlingly similar to McKinsey's own language in its contracts. These two had lifted if not the exact language, then the very spirit of the firm that had provided both with great success. It was a clear breach of duty. What was even more shocking is that InfoUSA was an existing McKinsey client. In fact, when the extent of their activities with Mindspirit became clear in 2010, after Anil Kumar's arrest, McKinsey issued a rare on-the-record statement referring to Mindspirit and repudiating the actions of the two. "It has always been a clear violation of our values and professional standards for any firm member to provide consulting or advisory services outside McKinsey's for personal monetary gain." The statement was issued by McKinsey spokesman Michael

Stewart in a sad denunciation of Rajat Gupta, a person who had achieved tremendous success for McKinsey built on a personal reputation widely believed to be pristine.

While the U.S. press was strangely silent about Mindspirit, the Indian press picked up the truth about Rajat and Anil's surreptitious activities. In numerous articles, the Indian press was shocked that Rajat Gupta and Anil Kumar would moonlight while earning multimillion-dollar salaries as senior partners at McKinsey. On May 17, 2011, BusinessInsider.com, a popular Indian website, broke the news: "Rajat Gupta BOMBSHELL: He and Anil Kumar ran secret side consulting business while at McKinsey."

InfoUSA is one of several examples. I heard personally from many entrepreneurs of Indian origin, both in the United States as well as in India, that Anil and Rajat would routinely approach them with offers to provide their companies with strategic advice in return for an equity stake in their private companies. Because these companies, unlike InfoUSA, were private, there are no records or public filings disclosing their equity holdings.

ANIL'S LIES ABOUT MINDSPIRIT

AT MY TRIAL, WHEN QUESTIONED under oath, Anil lied blatantly and repeatedly about Mindspirit. He claimed that Mindspirit was an investment company, which it was not.

The distinction is not subtle. An investment company makes investments. It provides financing to another company. It *invests* in other companies. And then, over time, an investment company generates returns on its investment. It does not receive options as compensation for providing consulting services. A consulting company is paid for providing these services.

Q: Mindspirit was a consulting company you set up so you can moonlight, correct?

Kumar: Mindspirit's operating agreement and operating articles of incorporation say it's an investment company. It's not a consulting company. And it made only one investment.

At this point, John Dowd showed Anil Kumar the consulting contract between Info USA and Mindspirit and the compensation of two hundred thousand options of InfoUSA for providing "strategic advice" to its CEO.

Q: And in fact, Mindspirit was compensated with two hundred thousand stock options as reflected in this consulting contract, correct?

Kumar: Mindspirit was not, sir, and it went directly to my wife.

Anil Kumar presented Mindspirit as an investment company, not as a consulting firm, somehow believing that the nuance manipulation would either absolve him from wrongdoing or have the jury accept his version of the facts.

Recall that Anil Kumar's entire testimony hinged on persuading the jury that it was I who had corrupted him. However, there was no way for him to blame me for his and Rajat's involvement with Mindspirit. They started the firm well before I was introduced to Rajat, and they had made their wives co-conspirators to evade McKinsey's oversight. They received compensation from InfoUSA more than two years before they approached me for support for ISB and long before Anil Kumar had any business dealings with Galleon in 2003.

John Dowd failed to follow up. He did not ask about:

1. As a publicly traded company, InfoUSA filed all the documents with the SEC reflecting exactly their understanding of their own contract with Mindspirit. Their documents clearly stated that Mindspirit was serving as a consultant to InfoUSA.

2. What "services" did Mala Kumar and Anita Gupta, homemakers, provide to InfoUSA, a publicly traded company with accountability to outside shareholders and an independent board of directors? Why would such a company deem it fair and proper to pay almost $2 million for Mala Kumar's and Anita Gupta's "advice"?

Anil Kumar's overarching premise that I was the Machiavellian force in his life, corrupting him beyond repair, is, of course, a wild fabrication in light of his deviousness and greed. Anil was trying to run away from the fact that he was corrupt well before he approached me at Galleon in 2003 with an offer to consult for Galleon.

ANIL'S CONSULTING FOR GALLEON— OCTOBER 2003 TO OCTOBER 2005

AROUND OCTOBER 2002, ANIL KUMAR came to me with the idea of McKinsey doing some consulting work for Galleon. He was attempting to turn a purely social relationship into a business relationship. I was not interested. Ours was a real-time business and my understanding was that McKinsey was a long-term strategic consulting firm.

In May 2003, slightly more than six months later, Anil tried again. He now had his colleague, Tom Stephenson, a McKinsey consultant, send me an email on May 15, 2003:

> Anil asked me to send you 2 documents. One is our original
> discussion document on how we might be helpful to you at Galleon;
> the second was the potential topics we pulled together in October.
> Please feel free to call either Anil or myself to discuss. Thanks Tom.

> I was not still interested.

That very same month, in May 2003, Infosys, one of the leading Indian IT service companies, announced that they were offering ADRs (American depository receipts: in essence, a security that represents the shares of non-American companies that trade in the U.S. financial markets) to American investors by listing on the NASDAQ stock exchange.

I had limited knowledge of Infosys. When I was reading the prospectus, it seemed that the company was growing very rapidly. At that time, we had no analyst covering Indian technology companies. I called Anil to get his thoughts on Infosys, remembering that he was an expert on the Indian BPO sector. He told me it was a well-run company, a leader in the outsourcing business, and that the CEO was highly regarded in India. After additional internal analysis at Galleon, we decided to invest approximately $40 million in Infosys, which turned out to be a good investment, making over $10 million for our investors over a three-month period. I called to thank Anil for his input.

The next time I saw Anil was in New York at a charity dinner for the Indian School of Business. Having already successfully executed a secret side consulting agreement with InfoUSA through Mindspirit well before he reconnected with me, Anil now chose me, a South Asian running his own company, as his next target.

Anil approached me at the dinner. He and a friend in India had formed a company called Pecos Trading to provide consulting services to American clients on Indian companies. By now, there were a handful of Indian IT companies that were listed on the NASDAQ including Cognizant, Wipro, and Satyam. They were among the fastest growing companies in the technology sector. We did not yet have an analyst covering the Indian IT sector, and this time, I agreed to hire him and his company, Pecos Trading, as consultants to Galleon on non-U.S.-based technology companies.

Anil was now getting bold. He was using Pecos Trading (also formed before we had reconnected in 2002) instead of Mindspirit, to cut out his McKinsey partner and also his mentor, Rajat Gupta. He took his greed to an even higher level by having all the consulting fees paid to Pecos's offshore bank account to avoid paying taxes on that income. Effectively, he cut out Rajat Gupta using Pecos Trading and avoided paying taxes using an offshore account. He wanted it *all*—and all to himself.

We executed a consulting agreement on "non-US-based technology companies" between Galleon and Pecos beginning October 1, 2003 for $125,000 a quarter, which was in the normal range that we paid our outside consultants. The consulting agreement called for Pecos Trading to provide consulting services to Galleon on non-U.S.-based technology companies. At Galleon, similar to other investment firms, we routinely hired external professional consultants to share their knowledge of particular fields. These consultants provided expert advice on new products or foreign markets where we had no in-house expertise. In fact, most years we routinely paid over $10 million annually to outside consultants. It was a completely normal business practice, and I did not think more about it.

In hindsight, perhaps I should have asked a few questions, considering his role at McKinsey, but I just assumed that a professional of his rank and status would have the clearance from McKinsey to operate Pecos Trading. Galleon's back office handled all the paperwork and kept meticulous records of quarterly payments to Pecos Trading. I signed the consulting agreement on behalf of Galleon, as I did all other consulting agreements at the time. We had nothing to hide.

Between 2003 and 2005, Galleon made approximately $34 million investing in Indian IT stocks, as was later independently determined by Shearman & Sterling, the law firm that represented Galleon. At the time, as our trading in Indian stocks increased, I realized that we needed a full-time, in-house analyst to follow the Indian IT sector. In 2005, we hired an analyst to follow this sector. We did not need Pecos Trading anymore. We terminated our consulting agreement with Pecos.

In retrospect, my lawyers and I learned that Anil did *not* declare this consulting income on his taxes, and it became the central issue in his case, and one of the reasons the FBI could co-opt him to become a government witness. Obviously, it was not at all my concern or my business to determine whether any of our Galleon outside consultants filed or paid their taxes properly. I had no idea whether Anil Kumar paid his taxes on the consulting fees or not. We had multiple consultants, and their tax situation never entered my mind.

Caught in a real bind when questioned by the FBI, Anil insisted it was my idea for him to evade taxes. Absurd. Completely absurd. Here was a partner at McKinsey telling prosecutors that I had somehow coerced him to evade taxes and that the firm, Pecos Trading, which he owned with another person, was somehow my idea. A mere online corporate search would have indicated that Pecos Trading was set up well before 2003, refuting Anil's lie.

But the prosecutors were eager to hear anything that would help them and conveniently "believed" his lies. Anil said that this was a secret consulting contract and that by using Pecos Trading, I was 1) trying to cover up the consulting agreement and 2) the consulting fees were for him to provide inside information to me. What he did not bargain for was that Galleon meticulously kept all records, and there was no attempt to cover up anything. This is not what you do if you wanted to hide something.

Anil was now compelled to invent the secret inside information he allegedly gave me.

And in his testimony at the trial, Anil got caught in his own web of lies.

Lie #1: First he said that the initial consulting agreement was legitimate and that if I had asked for inside information, he would have never agreed to it.

Q: There was nothing inappropriate or improper about that proposal he made to you, correct?

Kumar: That's correct, sir.

Q: You testified that before 2004 you only provided Mr. Rajaratnam with legitimate insights about the industry, correct?

Kumar: About the technology industry in general.

Q: That's fine, technology industry. And that's the kind of information you and Mr. Rajaratnam discussed before 2004.

Kumar: That's correct.

Q: And that's what you understood you'd be doing when you agreed to provide consulting services through Pecos Trading, correct?

Kumar: Correct, sir.

Q: You didn't propose to pay—you didn't—Mr. Rajaratnam didn't propose to pay you in exchange for inside information on McKinsey clients in 2003, did he?

Anil Kumar: He didn't ask, say that, otherwise I would have said no.

204

If, as Anil Kumar himself testified, the consulting agreement was legitimate, why was there any reason for Galleon or for me to disguise payments to Pecos Trading? Anil Kumar had cheated on his taxes—and was blaming me for it.

LIE #2: FABRICATING "INSIDE TRADES"

IN HIS PRETRIAL MEETINGS WITH the FBI, Anil conjured up some inside information he supposedly gave me between 2003 and 2005, the period of the consulting agreement between Pecos and Galleon, to justify his story. The only thing he could come up with was that he gave me inside information on AMD, one of his clients, on three separate occasions. Here again, the Galleon trading records would not support his assertions. In fact, our firm's trading was in the opposite direction of his "alleged" tips.

The following is a segment of Anil Kumar's testimony regarding AMD. John Dowd posed the questions.

Q: Let me read to you a quote from the FBI interview on December 16, 2009. Rajaratnam knew AMD's finance numbers, which Kumar was clueless about?

Kumar: Yes, sir.

Q: Did you tell the FBI that?

Kumar: If it's in the written narrative that you have, it's got to be correct, sir.

Q: And that was true, wasn't it?

Kumar: I was clueless about AMD's financial results because when you talk about financial results it means all the details, sir. Revenues, profits, margins. How each line of business is done. I was clueless about what the financial officer at AMD would say was the financial results. I maintain that to this day, sir.

If Anil Kumar were "clueless" about AMD's financial results, how could he then legitimately claim that on three occasions he provided me with information on AMDs quarterly results? Again, Anil was lying. The only truthful thing about this testimony was that he was indeed "clueless" about AMDs financial results.

LIE #3: AMD & HEWLETT-PACKARD

ANIL KUMAR CLAIMED HE TOLD me about AMD's strategic partnerships with Hewlett-Packard before it was announced.

Q: And you testified that in 2004 that you provided Mr. Rajaratnam with material nonpublic information about Hewlett-Packard's plan to use AMD chips in some of its computer lines, correct?

Kumar: Absolutely, sir.

Q: There were two announcements about that deal?

Kumar: Actually, over time several announcements, but two main ones.

Q: Two main ones we focused on, correct, in your direct testimony?

Kumar: Yes, sir.

Q: And the first announcement was made by Hewlett-Packard on February 24, 2004?

Kumar: Yes, sir.

Q: And you're aware that Mr. Rajaratnam had *no* position in AMD stock at all at the time of this announcement?

Kumar: I was never aware of Mr. Rajaratnam's exact position in the stock. I would be aware from time to time that he actually held some stock. But I wouldn't know how much or when he bought it, how much he bought it for or when he sold it, Mr. Dowd.

If Anil had actually given me MNPI about this and I was in a conspiracy with him as he claimed, why would I have no position in AMD stock at the time of the announcement? He was lying again. It would get worse with the second announcement.

Q: And you told him with respect to this announcement that you thought this would be a fabulous thing for AMD, correct?

Kumar: I told him that in 2004, sir.

Q: And are you aware that Mr. Rajaratnam was *shorting* AMD stock at the time of this announcement?

Kumar: I have no idea.

Q: You understand when someone shorts the stock, he's betting that the stock will go down, correct?

Kumar: I am very aware of that, sir.

Galleon records show that I was indeed shorting the stock, *betting heavily that AMD's stock would decline at the very same time that Anil claimed he told me that the announcement would be fabulous for AMD.* His lies did not make sense. Once again, I was hoping that the jury would be able to follow these details and be able to identify Anil for the liar he was.

Kumar also testified that he told me about the spin-off of AMD's flash memory business into a company called Spansion and that it would be great for AMD. Once again trading records show that *I did not have a position in AMD* before the spin-off was announced.

If you believe Anil Kumar, in almost two years of consulting with Galleon, he gave me three supposed tips regarding AMD between 2003 and 2005.

Galleon records show that we had no long positions and one short position in direct contradiction to Anil's alleged tips.

LIE #4: HIDING MONEY WITH THE HOUSEKEEPER TO AVOID TAXES

Impressed by Galleon's performance, Anil wanted to be an outside investor in one of Galleon's offshore funds.

In 2003, he asked Tom Fernandez, head of our investor relations team at the time, how to invest in one of Galleon's offshore funds. Tom told him he could not do so because these offshore funds could be invested in only by non-U.S. taxpayers. Attempting to evade taxes, Anil said that the investor would actually be Manju Das, the name of his housekeeper, an Indian national, to shield his own income from U.S. taxes. This was not specifically unusual, as many of our client accounts were opened for different entities, family members, and associates of various advisers and consultants. However, unbeknownst to me or our company at the time, Manju Das was actually the Kumar family's housekeeper in California, who lived with them from 1999 to 2009. Anil was using her name in an effort to shield his own money from American taxes.

Manju Das was an Indian citizen, and if she was residing in India, she would not need to pay U.S. taxes. On the Galleon subscription forms, instead of putting her real current address at the time in California, Anil put his in-laws' address in New Delhi to make it appear that Manju Das lived in India. However, Shireen Gianchandani, our Galleon investor relations manager, and Morgan Stanley, Galleon's fund administrator, were diligent and asked for proof that Das really lived in India.

Anil needed to create a new story for Manju Das. He came up with the idea that he would prove Das's residence by using a fake doctor's note and a fake affidavit. He persuaded Dr. Alok Mathur, who was also at one time the medical consultant to McKinsey employees in New Delhi, to write a letter stating "This is to certify Ms. Manju Das has been under my care since the last ten years and lives at the New Delhi address." Anil also had Manju Das sign a fake tax form saying she was a resident in India.

Fake affidavits, fake doctor's note, and fake tax forms were still not enough. Galleon and Morgan Stanley needed more official proof. They wanted a utility bill or a bank statement. In frustration, Anil sent an email to Shireen at Galleon.

"Dear Shireen, as we discussed, in India there are no utility and fuel bills in individual's names since the infrastructure is so weak. The same holds true for the financial banking infrastructure, many people have historically held money in other forms or joint accounts with other people in other cities. It's been a country where money matters are dealt with on faith. For example, you can buy jewelry in one city and pay in another, months later, based on good faith. Each country has its own customs. You can do the same in Japan. For example, this is why she got the letter from her long-term doctor and the notarized passport with address. Regards."

Shireen, who is of Indian origin, did not accept this rationale and needed more proof of Manju Das's residence. Anil gave it one more shot. This time, he opened a bank account in Manju Das's name in Bangalore. He asked the bank for a letter providing Das's supposed address in India, but HSBC included more information than Kumar had asked. HSBC noted the account had been opened only a few days earlier. The whole point was to make it appear that Das had lived at this address for ten years, so Anil told them to change the letter to delete when the account was opened, which the bank did.

When Anil was first cross-examined under oath, he lied and denied that these were fake documents. But when confronted with the evidence, he found out he could not get away with it any longer and confessed the truth. He admitted that all these were fake documents created to fool Galleon and Morgan Stanley and to evade taxes.

To avoid responsibility to his web of lies, Anil complained that he did all of this under my instructions. I was stunned. I had no knowledge of Anil's schemes. There is not a single email or any type of communication between us suggesting that I did. I was not copied on the emails between Galleon, Morgan Stanley, and Kumar, as these were routine compliance matters outside my daily role. Shireen never once discussed the numerous issues with me.

Galleon had many investors. I always had a list of our fifty largest investors and their contact details laminated and on my desk at all times. Our policies and procedures dictated that the investor relations team had a separate password-protected area on our network, to which I did not have access.

In preparation for my trial, Shireen met with the lawyers from Akin Gump and Shearman & Sterling on January 16, 2010. She told them that when the account for Manju Das was established in October 2003, she did not know who Manju Das was. She said that this was not an issue because many of Galleon's clients invested through different entities, such as trust accounts. In any case, she said there was never any question in her mind that Anil was the ultimate beneficiary of the account. Along with the original subscription agreement, a letter was also submitted (purportedly signed by Manju Das) that told Galleon to accept instructions from Kumar on behalf of the account, and further instructed that Kumar was to be copied on all correspondence.

Tom Fernandez also met with the lawyers a few days later, on January 20, 2010. He said that he never spoke to Manju Das himself, and had no understanding of the real relationship of Kumar to Manju Das. If Tom, the head of our investor relations team, did not know that the account was actually a front for Anil's tax evasion maneuvers, how could I, even further removed from such everyday investment relations matters, have known anything, especially since I never knew who Manju Das was either?

As I would learn before my trial, Anil was dishonestly fudging paperwork, illegally cheating on his taxes, and unethically fleecing his partners—worst of all, he also lacked common human decency. Many wealthy people in India and the world over treat and speak about their household help in a derogatory manner, but Anil was particularly heartless. The same housekeeper, Manju Das, under whose name he was hiding his money, was treated very poorly. She had come to the U.S. in 1999 and was paid a salary of $150 a month for working a full seven days a week. This translates to five dollars a day: completely illegal in the U.S. and equally morally bankrupt. After about five years, when Das asked for a salary increase, Kumar "generously" increased her salary to $600 a month—or twenty dollars a day.

Furthermore, Das had no health insurance. Once, she slipped and broke her hip, an excruciating injury. Rather than taking her to a doctor in California, Anil put her on a twenty-four-hour flight to Calcutta, India. Imagine being on such a long flight when you are in terrible pain. In Calcutta, she underwent an operation before coming back to the U.S. Why all this travel? Medical care in India is a fraction of what it is in California.

A few days after his arrest, Anil quickly dispatched Manju Das back to India, to the small village in Bengal where she was born. Today, I understand that she still lives in a small two-room house in the same village as her son. Manju Das told an investigative journalist that Anil Kumar had promised her $5,000 for ten years' work when she went back home, but had reneged on that promise.

She claimed that Anil would take her passport when she arrived in San Francisco and that his in-laws would take her passport when she arrived in Delhi.

As evidence of using Manju Das for the Galleon account, there is an email, dated December 12, 2005, Anil's mother-in-law, Reva Dayal, wrote to Anil that,

> "My concern is with Manju's mail [in reference to Galleon's statements]—there is always the possibility of it being handed over to one of her relatives by mistake/returned/handed over to others (they do ask and come here occasionally to get news of her). Perhaps some alternative can be found. We leave for Spora on the 31st but I have asked our *goofs* to keep our mail...."

Goofs?

LIE #5: ANIL KUMAR'S LIES ABOUT MANJU DAS

AT TRIAL, ANIL KUMAR TOLD the jury that investing in Manju Das's name was my idea because I wanted to disguise the consulting agreement. During cross-examination, Anil was finally forced to admit the truth about the fake documents.

Q: Your wife didn't know how adept you were at faking paperwork did she?

Kumar: Do you want me to answer that sir?

Q: I sure do.

Kumar: Yes, my wife did not know how adept I was.

Q: You also provided Morgan Stanley with a false tax form, didn't you?

Kumar: Are you referring to 04?

Q: Yes, sir. Thank you.

Anil Kumar: Yes, sir.

Referring to the original subscription agreement that Kumar falsified in 2003, Dowd asked:

Q: You filed out the form and you signed the form, correct?

Kumar: Yes, sir.

Q: And you did it in order to avoid reporting your income and paying your taxes?

Kumar: I did it to avoid McKinsey knowing about it, sir.

Q: So, the phony affidavit and the phony doctor's note and the phony tax form didn't cut, did it? Morgan Stanley told you that the proofs of Das's residence you provided were insufficient, correct?

Anil Kumar: Yes, sir.

Anil's main contention that this was all my idea is utterly false. I personally had no basis to even make such suggestions. I had no Swiss bank accounts. I have a housekeeper in New York whom I pay a fair market wage. I never tried to use my housekeeper's name to try to avoid taxes. It was pathetic to see a senior partner at McKinsey blame his life of greed and crime on me. Abdicating all personal responsibility and simply claiming "Mr. Rajaratnam made me do it" was his default defense.

CHAPTER 16

ANIL KUMAR AND NEW SILK ROUTE

In mid-2005, Rajat and Anil together approached me with a new business idea. They wanted to launch an investment firm focused on the Indian subcontinent with two distinct silos—one private equity, the other a hedge fund. With both silos under one umbrella, they envisioned the new fund to be called New Silk Route (NSR). By this time, Rajat Gupta had stepped down from his day-to-day duties as managing partner of McKinsey & Partners and was sorting out his next steps. Rajat's goal was to bring together a group of experienced South Asian investment professionals to make his vision a reality. Rajat asked me to run the hedge fund and Parag Saxena to run the private equity side.

I had known Parag for a long time as we had overlapped at Wharton. Three of us—Rajat, Parag, and I—came to an agreement quickly and easily. We would each have equal equity stakes, with Rajat serving as NSR's chairman. The fourth, Anil, was the holdout, hedging his bets and unwilling to commit one way or another. After some deliberation, Anil finally informed us that he would remain at McKinsey through 2010, citing the lifetime family health care coverage that he would attain at his twenty-five-year mark. We were perplexed. Rajat outlined the many health care options available to him but to no avail—Anil remained at McKinsey. He would not step away until it was clear that NSR was a success.

Ironically, Anil's aversion to risk was no deterrence to his entitled and aggressive push to be included as a founding member of NSR, which would include an equity stake in our venture. He appeared to overlook the fact that he was taking no risk and that he remained employed by McKinsey. Anil negotiated a compensation package for himself and Rajat consisting of a cash compensation of $400,000 annually (translating to $4 million over ten years), carried interest on $10 million, and 6 percent ownership of the private equity side of NSR. Parag and I calculated the overall potential value of this package as approximately $30 to $40 million over ten years, assuming New Silk Route performed well. We were both surprised. This was a very rich package for someone with no professional investment experience and who was still working full-time at McKinsey and continuing to receive a multimillion-dollar salary. In hindsight, I wonder why Rajat, McKinsey's former managing partner, saw no conflict of interest in any of this.

Incredibly, Anil would soon begin to push for even more equity, wanting an additional 2 percent equity on the private equity fund side. He just would not stop. A year and a half after NSR launched, he was still negotiating and still at McKinsey. Was this entitled or delusional? Rajat and I discussed this specific issue, which the FBI captured on a wiretapped call on July 29, 2008:

Rajat: I look at how he was fighting for this 2 percent in NSR equity, I mean it was kind of, you know…

Raj: You know, without, without a leg to stand on. I mean you know, I think everybody was doing it because they were magnanimous, good people.

Rajat: Look, his overall deal in NSR, as you were agreeing, it is very good. I mean, you know, he gets four hundred thousand in cash, ten million, in, you know…

Raj: Carry

Rajat: Carry

Raj: Uh-hum

Rajat: And you know, 6 percent equity, I mean...

NSR's first phase was developing an action plan with marketing documents. Given that Parag and I were busy during the weekdays running our own firms, we decided to hold conference calls regarding NSR on Saturdays. Anil would call in from California. He assumed the administrative role of coordinating the weekly calls, identifying the action steps to be taken, and distributing all subsequent action steps and the agenda for the following week. Anil also took responsibility for developing the marketing power point presentation we needed to take NSR on the fundraising marketing "road show." In mid-July 2006, Rajat, Anil, and I flew to India on an exploratory trip. I did not know many people in India; the meetings were set up by both Anil and Rajat. We met with the most senior leaders in business and in government.

While NSR was well received by institutional investors, many larger investors were not as receptive to the concept of a hedge fund and a private equity fund coexisting under the same umbrella. Their respective mandates were opposite in terms of timing as well as their use of capital. One was liquid; the other was locked up, long-term. After some discussion at the end of the summer of 2006, we decided to split NSR into two entities. The hedge fund side became Galleon International and the private equity side continued as New Silk Route. I gave up my equity stake in the NSR. Parag, Rajat, and Anil gave up their equity stake in what was now Galleon International. We were going to move forward as two different entities.

On January 1, 2007, we formally launched Galleon International with assets of $1.2 billion. The NSR private equity fund had also raised around $1.2 billion. The two funds began on par. I moved forward with Galleon International. During the previous two years—2005 and 2006—we had seeded Galleon International with partner capital of $200 million. Under the umbrella of Galleon International, we built out an equity research and trading team in Singapore, complete with a full back office and support staff. Leveraging the same disciplined investment process as with the rest of our Galleon funds, we achieved returns of over 25 percent annually at Galleon International.

Not long after we had decided to split the hedge fund from the private equity fund, Anil approached me wanting to be paid for his efforts in 2006 in coordinating the launch of the hedge fund side. I discussed this with both Rajat and Parag and agreed to pay him $1 million. It was generous for what amounted to administrative work, but I wanted to move on.

Around the end of 2006, the time of year that we typically determine and pay bonuses, I told our controller at Galleon, Yoga Kumar, to send out Anil's $1 million payment for his work in setting up the hedge fund. On January 4, 2007, Yoga emailed Anil to confirm the wire instructions. On file, we had instructions for Pecos Trading. Anil's reply to Yoga arrived more than ten days later—on January 15, 2007. Anil instructed Yoga to wait. He was looking into a "better option." Several days even later, Anil followed up, this time attaching a signed letter of authorization to wire the funds not to Pecos Trading but to an account in his own name in India. George Lau (Galleon's CFO) and I signed the authorization to wire $1 million from Galleon to this new account per Anil's instructions. As with all of our company's dealings, we had internal policies and procedures to fully account for and document our operations. We had nothing to hide.

Later, on a conversation recorded by the FBI and manipulated at the trial, Rajat and I discussed this very topic—the topic of my having paid Anil $1 million for coordinating the phone calls and administrative work of setting up the India fund.

Raj: Then he [Anil Kumar] was trying to talk about whether he can participate in Galleon International, and you know, at some point you know, I'm running a business for people who work hard and uh…

Rajat: Yes

Raj: You need to be compensated and you know you can't just keep giving, right?

Rajat: Yeah, yeah.

Raj: And you know, honestly Rajat, I'm giving him a *million dollars a year for doing literally nothing.* Just because....

Rajat: I know, you're being, I think you're being very generous.

At the time of this conversation, neither Rajat nor I had any inkling that the FBI were recording our calls. We were discussing the exorbitant sum I had paid Anil Kumar for his self-proclaimed and inflated role at NSR and Galleon International. My words and Rajat's acknowledgement reflect mirrored frustration about a colleague's overreaching greed.

Later on, at the trial, the simple conversation above was twisted into something sinister. In order to condense the facts into his fabricated testimony, Anil reversed course—he actually minimized his role at NSR and Galleon International and instead manipulated the facts to accuse me of paying him not for administrative work, but for inside information. The FBI and the prosecution allowed the fabrication to proceed. They turned a blind eye despite having access to all of Galleon's records, including the email exchange between Yoga and Anil and the recorded phone call above between Rajat and me. They *knew* Anil was lying under oath. They needed and encouraged Anil to continue inverting the facts into their framework of insider trading. Winning was more important than the truth.

ANIL'S UNBRIDLED GREED

BEING PAID $1 MILLION FROM Galleon International and retaining his equity in NSR was still not enough to satisfy Anil. He continued to dig, to find angles to try to benefit from the success of Galleon International. He told me that he could help attract significant new investors for Galleon International from his contacts in India. Two months later, on March 12, 2007, to further his case, he sent me an email with a link to an article headlined "36 Indians Among the World's Richest," which listed Indian billionaires:

"Fortunately know half or more of them—but clearly more to get to know—good starting point. Will work on it over the rest of the year. Let's plan an India visit together to spend at least a week there. Let me know which period would work best for you? Best, Anil"

Establishing relationships with billionaires and keeping score seemed to be Anil's favorite sport. He had not changed from the Wharton days when he spent time tracking everyone's grades. Anil raised no money for Galleon International. None of his contacts in India materialized. His efforts resulted in a total lack of success. And yet, none of the failures prevented him from asking for bonuses and equity positions in the fund time and time again. Except for that one payment for helping with the administrative setup in 2006, I did not pay him anything else—no other bonus or any equity position in Galleon International.

The digging was not just from Anil. Rajat would also jump onto the chorus for inclusion into Galleon International. They kept wanting more, both ignoring the fact that I had given up all equity claim to the private equity side. I wanted to focus entirely on building out the hedge fund. Rajat and Anil would continue a relentless effort to become a part of Galleon International's equity and profit-sharing program.

Finally, tired of the endless conversations about equity percentages and ownership, I asked Anil to talk to Rajat and to spell out exactly what they wanted. How would they add value to Galleon International? On October 2, 2007, Anil sent me an email outlining his vision of what he called "Galleon Global Group" or "3G." In the outline, he appointed himself and Rajat as "co-founders," allocating each a 30 percent stake in 3G. To me and my entire team, he allocated 40 percent. The email spelled out what they considered would be our respective roles:

"RR [Raj] to mostly focus on investments, risk management; strategy; key employee retention; fundraising; investor relations."

"RKG [Rajat] to focus on strategy, growth, network/ecosystem development, fundraising, investor relations."

"AK [Anil] to focus on strategy, talent acquisition, operating policies, *investment opportunities in India*, late-stage private investments, RKG follow up. Post 2010 also on investor relations, private equity investments."

"Post 2010" was Anil's reference to his plan to leave McKinsey. The email also dictated that "all new Galleon funds outside the U.S. will be within the 3G umbrella."

I was shocked by the audacity. This was a land grab of enormous proportions: Between them, Anil and Rajat wanted 60 percent of the equity of the Galleon Global Group while offering 40 percent to me and all the Galleon employees who spent their days doing the actual research and trading. I told them this was a nonstarter. I gave them no equity and no profit sharing. Profit sharing was reserved for those who actually did the work.

Anil's vision as laid out in his outline for 3G was, in fact, a window into the mindset of a man who spoke in words of smoke and mirrors. "Policies." "Ecosystems." "Key employee retention." We were running a multibillion-dollar fund and he had no idea what it meant to go to war each day and be measured by the returns produced for our investors. He was attempting yet again to get as much as he could from Galleon International while still staying firmly rooted to his multimillion-dollar job at McKinsey.

It was then that Anil informed me he had informed McKinsey he would be leaving in 2010, and had worked out a transition plan with them. As part of this plan, he would move from California to New York in early 2008. He said he had also told McKinsey that during this transition period he would be working with NSR and Galleon International and allocating one day a week, Fridays, to this effort. I believed him because he actually did relocate to New York.

THE INDIA BOOK

I CAME UP WITH A solution that would benefit both of us. In his 3G vision email, there was only one area in which I saw an overlap between Anil's stated interest and where he may benefit Galleon International. Anil alluded to uncovering "investment opportunities in India," as one of his responsibilities in his 3G email. Anil had spent several years in India while at McKinsey and claimed to knew the corporate business sector well. So I carved out a $25 million portion from Galleon International and called it the "Asian Special Opportunities Fund." Internally, we referred to this sleeve of Galleon International as "the India Book." Anil was assigned to manage this subfund. The India Book was prime brokered at Morgan Stanley, which also held the bulk of the Galleon International assets.

Anil was somewhat nervous. During his career as a consultant, Anil was used to being paid for giving advice; he had never been paid directly for contributing to a firm's bottom line. We in the investment world were paid on direct, measurable results, not on words of advice. He and I agreed to the same performance-based arrangement Galleon had with every other Galleon portfolio manager: Anil would make all buy and sell decisions and would be compensated with 10 percent of the total profits Galleon made on the India Book. I was explicit: he would get paid only if he made money. Anil would spend every Friday working on the India Book, researching Indian stocks. Although Anil was knowledgeable about the Indian market and Indian companies, the active, daily management of money was very different. I was not sure whether he had the capability to manage money.

I told Anil that 75 percent of the India Book had to be in Indian equities, and the other 25 percent could be invested opportunistically in any stock. Every Thursday, my administrative assistant would fax a copy of the India Book's holdings, with the individual positions held at Morgan Stanley, to Anil's fax machine. On Fridays at 10:30 a.m., Anil and I had a standing appointment for thirty-minute conference call to discuss the India Book's stock positions. This was exactly my practice with all the Galleon junior portfolio managers. We generally touched base once a week. As the portfolio manager, Anil had full discretion to buy and sell stocks. Over the course of the next year, Anil placed orders for over one hundred transactions. All of this is corroborated by fax, email, and phone records, as well as by the separate prime brokerage account records at Morgan Stanley.

Although the majority of Anil's positions were in Indian stocks, he also invested in AMD. He purchased two hundred fifty thousand shares in October 2007, followed by another two hundred fifty thousand shares in November 2007, and two hundred fifty thousand more in January 2008. Anil's rationale for buying AMD was his analysis that because AMD was about to spin off its manufacturing operations, its financials would immediately improve and the stock price would appreciate. The volatility in the stock market due to the financial crisis in 2008 panicked Anil. In March 2008, he sold the full position of seven hundred fifty thousand shares for a combined loss of 42.8 percent, over $3.4 million. During our weekly Friday calls, as I did with all our junior managers on underperforming positions, I asked him to explain his thinking about AMD.

By late 2007 to early 2008, there were several news articles and analyst reports that AMD had decided to outsource its manufacturing operations to the sovereign wealth fund of Abu Dhabi, ADIC (Abu Dhabi Investment Council). In January 2008 on an earnings call with analysts, AMD publicly discussed pursuing an "asset-lite" strategy, which involved divesting its many physical manufacturing assets to an investor who would infuse AMD with much-needed capital. For those of us who followed the company closely, it seemed likely that this investor was ADIC, which already owned 10 percent of AMD and was flush with cash. Anil and I would discuss all of these factors influencing AMD on our weekly calls.

On July 28, 2008, there were additional media reports that Dirk Meyer, AMD's CEO, had confirmed the asset-lite deal would probably be an Abu Dhabi entity. This was not a surprise to us at Galleon. ADIC was one of our investors. On June 5, 2008, less than two months earlier, a team of Galleon analysts and I had a conference call with ADIC at their request with a PowerPoint presentation giving them our opinion of AMD as a standalone company.[43]

Throughout 2008, I had maintained a long position in AMD in the Galleon funds. I did not panic and sell. Around August 2008, news articles about the impending deal with ADIC were swirling. On August 11, 2008, *Business Week* published an article stating "AMD will sell its lab and equipment in them to a third party…a leading candidate might be a sovereign wealth fund like ADIC."

Several days later, on Friday, August 15, 2008, in the course of one of our weekly India Book calls and refereeing to AMD and ADIC, Anil said "Yesterday, [I] had a handshake agreement, and now you can buy AMD in the India Book." In turn, I asked him how much he wanted to buy for the fund. He said one million shares. On Monday, August 18, 2008, the trade was executed according to Anil's instructions. This call was wiretapped by the FBI. The FBI and the prosecutors knew well the context of this call and that it was regarding the India Book, which Anil managed. Once again, they told the press that this was inside information. They press trumpeted this as the classic "handshake call" of Anil's giving me "hot" inside information. The reality is that the AMD/ADIC transaction happened over two months later, during which time AMD declined from $5.80 to $1.80, losing $4 million in the India Book. None of this was reported by the press.

In the twelve months ending in October 2008, the India Book, managed by Anil Kumar, lost 25 percent of its capital. That was it. I pulled the plug. A 25 percent loss was typically the trigger point, the stop point, for all Galleon portfolios. Anil and the India Book were no exception. I liquidated the positions and closed the India Book. Despite losing 25 percent, Anil once again asked to be paid anyway—he wanted to be paid for the time he spent on the India Book. He was trapped in the mind of a consultant, being paid for time rather than for profits. I did not pay Anil anything for his efforts in 2007, 2008, or 2009. He did not perform.

LIE #6: ANIL KUMAR'S LIES ABOUT THE INDIA BOOK

UNDER OATH, ANIL MINIMIZED HIS involvement with the India Book. He told the jury that the wiretapped August 15, 2008, "handshake" call was an example of his feeding me inside information. He said AMD and ADIC had a "handshake agreement" the prior day, ignoring the fact that many details of the deal had already been publicly reported on since the beginning of that year. Both AMD and the ADIC themselves had made significant disclosures about the impending deal, not the least of which was the ADIC's own request to Galleon in June 2008 for a presentation giving our view of AMD as a standalone company. Even more importantly, the jury ignored that on that very same call, it was Anil who had directed me to buy the one million shares of AMD for the India Book, the portfolio for which he was responsible!

John Dowd cross-examined Anil:

Q: And you advised Raj on the India Book beginning around September 2007, correct?

Kumar: That's what I wanted—he told me he had put a little money aside and he wanted my thoughts on India, yes, sir.

Q: The answer is yes?

Kumar: Yes, sir.

Q: You participated in weekly conference calls with Mr. Rajaratnam concerning the India Book?

Kumar: That is completely incorrect, sir.

Q: Okay, let's look at defendant's Exhibit 1363 and tell me whether you recognize it?

Kumar: Yes, sir.

Q: Wha. is it, sir?

Q: It is an email from Anita Teglasi to myself, Mr. Bahra Vakil, Ms. Ruth Dionisio, dated January 5, 2008.

Q: And the subject is what?

Kumar: Weekly conference call today at 10:30 a.m.

Q: Before these conference calls, you received a fax transmission from Mr. Rajaratnam's secretary, is that correct?

Kumar: Occasionally.

Q: And those transmissions would contain a breakdown of the current positions and holdings in the India Book, correct?

Kumar: Yes, sir.

The email and telephone records of weekly conference calls at 10:30 a.m. on Fridays and faxes beforehand were irrefutable evidence of the conference calls.[44]

Anil Kumar then testified that he did not get the bulk of the faxes because he was travelling extensively. He was doing his best in the courtroom to distance himself from the India Book and the AMD trades he did for it. Trading records also show a purchase of one million shares of AMD in the India Book soon after the wiretapped call in which Anil had directed me to buy AMD for the India Book.

Under oath, Anil disingenuously questioned even the existence of the India Book:

Q: And the reason you didn't get paid is because the India Book didn't make any money? Isn't that a fact?

Kumar: From the statements, if the India Book existed—which I wasn't even sure—the pages that Mr. Rajaratnam would send me showed abysmal performance that was unbelievable.

What was really unbelievable was the enormity of Anil's lies and evasions. He was running the India Book. He knew exactly how abysmal the performance was. Although John Dowd did a great job pinning Anil down, he should have taken the examination one step further and questioned him about the August 15 "handshake" call, which would have once again demonstrated the extent of Anil's lies.

LIE #7: ANIL'S LIES ABOUT EBAY

ON ANOTHER OCCASION, OCTOBER 3, 2008, Anil called me about eBay. This call was also wiretapped by the FBI:

Anil: Ah Raj, eBay is going to do a massive layoff on Monday

Raj: They're going to do what?

Anil: Layoffs on Monday

Raj: Okay

Anil: Now the problem again as usual is [that] it will mean everyone will say, "Shit this company is in trouble," or will it be good news?

Raj: Right

Anil: But the only thing I know is, I tried to get the percentage. I couldn't.

Raj: Okay

That was the sum total of the phone call. My monosyllabic responses reflected my lack of interest.

We were already short eBay since before August 3, 2008, based on the recommendation of the Galleon analyst Steve Pasco. On that same morning of October 3, 2008, TechCrunch, a widely followed website, had already published an article stating, "Last month reports started to emerge that eBay was poised to cut 1,500 jobs or 10 percent of its work force globally…my sources tell me the process will start on Monday next week…"

This public information about the layoff was more specific and precise than Anil's alleged tip. I was already aware of Anil's information and in greater detail. He was shedding no light on already public information. Additionally, on August 20, 2008, Steve Pasco sent me an IM about eBay stating, "I have heard 10 percent head-count reduction." This was well before Anil's October 3 call about the head-count reduction.

When the FBI interviewed Anil on December 17, 2009, the FBI agent's handwritten notes read "Kumar told Rajaratnam about some eBays layoffs

Kumar read about" and "Kumar did not recall giving Raj inside information about eBay." However, Anil changed his story, and under oath in court, he claimed this was somehow inside information.[45]

When giving his general jury instructions, Judge Holwell stated that alleged inside information was not MNPI if it were "publicly available through sources such as press releases, Securities and Exchange filings, trade publications, analysts' reports, newspapers, magazines, television, radio, or word of mouth." Despite knowing this, the prosecutors went ahead and charged me with alleged insider trading on eBay. The guilty verdict on the eBay charge demonstrated the jury's fundamental misunderstanding of what MNPI was (and was not). It also illustrates the case that can be made for juries with domain expertise for complex cases such as mine or medical malpractice.

REFLECTIONS

IT WAS A SURREAL EXPERIENCE for me to hear Anil's false testimony and to watch his evasive eyes. As I listened to him, I reflected on my relationship with him through the years. I had taken his words of friendship seriously and reciprocated the sentiments. At the courthouse, he appeared to be an outcast, disassociated even from himself. I felt no pity for him. When I saw him leave the courtroom for the last time, bowed by the battering that Dowd had given him, I hoped that I would never see him again.

His cheating was ubiquitous. During the discovery process of the case, McKinsey gave us documents they had obtained from Anil's computer related to Galleon. As I read these, I was shocked that Anil lied even on an internal expense report he had submitted to McKinsey on June 13, 2009. In it, he billed a May 13, 2009, dinner with me to a client development number—at that time, Galleon was not a client of McKinsey and there was no prospect of our becoming a client. Additionally, according to my calendar, on that very day, I was flying back from England. It was impossible for me to have had dinner with him. This was a small incident involving a few hundred dollars, but gives a much bigger insight into the ethics of a man who at the time was making millions of dollars as a partner at McKinsey.

Anil fooled the prosecutors, the jury, and the media, which basically parroted the prosecutors' commentary. The media in India, however, saw through Anil's lies.

"STOOP LOW AND WALK FREE"

IN AN ARTICLE HEADLINED "STOOP Low and Walk Free" that appeared a few days after Anil received his wrist-slap of a sentence, Sandipan Deb, a senior journalist and editor of a popular Indian website, wrote about Anil's seventy-two-page sentencing memorandum submitted by his lawyers in their appeal for leniency: "This document is the biography of a saint who, right from childhood, beat seemingly insurmountable odds, sacrificed his own happiness for the greater good, and devoted his life to philanthropy. But any intelligent Indian reading the document can have either of only two reactions: a hearty laugh, or lock-jawed amazement at the sheer misinformation and hypocrisy."

Deb goes on to say later in the article that "the document claims that Kumar was repeatedly treated unfairly by McKinsey, which directly resulted in him being vulnerable enough to be manipulated by Rajaratnam (Yes, it was McKinsey's fault). It provides an alarmingly long list of Kumar's philanthropic activities. Except for a few of the initiatives Kumar takes credit for were Gupta's projects, and Kumar only handled operational details. And later, the lawyers let slip that Kumar was getting paid for some of his 'contributions to India.' Oops."

Deb ends his piece with the following: "However, the most interesting argument that Kumar's lawyers make is that his going to prison would 'harm' India. Describing India as an 'unforgiving' society, the document quotes a friend, 'incarceration will make it considerably more difficult, if not impossible for Anil to continue pursuing [his] initiatives...Indian culture tends to ostracize individuals sentenced to prison.' But the document also admits that 'in the US, Anil is regarded as so toxic that the most companies and even non-profit institutions will not associate with him.' This, when Kumar hadn't even been sentenced. And he has the gall to suggest that Indians have a 'cultural' problem with jailbirds. The memorandum also suggests that 'the vast majority of work, both paying and charitable, that Kumar has been able to obtain [post-arrest] is in India.'" Deb concludes, tongue-in-cheek, "Kumar must be kept out of prison for the sake of those ungrateful merciless Indians. And because Indians are the only ones who will pay for his services anymore."

Later, Anil would turn on his mentor, boss, and friend, Rajat Gupta, and testify against him, leading to Rajat's conviction. For his tireless and unscrupulous efforts against Rajat and me, Kumar got what he wanted: no jail time. He was sentenced to two years of probation and fined a paltry sum of $25,000. However, he was now a publicly self-admitted tax cheat, thief, and snitch.

THREE YEARS LATER: ANIL KUMAR'S LIES EXPOSED BY ANIL KUMAR HIMSELF

MORE THAN THREE YEARS AFTER my conviction, Anil was once again on the witness stand. This time it was the trial of my younger brother Rengan. Rengan was tried on charges of conspiring with me to violate insider trading laws on several stocks, including AMD (see Chapter 18). The prosecutors called Anil to be their chief witness, and covered the same territory, the same events, and even some of the same taped conversations as in my trial. This time, however, there were stark and irreconcilable differences in Anil's testimony.

By the time of Rengan's trial, Anil had already completed his extremely light sentence of two years of probation (and no jail time), so he was no longer on the prosecutor's leash. He did not meet with the prosecutors even once before Rengan's trial. As Anil himself put it, this time he was testifying for his "peace of mind," not leniency:

Q: Are you receiving any benefit for coming to testify?

Kumar: Peace of mind.

Anil then went on to state "my life has been destroyed. It's been destroyed for five years. I can't sleep. I can't…. It's affected my family, my wife, my son. I've lost my reputation, my money, my friends, my family, all because of this. I'm kind of done, sir."

True to form, Anil oscillated between delusion, self-pity, and lies with effortless ease yet again.

A sample of Anil's contradictory testimony includes the following:

○ Anil testified at my trial that "McKinsey does not permit consulting work on the side" and that "I could not accept money because McKinsey doesn't allow me to do consulting."

○ He testified at Rengan's trial that side consulting "wasn't prohibited at McKinsey" and that "whatever you do on the side is okay," absent a conflict of interest with the firm (also a lie according to published McKinsey statements about company policy).

○ Anil falsely testified at my trial that it was I who proposed concealing the consulting fees he received from Galleon by using his housekeeper's name (Manju Das) for the Galleon account.

○ At Rengan's trial, Anil admitted that he was the one who did not want his tax returns to reflect the income from the consulting agreement.

○ Anil falsely testified at my trial that I bullied and bribed him into providing inside information. He stated that he had been "pressed and made to feel that [he] owed [me]."

○ At Rengan's trial, Anil claimed that the reason he shared inside information with me was somehow to help AMD survive and defeat Intel, and to help McKinsey obtain and keep Galleon as a client, which was simply ridiculous.

○ Anil falsely testified at my trial that the information he provided me with was material. He said he furnished me with the "what, how much [and] with whom" that provided certainly (which meant it therefore qualified as MNPI).

○ At Rengan's trial, Anil admitted struggling to convey any information that I did not already know, and conceded that he himself did not believe he was providing enough information to trade on.

○ Anil falsely testified at my trial that he provided information to me about the AMD/ADIC deal that was "better than what was available from other sources."

○ At Rengan's trial, Anil admitted that even before he reported the handshake agreement to me, rumors in the marketplace had advanced to "actual conversation, because of AMD's own disclosures to hundreds" of parties, including Galleon.

○ Anil falsely testified at my trial that Rengan was a member of a conspiracy with myself and him.

○ At Rengan's trial, he flatly denied that Rengan was involved in any scheme to trade on illegal inside information with myself or him.

○ At Rengan's trial, Anil had stated categorically that "I don't *ever* recall giving him [Raj] enough information which to trade on."

In other words, Anil finally exposed his own lies when he admitted that the consulting agreement was legal, and that he did not recall ever giving me information on which to trade. Basically, the government's star witness admitted that he had made it all up. Although it was too late for me, the truth finally came out. I did not receive any inside information from Anil. The court records are available for everyone to see.

Unlike Judge Holwell who remained silent at my trial, Judge Buchwald, who presided over Rengan's trial, stated that Anil Kumar had clearly admitted that there were "no secrets" and nothing that was "not generally known by the time the handshake agreement was announced." Even the prosecutors recognized Anil's duplicity, and they sought to impeach him claiming "direct conflict" with his prior testimony.

Anil's falsehoods, aided and abetted by the FBI and government prosecutors, beg the question: in how many other trials did the FBI and the government act in this way? How much harm has been wreaked on other defendants?[46]

CHAPTER 17

Rajat Gupta:
The Public and the Private Man

O ver time, I began to learn there were two Rajats. The public Rajat and the private Rajat. The public Rajat was expansive, altruistic, gracious, and structured. The public Rajat was one of the most distinguished leaders McKinsey had produced. He was a hero in India and among South Asians in the U.S. The private Rajat wanted more. More recognition, more glory, more wealth. His projected self-image was simply not enough. Something had to give somewhere. In 2001, with Mindspirit, the private Rajat made a formal and clandestine split with the public Rajat. Mindspirit was a secret "side consulting business" that offered some of McKinsey's Indian clients discounted consulting fees and diverted these funds into Rajat's wife's bank account. (As outlined in Chapter 15 and verified by public documents.)

I am still shocked.

Rajat Gupta stepped down as managing partner of McKinsey in 2003 after serving the maximum three terms. Rajat was well connected and took great pride in his global network of high-level business and political leaders. He was publicly passionate about a number of charities and lent his name and network to many worthy causes. Soon after he retired from McKinsey, Rajat joined the boards of several companies, both public and private. From the onset, it seemed that Rajat was unable to say no to business opportunity.

He began spreading himself too thin. Despite being technically retired from McKinsey, he continued to maintain a furious pace. One day, he showed me his weekly schedule—each day of that week listed at least eight to ten meetings or conference calls. I was amazed. He appeared to be able to truly multitask; between meetings, he would make additional calls and return messages.

However, Rajat was somewhat naive when it came to dealing with Wall Street and how to focus his efforts therein. After thriving in the structured world of McKinsey, he seemed scattered and a little lost, unclear how to navigate Wall Street and what now composed his new world. He quickly agreed to many roles with numerous firms, but he did not—could not—always deliver.

At one point, Rajat told me NSR would be his only interest in the financial world and told investors that he would spend 80 percent of his time on NSR and the remaining 20 percent on his various charitable and philanthropic works. I quickly found out Rajat overpromised and underdelivered.

Soon after the launch of NSR in 2007, with its fundraising complete, Rajat began talks with AT&T about launching another private equity fund, with AT&T as an anchor investor contributing $200 million. In mid-2008, he started talking to KKR, one of the world's leading private equity funds, about joining them as an adviser for their Indian business. Rajat was extremely well connected in India, and understandably, KKR wanted his input, access, and relationships. There appeared to be an obvious conflict of interest for Rajat to serve both as chairman of NSR and adviser to KKR in India. He explained away the conflicts by defining NSR as a venture focusing on India deals below $100 million and KKR focusing on deals over $1 billion. In deals that fell to the middle, he would assure that both NSR and KKR would have an opportunity to invest. Rajat seemed to always come up with a business rationale to suit his purpose.

By 2008, Rajat was on the boards of Proctor & Gamble, Goldman Sachs, American Airlines, Sperbank (a Russian bank), and GenPact (an Indian consulting company) among others. Unlike Rajat, Lloyd Blankfein, CEO of Goldman Sachs, believed Rajat's involvement with KKR would be a conflict of interest. McKinsey had made a large and successful practice of sometimes advising all the leading companies in a given sector, but Wall Street is not so egalitarian—you need to pick the horse you want to ride. Rajat seemed to have difficulty understanding that he could not ride them all.

Rajat now had to choose between Goldman and KKR. He asked for my advice and I said (in a recorded call on July 29, 2008), "I would join KKR in a heartbeat," because I knew his passion for working with Indian companies. This conversation was in July 2008, well before the prosecution alleged that Rajat Gupta gave me inside information on Goldman Sachs in September and October 2008. Rajat submitted his resignation to Goldman, but because of the financial crisis, Blankfein wanted to show continuity and asked Rajat to remain on the board until the crisis of 2008 was over.

If Rajat were actually involved in an alleged conspiracy to provide me with inside information on Goldman, I would much rather have had him stay at Goldman than leave for KKR. Once again, the prosecutor's allegations simply do not make rational sense.

Characteristically, Rajat wanted to profit from the success of Galleon International. He offered to raise money for and to serve as chairman of Galleon International. He explained this would give him credibility to raise money from his contacts. He committed to leading this effort by spending at least 20 percent of his time, or one day a week, on the project. Having observed him, I was skeptical about his ability to make the effort or to carve out the time from his many other obligations. I structured a deal in which Rajat would be paid the normal market rate for raising capital for Galleon International. If he were successful, it would free my time away from fundraising.

In reality, Rajat met with our marketing group just once or twice in early 2008. In April 2008, he was in the Middle East and he met a few of our investors in the UAE alongside the Galleon marketing person who covered that region. As it turned out, I was accurate in my assessment of Rajat Gupta—he could not and would not devote the time required for raising funds for Galleon International. He did not raise any money and I did not pay him. He would have to earn his compensation like the rest of us. Time and effort are subjective; results are not.

Rajat did a lot of good philanthropic work. In addition to the Indian School of Business and the American Indian Foundation (AIF), of which he was part of the founding group, he was chair of the International Chamber of Commerce, chairman of the Public Health Foundation of India, and on the advisory board of the Gates Foundation, among others. I respected him for that.

Rajat did not seem interested in smaller charities that were local or did not have a large, publicly visible footprint. One day, I got a call from Annetta Seecharran, director of a local New York City charity called SAYA (South Asian Youth Action). Based in Queens, New York, SAYA worked with South Asian youth from economically disadvantaged, less educated families and helped address the real racial, religious, and cultural challenges these young people faced as recent immigrants to the United States. She wanted to meet with me for fifteen minutes. I agreed, although it was in the middle of the trading day. She told me that at that time, they were operating on a budget of about $1 million a year, and she was constantly fundraising. She was having difficulty getting the more affluent South Asians in the area to support SAYA. I asked her how I could help. I was impressed with her determination, passion for the kids, and the quality work her team was doing. She asked for three things, like three wishes: $250,000 a year for three years; be the keynote speaker at the first gala dinner they were planning; and serve on the board of SAYA. I agreed to the first two but not the third. SAYA's first gala raised over $400,000. Rajat Gupta came to the gala and according to Annetta, pledged $25,000, but he never sent the money, despite repeated requests. She later asked me to call Rajat Gupta about his pledge, which I did not do. I told her that it was not for me to do that.

VOYAGER CAPITAL PARTNERS SEPTEMBER 2005 TO SEPTEMBER 2008

IN MID-JULY 2005, RAJAT APPROACHED me with a proposal to create a new fund, Voyager Capital Partners, a highly leveraged fund of funds that invested in the various Galleon groups. The deal was structured by Ravi

Trehan, the founder of Broadstreet Capital, and involved Lehman Brothers as the prime broker. Essentially the deal was that if we put up $50 million in equity, Lehman would put up $350 million, making the fund highly leveraged at seven to one. Any investment returns above the interest rate charged by Lehman for its $350 million loan would accrue to the equity owners. While individual funds at Galleon have lost money in any given year, we did some simulation analysis showing that if we invested one dollar equally across all the Galleon Funds since inception, we would have made money every single year.

From Galleon's standpoint, this was an attractive opportunity. Our portfolio managers would have an additional $400 million to manage at full fees on gross returns. The Lehman loan interest payments would be paid by the equity owners of Voyager. Galleon would conduct business the same way as Voyager was an outside investor.

In September 2005, Rajat, Ravi Trehan, and I launched Voyager Capital Partners. At the outset, Rajat and Ravi Trehan would each personally invest $5 million and I would invest $40 million. The profits would be divided in proportion to our investment—with Rajat and Ravi each receiving 10 percent of the profits and I receiving 80 percent. Galleon would charge its normal management fees, which reflected the industry standard: 2 percent of total assets and an incentive fee of 20 percent of any profits. I, as the 80 percent equity owner, would be paying 80 percent of the fees.

In December 2006, Ravi indicated he wanted to cash out. The fund had returned 60 percent over the previous fifteen-month period. Rajat indicated he did not have the funds readily available at that time. So I decided to buy Ravi's stake for $8 million, which was the net asset value (NAV) at that point of his 10 percent stake. Ravi had invested $5 million in September 2005. He made a profit of $3 million, or 60 percent, in fifteen months.

In the fifteen months from the launch of Voyager through to December 2006 when Ravi exited, Ravi and Rajat repeatedly approached with me with a slew of potential deals. All these deals had one thing in common—*their apparent smarts and my real money*. One deal was to buy a fund of funds in Florida; another deal was to buy an internet bank; and yet another idea was for me to invest $100 million in a life insurance product whereby we would benefit if the policy owners died ahead of the target established using actuarial tables. These deals were beyond my area of expertise. I turned them all down.

In mid-July 2006, with Voyager doing well, Rajat Gupta approached me with another project. This time, he asked for a bridge loan of $25 million, explaining that he and his friend Ramesh Vangal wanted to buy a bank in India called the Tamilnad Mercantile Bank through an entity called Katra Finance. I was reluctant—I did not know Ramesh Vangal. Rajat said that he would personally vouch for the loan. Up until then, my dealings with Rajat had been good. Based on just that, my past experience with Rajat, I agreed to provide $25 million bridge loan to Katra Finance, but with an emphasized caveat: I needed all the funds back by December 1, 2006. The deal was done on a handshake.

By December 1, 2006, we had not received repayment from Katra Finance. The Galleon CFO, George Lau, and I were concerned. I called Rajat Gupta a few times and was getting a familiar bait and switch routine. Three weeks later, on December 21, 2006, I sent Rajat an email:

> We still have not received total payments for Katra Finance nor has Mr. Vangal contacted me as he had indicated to our CFO yesterday. Under the circumstances I am not able to meet you for lunch today and I am cancelling all further meetings.

Soon after, I left with my family for our planned Christmas vacation. I vowed to come back and pull out of both Voyager and NSR. Before leaving, I asked George Lau to take care of the matter with Rajat Gupta. After waiting a week and still receiving no communication about the loan repayment, George Lau sent Rajat Gupta an email on December 28, 2006:

> Our team has been chasing Ramesh's team on a daily basis and we still have not received 100 percent signal that the wire has been sent out. Tomorrow is the last day of the month and the funds have to be in our account. Please advise what else I can do.

Rajat Gupta replied:

Rest assured please tell Raj that he should also believe I have been working nonstop the past 7 days to make this happen.

Eventually, Katra Finance repaid the loan in full. My natural tendency to work on a handshake would be curtailed in any future dealings with Rajat Gupta.

After deducting Galleon's customary fees (both management and incentive) and paying Lehman the interest on its loan, Voyager's net performance in 2007 was essentially flat. In December 2007, Rajat indicated that he wanted to increase his stake by 10 percent to 20 percent by investing an additional $5 million as of January 1, 2008. The Voyager documents had provided for the option for Rajat to increase the stake to 20 percent but did not specify at what price.

Rajat and I had a difference of opinion. My position was that any transaction had to take place at the current NAV. Rajat's position was that he wanted to invest his $5 million at the NAV at inception. That did not make sense. I had just paid $8 million to buy Trehan's 10 percent stake a year earlier. It was just not fair to me to turn around and sell the same 10 percent stake to Rajat Gupta for $5 million. Essentially, what he was asking for was to buy $8 million for $5 million. It did not make sense to me; obviously, it did to him.

The only feasible option was to reduce my capital stake to reflect the new eighty-twenty split going forward. At this point, Rajat's equity capital was worth $13 million (original $5 million plus $3 million appreciation plus the second $5 million). To make it an eighty-twenty split, my stake would have to be $52 million, which was exactly four times Rajat Gupta's stake of $13 million. It was very simple. In January 2008, I reduced my equity capital to $52 million by withdrawing the excess funds.

Rajat Gupta continued to argue that although he had not put up the second $5 million in 2005 but in 2008, that any returns up until then should be credited to his second $5 million.

The fact that I had bought Ravi Trehan's 10 percent stake for $8 million in cash was essentially not his problem. In liquid securities—whether shares in mutual funds, exchange traded funds, or hedge funds—everything is done at NAV. Rajat's position was neither fair nor logical to me. Also at this time, we were having discussions about Rajat's role in Galleon International, and uncharacteristically, I succumbed to his demand. I moved $3 million from my equity capital account to Rajat Gupta. He got what he wanted—$8 million stake for a $5 million investment. I was prepared to move forward. He was pleased until six months later: September 15, 2008.

On September 14, 2008, Merrill Lynch was saved from bankruptcy by being taken over by Bank of America—a feat engineered by the government. On September 15, 2008, Lehman Brothers filed for bankruptcy and the next day, the Federal Reserve injected $85 billion into AIG to prevent the collapse of this global insurance firm. The markets were wild. I had experienced nothing like it at any point in my career. The financial system was frozen. Banks stopped lending to each other. Credit flow was sporadic. The entire market was in completely uncharted territory—much, much worse and deeper than those outside the markets ever truly understood.

The government pulled the plug on Lehman. They were allowed to go bankrupt. As a result, Lehman called our $350 million loan with Voyager. This was the worst possible time. Voyager's equity capital was wiped out. In one fell swoop, both Rajat and I lost our entire Voyager stake. Excessive leverage, which helps you on the way up, hurts exponentially on the way down. Yes, I was upset. But as a portfolio manager, I was accustomed to winning and losing on a daily basis. Rajat could not handle the fact that he had just lost his entire investment of $10 million. He began an irrational campaign again for me to personally partially or fully offset his loss. I had just lost over $50 million.

It was unbelievable. On the way up, he wanted more than what his investment earned and I accommodated that by transferring $3 million from my account to his. On the way down, he wanted a safety net, protection against any loss, as though investing in the market was the same as putting money into a CD and would yield guaranteed returns. This was not going to happen. It was a short conversation.

In a possible futile attempt to intimidate me, he told Anil Kumar that he was going to sue me. He felt I had dropped the ball. Dropped the ball on what? Rajat acted as if he were unaware that the Lehman Brothers bankruptcy had just precipitated the worst economic crisis in the United States since the Great Depression. Investing in the stock market does not come with a money-back guarantee.

After that, my relationship with Rajat was strained. In the months that followed, Rajat and I talked primarily about Voyager. Despite agreeing to it earlier and despite accepting my $3.5 million transfer to his equity account, he was now questioning the legitimate fees (management and incentive) Galleon had earned from Voyager and the withdrawal of my excess funds.

It was during this period that the prosecutors would allege Rajat gave me inside information on Goldman Sachs. However, despite extensive wiretapping, the prosecutors came up with no instance of Rajat tipping me on any MNPI. In fact, the thrust of his entire defense strategy during his trial was that he was so unhappy with me over Voyager that he had no incentive to give me any inside information.

After my conviction and before Rajat's trial, I spent four hours with his lawyers at the New York office of my lawyers at Akin Gump. We talked about the circumstances surrounding my trading on Goldman Sachs. Gary Naftalis, Rajat's chief lawyer, thanked me and said that he might use the notion that Rajat was upset with me and so would have no reason to give me any inside information. I just assumed that this was typical legal strategic maneuvering and thought no further about it. After that meeting, my lawyers assisted Rajat's efforts and provided a lot of documentation to his lawyers. Rajat told Samidh Guha, one of my Akin Gump lawyers, to tell me he "greatly appreciated all the help" and to thank me for my assistance.

So naturally I was flabbergasted yet again when Rajat's trial legal team claimed I had swindled Rajat in his Voyager investment in an effort to show that he had no incentive to give me any inside information! We were indignant at being Rajat's public scapegoat when simply showing the facts would have proven that Rajat provided me with no inside information. Terry Lynam, by now my chief lawyer, who had never engaged with the press up to now, sent out a strongly worded press release published in the *Wall Street Journal* on December 28, 2012:

> Counsel for Raj Rajaratnam strongly denies the public reported characterization by Rajat Gupta's appellate lawyer that Mr. Rajaratnam 'swindled' Mr. Gupta in any way in connection with the investment that Mr. Gupta voluntarily made in the Voyager International Fund. As well documented in this matter, Mr. Gupta and Mr. Rajaratnam jointly invested in this fund whose prime broker was Lehman Brothers. The fund was highly leveraged, with $50 million in equity and $350 million in debt through Lehman Brothers and others. Mr. Gupta initially invested $5 million to secure a 10 percent profit participation in the fund. As a partner in the fund and also someone with a sophisticated business background, Mr. Gupta was aware of the potential risk and rewards of this investment. As of December 31, 2007, the Fund was profitable and Mr. Gupta's investment had appreciated approximately 60 percent. On January 1, 2008, Mr. Gupta invested another $5 million to secure an additional 10 percent profit participation. At that point, monies that had been withdrawn from the fund consisted of the customary management fees that Galleon Management charges its entire fund that it manages (90 percent of which were paid by Mr. Rajaratnam). In addition, in January 2008, following Mr. Gupta's additional investment, a portion of Mr. Rajaratnam's share of the equity was withdrawn so that their respective profit percentages would reflect the new 80:20 split. In September 2008, Lehman Brothers collapsed. As a result, the fund collapsed as well and Mr. Gupta lost his investment of $10 million and Mr. Rajaratnam lost his investment of $40 million. No funds of Mr. Gupta were ever misappropriated and Mr. Gupta was not "swindled in any way."

Rajat Gupta went even further. He asked his friend Ajit Jain, an executive with Berkshire Hathaway, to testify on his behalf on Voyager despite the fact that Ajit Jain had no connection whatsoever to Voyager. I doubt Alit

Jain did any due diligence on Voyager before he testified, relying instead on Rajat Gupta's incorrect and self-serving version of the Voyager narrative.

As fate would have it, our paths would cross again. Rajat was sent to the Federal Medical Center in Devens where I was also housed. I asked him why he had claimed I "swindled" him when the facts were so clear—the only funds withdrawn from Voyager were the customary Galleon fees and my capital. First, he blamed the false claim on his attorneys. Later, he asserted that it was actually a "misunderstanding." My attorney, who knows his attorney, later found out that it was Rajat's insistence to push the defense argument that he was swindled by me and therefore had no incentive to provide inside information. Once again, a stark contrast between the public and the private Rajat Gupta. I told him that there could be no misunderstanding as the numbers were the numbers, referring to an old axiom on Wall Street: "Numbers don't lie; people do."

At Devens, we were civil to each other. He told me he was writing an autobiography that would invoke the virtues of spirituality as espoused in the Bhagavad Gita, and repeatedly denounced materiality. Once again, I was flabbergasted when, a week or so before he was scheduled to leave Devens, Rajat approached me again about the loss in Voyager. This time, he wanted me to simply give him money. Of the $10 million he had lost, he wanted me to give him at least $5 million. His argument was that the $10 million he had lost in Voyager was a greater percentage of his net worth than the loss of over $40 million was of mine. Huh? There was no logic—what logic? I shook my head. I said no. Never mind that he was the second-richest inmate in Devens. If I wanted to give $5 million to anyone, he would be below my last choice.

My mind wandered to the many conversations we had had about spirituality and materiality and this cemented my analysis of the wide chasm between the public and the private Rajat Gupta.

GOLDMAN SACHS

THERE IS ONLY ONE RECORDED phone call between Rajat and me that even mentions Goldman Sachs. It occurred on July 29, 2008. In it, I told Rajat about an upcoming normal meeting with Gary Cohen, the president of Goldman Sachs. I wanted Rajat's input on some of topics that I should discuss at the meeting. This was normal background work that any business person in any industry would conduct. Following that call, I did not trade in Goldman.

The prosecutors alleged that Rajat, a board member of Goldman Sachs, gave me information on Berkshire Hathaway's investment in Goldman on September 23, 2008, and also that he shared details of Goldman's financials on October 23, 2008, nearly two months prior to Goldman's quarterly earnings report on December 16, 2008. Despite the extensive wiretapping of my cell phone, there was no recorded call of Rajat ever giving me any inside information on Goldman Sachs. Ironically, I lost over $2 million cumulatively on these trades.

As the former head of McKinsey and a member of the board of several leading companies, Rajat was the type of high-profile person over whom the U.S. Attorney Bharara salivated. Rajat was charged with insider trading in a separate trial, in which he vehemently denied giving me any MNPI on Goldman Sachs.

Preet Bharara did not charge or even have any interest in interviewing some of the other alleged tippers in the Galleon case. These included Sunil Bhalla (Polycom), Shammara Hussain (Google), Kieren Taylor (Akamai), and Kamal Ahmed (Morgan Stanley). Bharara did not charge any of these people because they were not high profile enough. High-profile people generate a lot more media coverage. As we have seen over the years, a conviction, whether just or unjust, of a high-profile person enhances the career aspirations of any U.S. attorney. Preet Bharara understood this well.

BERKSHIRE HATHAWAY INVESTMENT: SEPTEMBER 23, 2008

By September 2008, there was real panic on the Street.

Given that the U.S. Federal Reserve had allowed Lehman to go under, what would happen to Morgan Stanley and Goldman Sachs—the two of

Galleon's prime brokers we felt were most vulnerable? Two days after the Lehman bankruptcy, on September 17, the Fed lent $85 billion to insurance giant AIG to help it avoid insolvency. On September 18th, Federal Reserve Chairman Ben Bernanke met with key legislators to propose the Troubled Asset Relief Program (TARP), a $700 billion fund to collectively purchase the toxic assets of the financial firms and bail them out. TARP would isolate the problems and inject liquidity into the markets, but not everyone was on board. "If we don't do this, we may not have an economy on Monday," warned Bernanke.

Financial stocks such as Goldman traded wildly, large swings based purely on the latest rumor and innuendo. On September 18, 2008, Goldman Sachs traded between $99 and $132, a one-day swing of over 30 percent. It was wild and unprecedented. These pricing fluctuations are exactly where traders make their money. I traded Goldman Sachs *every day between the day Lehman went bankrupt and before the announcement of Berkshire Hathaway's investment in Goldman.* In fact, between September 16 and September 23, I personally traded over eight hundred thousand shares, for a total value of well over $100 million. Our trading had nothing to do with Rajat Gupta.

There appeared to be some progress on TARP in Washington over the weekend of September 20. We worked with a consulting firm in Washington called Cypress Consulting, which monitored the likelihood of TARP passing. They sent us regular updates via email.

Believing the probability of TARP passing was improving, I bought one hundred thousand shares of Goldman Sachs on September 22. On September 23, I instructed Ian Horowitz, my trader, to buy an additional two hundred thousand shares of Goldman slowly over the course of the day. However, Ian had to go to a funeral later that morning, and I assumed he had delegated it to his assistant. Congress was in session through that day and the only thing the market was focused on was the passage of TARP.

At 3:29 p.m. on September 23, we received an email from Cypress Consulting stating "we remain committed to our view that the bill will pass in the coming days." I decided that if TARP passed, it would be extremely good for the entire financial sector. The U.S. financial sector would soar.

I walked over to the office of one of our financial services analysts to discuss which financial exchange traded fund (ETF) to buy. An ETF is a proxy for the entire sector and comprises the leading companies in that sector. We settled on the XLF index because it did not have any weighting to leading foreign banks such as Barclays, Deutsche Bank, or UBS. Foreign banks would not be eligible for TARP, and as a result, an index with these foreign banks would not move as much as an index which contained only domestic banks.

My assistant came running up and said I had a call from Rajat Gupta. The time was 3:54 p.m., six minutes before the market closed. Rajat was in a panic about his investment in the Voyager Fund, which was housed at Lehman Brothers. I hurriedly told him I had not heard from Lehman yet. I said it looked like TARP was going to pass and I was about to make some trades. I would call him after the market closed to discuss Voyager. I recall a casual comment about the passage of TARP being good for all bank stocks including Goldman. Rajat in his Wells submission, his initial response to the SEC's Wells notice about a possible civil action, suggested that he and I may not have even spoken directly at all. The duration of the incoming call was less than a minute, including the time my assistant ran over to find me.

Telephone records show that later that same evening, well after market close, I had called Rajat Gupta at home and had a thirty-four-minute call to bring him up to date on his investment in Voyager. This was only seven days after Lehman had filed for bankruptcy. I rarely, if ever, recall calling Rajat Gupta at home.

Turning back to the business at hand, I had six minutes left in the trading day. I asked for a recap. How many shares of Goldman had we bought through the day? Ian's junior trader mumbled something about not having bought any shares other than the fifty thousand shares Ian had bought earlier in the day. He said the stock had run away from him. He was a rookie. He looked frozen. If Ian Horowitz had been there, it would have been no problem. I was frustrated. I asked Gary Rosenbach, a founder of Galleon and the head of trading, to execute the order. I told him about the email from Cypress Consulting and that I was expecting TARP to be passed. In addition to buying 1 million XLFs and two hundred seventeen thousand Goldman for me, Gary bought half a million XLFs, fifty thousand Goldman, and two hundred thousand Morgan Stanley for portfolio he managed. This was four times as many Morgan Stanley as Goldman.

At about 5:45 p.m., the news agencies reported that Berkshire Hathaway was to invest $5 billion in Goldman.

The prosecutors alleged that in the 3:54 p.m. call, Rajat Gupta told me about Berkshire Hathaway's investment in Goldman and that was the reason I bought the additional shares. The alleged profits from this Goldman Sachs trade were only $842,000—which, while a sizeable amount, was only a tiny fraction of our daily profit and loss swings of up to $50 million during this very turbulent time. I had no idea that Goldman had had a board of directors conference call to approve the Berkshire Hathaway investment. There was no discussion of it when Rajat called me. Berkshire Hathaway was the last thing on my mind that afternoon.

News of the impending Berkshire Hathaway investment must have leaked into the market because Goldman Sachs stock had already begun to spike up soon after 3:00 p.m. that day. In fact, 20 percent of the Goldman stock that traded that day occurred between 3:00 and 4:00 p.m., the last hour of the market. Galleon financial trader McCowen Smith, capping up the day's action, stated in an email after the close that Goldman Sachs stock "had a big move right at the close rallying $7 in the last 10 minutes to close above $125 and up 3.5 percent." The market was well aware that something was afoot, most likely related to TARP, and possibly the pending Berkshire Hathaway investment.

The actual facts totally undermine the prosecutor's theory. Why did I buy Goldman Sachs that morning before any call from Rajat Gupta? The prosecutors ignored the million shares of XLF that I bought at the end of the day or the 3:29 p.m. email from Cypress. In addition, my trading between September 23 and October 2, when TARP was enacted, shows that I continued to build large positions in Morgan Stanley and Citicorp, demonstrating my positive view as to the potential impact of the passage of TARP on financial stocks overall, not just Goldman Sachs.

On that day, the only thing on Rajat's mind was Voyager. It was his single-minded focus. He was concerned about potentially losing $10 million. The first thing Rajat did after the Goldman conference call was to call me about Voyager. It was 3:54 p.m. I had no time to speak to him about Voyager. He then made another slew of calls to his bankers at JP Morgan. Less than thirty minutes after Rajat and I spoke, one of Rajat's personal bankers at JP Morgan, Jeffrey Wrobel, emailed Rajat's secretary, Renee Gomes, asking for the Voyager subscription document and partnership agreement. At the same time, another of Rajat's personal bankers at JP Morgan, Thorsten Dueser, reached out directly to Shireen Gianchandani in Galleon's investor relations department for the same information. At 4:49 p.m., Shireen responded to Rajat's bankers that she had not yet located the documentation. Voyager and the impending loss of his $10 million was the only topic dominating Rajat's thinking. Not Goldman Sachs. Not inside information. The prosecutors inserted their own interpretation of recorded facts.

DECEMBER 16, 2008, GOLDMAN'S EARNINGS RELEASE

THE PROSECUTORS FURTHER ALLEGED THAT a month later, on October 23, 2008, Rajat Gupta gave me information on Goldman Sachs's financial results, which were reported on December 16, 2008. Once again, they had no evidence on this.

Based on a recorded call of an internal chat with David Lau, the head of our Asia office, I speculated that Goldman would lose two dollars per share in that quarter. The prosecution alleged that I got this information from Rajat. This was nearly two months before Goldman's quarter had ended. It was a pure back-of-the-envelope calculation on my part. I was so wrong. When Goldman Sachs actually reported their quarterly financials on December 16, they reported a loss of five dollars per share. The prosecutors claimed that this was significant, since it was the first quarter that Goldman Sachs had ever lost money. What they did not tell the jury was that every single major investment bank also lost money that quarter during the worst U.S. economic crisis in eighty years.

Here again it is important the context in which I spoke to David Lau and based my decisions on trading Goldman Sachs. Goldman Sachs had a large investment in ICBC, the Industrial and Commercial Bank of China, that nation's largest bank. As of August 28, 2008, (end of Goldman's previous quarter), Goldman's holding in ICBC was valued at approximately $7.14 billion. This was Goldman's largest asset on its balance sheet. A 1 percent positive swing in ICBC's stock could add $71 million to Goldman's profits; conversely, a 1 percent decline in ICBC's stock would reduce profits by exactly that same amount.

Goldman had at that time approximately 395 million shares outstanding. A 1 percent move in ICBC stock could add to or subtract almost twenty cents from Goldman Sachs's earnings per share (EPS). ICBC's stock price was one of the biggest variables in calculating Goldman's EPS.

ICBC was slated to report its quarterly results on October 23. Our Asian financial services analyst was quite positive on the stock. Unlike the U.S., China was not in any type of financial crisis at that time and the banking sector was doing quite well. I chatted with David Lau, the CEO of our Asian business, about ICBC's prospects. Then I brought one hundred fifty thousand shares of Goldman Sachs at $120 per share, expecting that if ICBC reported strong results, its stock price would rise and would positively impact Goldman's profitability. For this reason alone, I bought Goldman Sachs on October 23, 2008.

ICBC's results, which were reported at 4:45 a.m. (EST) on the morning of October 24, were unfortunately not as strong as expected. The stock declined from $3.54 HKD at close of business on October 22 to $3.15 HKD at the close of business on October 24, a decline of approximately 11 percent. This resulted in a loss of approximately $786 million, or *two dollars per share to Goldman Sachs*. Rick Schutte, the president of Galleon, testified that he distinctly remembered my asking our financial service analyst at our morning meeting to calculate the impact of ICBC's stock price on Goldman Sachs's earnings that morning.

Others had figured out the impact of ICBC news on Goldman Sachs and the stock declined twenty dollars a share. It was a bad trade on my part. I sold the one hundred fifty thousand shares that I had bought the day before at $120 per share on October 24. We lost $3 million on that sale. When you're wrong, particularly in the investment business, it's best to cut your losses quickly. That's the reason why I sold the Goldman Sachs. It had nothing to do with Rajat Gupta.

The prosecutors alleged that I sold Goldman Sachs because Rajat had told me that Goldman would lose two dollars a share. They pointed to a call I had with David Lau on October 24 after ICBC had reported. David Lau had called me to get an update about the ICBC/Goldman trade we had executed together. I gave him an update on the U.S. market and told him that I had talked to Rajat about the 10 percent layoff at Goldman Sachs that was in the newspapers and that "today Goldman Sachs lost $2 per share," referring to the impact of ICBC on Goldman's profitability.

REFLECTIONS

Looking back, I have mixed feelings about Rajat. I respect him for the numerous charitable efforts to which he tirelessly gave his time. This was the public Rajat—the former global head of one of the world's most respected consulting firms. The private Rajat was constantly looking, scheming to increase his already large fortune by moonlighting with Anil Kumar in their own shadow consulting firm, Mindspirit, and attempting to piggyback on the work of others, cashing in on his public image.

Still, when faced with overzealous prosecutors, he had the courage to fight for his innocence. However, during his defense, he was quick to publicly throw me under the bus by falsely claiming that I had swindled him. Meanwhile, privately, he was seeking help from both me and my attorneys and thanked me for my help. I understand the need to employ creative legal strategies, but he followed no ethical boundaries.

Rajat Gupta vigorously maintained his innocence to the end. In an email to the board of directors of the Indian School of Business, he said, "Just to be clear. There are no tapes or any other direct evidence of me tipping Mr. Rajaratnam. I have spent my entire professional career zealously guarding the confidence of my clients. There is no reason for me to suddenly deviate from a lifetime of probity and honor."

The reality is that only Rajat Gupta and I know the truth. Rajat Gupta is innocent of passing me inside information on Goldman Sachs. He may have been technically convicted by a jury—but once again, the facts were misrepresented by an ambitious U.S. attorney who was seeking high-profile cases for his own political gain. Rajat Gupta did not cheat on his taxes or have secret Swiss bank accounts like Anil Kumar and Rajiv Goel. Rajat Gupta fought for his innocence and went to trial, but could not overcome the stacked prosecutorial deck and the false testimony of Anil Kumar. In his characteristically self-serving manner, Anil Kumar would turn on his own mentor and closest personal friend, testifying for the prosecution against Rajat.

Soon after my trial, one of the prosecutors approached my defense lawyer, Terry Lynam. He wanted to discuss my testifying against Rajat in exchange for a lesser sentence. I said no. I was not going to lie. I was not going to testify falsely against Rajat or become a puppet of the prosecutors.

Rajat Gupta was sentenced to two years in prison.

CHAPTER 18

MY TRIAL

*"Life is 10 percent what happens to me,
and 90 percent how I react."*

JOHN MAXWELL, Author

My trial began on March 8, 2011, almost eighteen months after my arrest.

The journey had begun with stunned disbelief in the fall of 2009. In the intervening days, weeks, and months, we prepared intensely. We built our defense. We transformed all the complex layers of information into simplified sound bites. The level of detail was mind-numbing. Each piece of information had to be considered and added like a building block or discarded. We had one single-minded purpose: to engage a jury of laypeople to absorb our story. We pored over hours of wiretapped material. We read through thousands of pages of wiretap transcripts, emails, instant messages, and analyst reports. The journey had been arduous. We were all well aware that public opinion was very much against us, against me. The Occupy Wall Street movement around the country was in full swing and most intense on the streets of New York. My photograph, centered in the bull's-eye of an elaborate ring of conspiracies, was everywhere. By the spring of 2011, the vitriol had reached a fever pitch and yet I was confident. I had no doubt we would prevail. We had everything right there in black and white to support our case.

To the core of my being, I trusted the American justice system. I believed that once the facts were established, the jury would understand. I was innocent. I went further—I believed not only would the jury understand my innocence, they would also understand that with the illegal use of wiretaps, my basic civil rights had been violated.

I was well aware of the level of attention my case was getting. There was no avoiding the fact while listening to the top news stories or opening up any newspaper. I understood not to react to any comment from the media at any time. Any response from me could and would be used against me. I was going through two trials: one official, one not. The first was about to begin, led by a judge in a courtroom. The other had begun months ago. The unofficial trial—conducted on radio, television, newspapers, magazines, and the internet—was orchestrated not by a dispassionate judge, but by the prosecutors conducting the press and therefore the public with sensationalized and distorted facts.

Finally, the day arrived. We drove to the courthouse. I saw only rows of white and black vans with satellite dishes. Cameras everywhere. We stepped out into a swarm of photographers, faces covered by enormous lenses. All of them called out my name, pushing at each other to get to me. In their attempt to get close-up shots, they pushed their cameras into my face, blinding me with flashes. We got out of the car and began to walk to the courthouse. The photographers sprinted ahead of us, turning right back around to take more photographs. "Raj!" "Raj!" They asked silly questions: "How does it feel like to be on trial?" or "'Are you prepared?" For the entire length of the trial, they persisted. Day in, day out. Morning and afternoon. The reporters tried in vain to provoke a response from me. Any response. I kept my expression noncommittal. I walked slowly and calmly through the crowd. There was no way I would engage.

The attorneys took three full days to select a twelve-person jury from a pool of three hundred people. The process here was also painstaking, detailed, and yet cookie-cutter in its approach: the attorneys had the freedom to vet the "qualifications" of each person. The judge had the freedom to shape or tilt the direction of the choices.

One of the first statements from the judge was to let everyone know that the trial would take up to three months. The response was immediate. Many potential jurors bowed out. Only a select few who could afford "the luxury" of being away from work for that long or who had the support at home to commit to that kind of time remained. We were left with people for whom going to work every day was not an imperative. How could this be a "jury of peers" if most of my peers could not afford to serve on a lengthy trial?

Three days later, we had a jury of nine women and three men: postal workers, Central Park employees, cafeteria workers, elementary school teachers, nurses, and housewives. They appeared to be decent, honest, and hardworking people and yet, for me, each was missing a critical element. Not one had personally invested in the stock market. How was it possible that decision-making power was in the hands of a group of people who had no idea about the subject matter? Without some understanding of the market, how would these individuals evaluate the information or decisions on the volume of complex information presented throughout the trial? They could be easily misled and manipulated. These were the twelve people in whose hands my fate would lie.

I was curious. How would the defense, or the prosecution for that matter, convey to the jury in simple sound bites volumes of dense financial data and stock market activity? How could one convey as "normal" the enormous dollars at stake in the middle of a global financial meltdown? Why, for intricate financial cases, or for complex medical malpractice cases, do we not have a specialized jury system? A specialized jury versed in finance could realistically assess evidence presented by both sides. This is even more important because under the current system, a defendant cannot appeal on the facts, only on the matter of the law. I was slowly absorbing the reality of my situation.

Just as my trial commenced, the government dropped their charges on twenty-five of the thirty-four stock trades. From thirty-four to nine. In the instance of a brief statement, twenty-five charges evaporated. Months of intense preparation. Millions of dollars spent preparing to defend each of those twenty-five stocks. Outwardly, the decision seemed curious, even arbitrary. The reality is almost mundane, a strategic maneuver to maximize media sensationalism, confuse the public, and force me to capitulate. I did not capitulate. They dropped charges; the prosecution had no basis for any of them. A common prosecutorial tactic: "stacking the deck," casting a wide net specifically intended to intimidate and stretch the defendant's resources during the pretrial phase. Prosecutors face no penalty or downside for dropping charges. Instead, the defendant is faced not with "Innocent until proven guilty" but "Guilty until proven innocent." It was a routine, dirty tactic employed by overzealous prosecutors to force a specific outcome: a victory for themselves.

The first day of a trial is reserved for opening arguments from both sides. The government always goes first. The relative quiet of the jury selection inside the courtroom proved to be a brief respite. As soon as the opening arguments began, the atmosphere became impossibly more charged. The drama, long anticipated and fanned to a crescendo with months of intense media coverage, peaked to virtual hysteria. Hordes of people arrived to watch the spectacle. There was no way to fit them all into the courtroom. Security needed to open two other courtrooms, each fitted with live TV feeds into the action next door. The crowds filled up the first extra room and then overflowed to completely fill up the second. They were all hungry and ready for a good show, and that's precisely what the prosecution fed them.

"Greed and corruption—that's what this case is about!!" The prosecutor set the stage, shouting out theatrical words, strategic in his use of pauses to heighten the drama, all the while pacing, snarling. The performance harkened to the stage established in the 1980s by Rudy Giuliani in his own media-frenzied prosecution of Mike Milken. As Guiliani did then, Jonathan Streeter did now. He presented as fact to the jury the long list of allegations against me, basically confirming my guilt to a group of jurors who had no experience to ask questions or to ferret out the truth. Streeter had a lectern placed squarely in front of the jury. When he was not pacing, he returned to the central spot and spoke directly to them. They were riveted. I sat still, listening.

Since the 1980s, U.S. attorneys have targeted Wall Street as the epicenter of corruption and greed. Fighting Wall Street was presented by prosecutors as an epic battle, a crusade to be fought with religious fervor. Good versus evil. The general public had no way of contextualizing the enormous dollar amounts in the world of banking, much less the world of hedge funds. The prevailing view of general public, which included the jury who were supposed to be dispassionate about the trial, was what was being chanted on the streets at that time: It was not just an Occupy Wall Street movement, it was Take Down Wall Street. On every newspaper or TV show, I was the face of the greed of Wall Street, the epitome of evil, and there was nothing more prejudicial in this context than to hear an ardent prosecutor proclaiming, "Mr. Rajaratnam exploited a corrupt network of people to get access to secret, sensitive corporate information to make tens of millions of dollars." The jury was mesmerized. They had no experience or knowledge to do otherwise.

Right from the start, the prosecution began misrepresenting the facts and the numbers. They began from the onset to throw out a vast number of inaccuracies—each of which, when introduced to inexperienced and unsuspecting jurors, assume a deeply prejudicial overlay to all subsequent information.

For example, $63 million—the number I was alleged to have earned personally off my "illicit trades." Instead, the reality: $63 million was, in fact, an aggregate number, a total gain accruing to the Galleon funds and to all the hundreds of investors in the funds, not to me personally.

Another example: the prosecution spoke only of gains generated by the alleged illicit trades. They made no mention of losses. Not once. What was reality? The total gains to all our investors did amount to $63 million but total losses were higher. These were $67 million. If the total losses from the nine charges were subtracted from the gains, the net would be an overall loss! The layperson, his or her head already reeling with astonishing numbers, would never think to question the allocation to me, personally, of a number as improbably large as $63 million.

Sadly, predictably, and irresponsibly, the media actually compounded the false narrative presented by the prosecution. Not only did they embellish the alleged dollar amounts, they also misled the public by perpetuating the insinuation that I had personally taken all this money. "In the Galleon case, the government alleged that Rajaratnam pocketed as much as $75 million from his illegal trade compared to Rajaratnam's net worth of $1.3 billion."[47]

The prosecutors alleged that I was fully aware of my own criminal actions. They highlighted wiretap conversations—snippets of innocent conversation taken totally out of context—showing "Mr. Rajaratnam committing his crime in real time." The government strategy was to deceive the jury into viewing each conversation in isolation, ignoring the very real facts that it was all available in the domain of public information.

Then it was the defense's turn for an opening argument. Doing a solid job of presenting the facts, John provided an overview of Galleon. He went into necessary detail about the firm's rigorous research process and outlined that gathering information was part of our daily job as professional investors. He emphasized that the defense would show that all information discussed in the case (including that recorded in the wiretaps) was public information, available in articles, financial websites, sell-side analysts' reports, and in Galleon's own analyses. John told the jury, "Ask yourself: was the information already public? Has the company announced it? Has it been reported in the newspapers? Because if the information is public, then there is no case here. It's over."

John also made a full-frontal attack on the three cooperating witnesses, Anil Kumar, Rajiv Goel, and Adam Smith: "Each one of these government witnesses is here because they committed their own crimes . . . each of them faced twenty-five years or more in prison. The prosecutorial leash for each witness enabled the government to guide their testimony."

Unfortunately, in this day of sound bites and social media aesthetics, John Dowd lacked the visual appeal, the verbal drama, and the theatrics of the prosecutor. John fell short of the expectations implicit in the heightened drama required for this trial.

The heart of the government's case revolved around the false testimony of the three cooperating witnesses: Anil Kumar, Rajiv Goel, and Adam Smith. Not one of them made eye contact with me throughout his testimony. The cooperating witnesses were well coached. The prosecutors had coercively told each of them that they would have to incriminate me convincingly if they wanted a deal to offset their own crimes; they had every incentive to perform well.

Early in the trial, I received an anonymous email from an unknown person stating one of the jurors was a relative and suggested that if I sent $200,000 to an account, that juror would vote to acquit me. The email was heavily encrypted, sent by someone with a computer background. They wanted me to make contact with them through some encrypted instructions. I immediately informed John, who in turn brought it to the judge's attention. The judge alerted the FBI, which tried unsuccessfully to make contact with the anonymous person, who did not take the bait. We speculated that it could have actually been the FBI itself that had sent this email in an attempt to charge me with jury tampering.

DECEPTION #1: CONFIDENTIAL INFORMATION VERSUS MNPI

THE ISSUE OF CONFIDENTIAL INFORMATION is a subtle, crucial point essential to understanding my case. Confidential information and MNPI are not one and the same. *According to the law, "Confidential information" is not necessarily material, nonpublic information, and talking about and trading on confidential information is not a crime.*

Take, for example, Apple and the hype leading up to an announcement of the latest advancement in their iPhone. Weeks before Apple formally introduces their latest iPhone, many of its features are widely reported in various blogs, technical journals, and mainstream magazines. This information is what Apple would consider *confidential information* before the formal introduction of the new iPhone. However, once the information comes into the public domain it is *not MNPI*—and therefore it is fully legal to discuss and act on that information.

The distinction between "confidential" and MNPI is very important. The prosecutors did not even try to prove that the information in my case was *material and nonpublic* information, as required by the law. Instead, they focused on whether the information was "confidential" in an attempt to deceive the jury. The distinction was lost on a jury of laypeople as was the corporate reality of the word "confidential."

In his closing remarks, John tried again to differentiate between the two. He said "The government cannot prove that this information was non-public, so it has tried to prove something else. This is an example of the government relying on fiction to mislead you. The fiction is that everything that goes on inside a company is confidential...until a company issues a press release about out it. But in the real world, information can become public whether a company wants it or not. In the real world the information can become public in all kinds of ways."

I watched the jury as these distinctions were being made. To me, it was clear. The law allows you to trade on information that a company considers confidential if that information is already public, whether in the newspapers, in a trade journal, or in a snippet of research disseminated to clients. *"Confidential" and "nonpublic" are not the same thing.*

Did the jurors actually appreciate the differences? What is "confidential" under various corporate policies and what is "material nonpublic information" as defined by the law? It was an important point to be highlighted by Judge Holwell to the jurors. This was the whole point of my trial, the major thread running through every charge against me. But Judge Holwell said nothing. Judge Holwell said nothing to clarify the topic to the jurors.

DECEPTION #2: NOT ONE OF THE ORIGINAL ALLEGED TIPPERS WERE CALLED TO TRIAL

THE GOVERNMENT RESTED ITS CASE without calling a single one of the original alleged tippers to testify: Kieran Taylor (Akamai), Sunil Bhalla (Polycom),

Shammara Hussain (Google), Deep Shah (Hilton), Kamal Ahmed (AMD/ATYT, IDTI/ICST), and Rajat Gupta (Goldman Sachs). Not one of them was called to testify against me at the trial. Yet, these were the very names the FBI and Bharara's SDNY trumpeted for months to substantiate their case. I knew Rajat; I had no idea who the others were. I had never met them. Until my case, I had never heard their names. Yet the government alleged that I was the leader of this alleged "insider trading ring."

The prosecution of insider trading requires proof that the tipper wrongfully disclosed secret information in breach of duty to his or her employer. In other words, if the source did not break the law, no one who trades on the information can be held liable. Through their lawyers, Kieran Taylor and Kamal Ahmed strongly denied any wrongdoing. Sunil Bhalla from Polycom in his SEC deposition under oath denied giving any inside information to Roomy Khan. Rajat Gupta vehemently denied having done anything wrong and subsequently went to trial in an attempt to prove his innocence.

There was a very good reason the prosecutors did not call any of these alleged tippers: the government's case was built on innuendoes and speculation. There was nothing tied to fact. *The government was afraid of the truth.*

In addition to the three cooperating witnesses, the government subpoenaed several senior executives from Polycom, Akamai, Intel, and Hilton. Each was to confirm under oath that at least some of the information discussed on the wiretapped calls was confidential to the specific company. However, in the instance of Goldman Sachs, the prosecutors brought in Lloyd Blankfein, CEO and most prominent of the senior executives to be subpoenaed. This was yet another shrewd move by the media-savvy U.S. attorney. Why not the CEOs of the other companies? Why specifically Lloyd Blankfein?

Given the extremely charged environment of the financial crisis, the prosecution understood that the CEO of Goldman Sachs would generate maximum media coverage. What they did not count on was Lloyd's capacity to articulate in layperson's terms the nuanced and subtle distinction between "confidential" and "nonpublic" information: the two essential elements of my trial. Finally, the jury—and, in fact, the media—had information conveyed in words they could understand and digest. The jury and the world began to see through the obfuscation presented in confusing detail by the prosecution. Lloyd's testimony was a high point for the defense.

Lloyd and I knew each other through our professional roles. After his testimony, he made it a point to walk over to my table and greet me. Some have speculated that he was walking a tightrope—the government was eager to find individual and corporate scalps to atone for the financial crisis. At that time, Goldman Sachs was under investigation on many fronts. Rajat Gupta told me later that the Goldman Sachs board had been so concerned about Lloyd's having been subpoenaed by the government for my trial that they had asked him to secure personal counsel for himself. Had he chosen not to testify for the government at my trial, and knowing what I now know about government tactics, it is within reason to speculate that Goldman Sachs may likely have suffered some consequences for their role in the financial crisis.

The questions to Blankfein focused on a telephone conversation I had on July 29, 2008, with Rajat Gupta ahead of an in-person meeting with Gary Cohen, president of Goldman Sachs, on July 31. Blankfein testified my conversation with Rajat covered topics that, while confidential to Goldman Sachs, were already in the public domain. This is the single most important point Lloyd could make: the information was confidential to Goldman Sachs, but was already in the public domain. This was exactly what we on the defense team were attempting to communicate. On the call, I asked Rajat about topics I should discuss with Gary Cohen. At that time, I was more worried about our prime brokerage balances at Goldman Sachs and the solvency of that firm than anything else. There was *no subsequent trading* by me in Goldman Sachs or any of the other companies that Rajat and I talked about.

Confidential information recognized as already out there in the public domain was the significant point—and the distinction made by the CEO of Goldman Sachs that the exchange of information was straightforward and also that there was an important distinction to be made between confidential information and MNPI.

Unlike the senior executives testifying at my trial, *Blankfein was the only one who had significant Wall Street experience.* He was the only executive called to testify who understood and made it a point to differentiate between confidential and nonpublic information. He elevated this point as a crucial distinction. Would the jurors understand the distinction? Or would the jurors continue to be blinded by the deception presented by the prosecutors?

THE DEFENSE'S CASE

IT WAS THEN OUR TURN to present the facts. There is one important word that distinguished the testimonies of the three government witnesses from all the defense witnesses: motivation. Each of the three cooperating government witnesses (Anil Kumar, Rajiv Goel, and Adam Smith) had already pled guilty to a completely separate crime that was not associated with me or Galleon. Testifying against me for the government was their fervent effort to earn a Get-Out-of-Jail-Free card. Each had every incentive to lie. In fact, Anil Kumar got to lie at my trial and then do a 180-degree reversal at my brother's trial on the same topic. Both accounts were accepted by the court. One denied freedom; the other, granted freedom. At the same time, not one defense witnesses was coerced or accused of any crime and therefore had no incentive to lie. If they lied under oath, they could be and would be charged with perjury and go to prison.

We had planned to put on a substantial case with a number of witnesses to rebut the prosecutors' narrative. However, at the last minute, John Dowd decided to cut the defense witnesses down to just five. I disagreed. We had prepared well, and I wanted to demonstrate my innocence to the jury. John's rationale was that the jury was tired and wanted to go home.

The first witness for my defense was John Pernell. John was an early investor in the Galleon technology fund and stayed with us to the end. John was the seed investor in Adam Smith's new fund Rose Lane Capital, which Adam established in 2010 after Galleon was dissolved. John testified about his breakfast meeting with Adam Smith on February 2, 2011, in which

Adam related being intimidated by the FBI into pleading guilty to insider trading and implicating me.

Incredibly and inexplicably, Judge Holwell did not allow the memo that John Pernell had written to John Dowd about the breakfast meeting into evidence, so the jury was not able to see a very important document. The judge had earlier allowed the prosecutors to introduce any and all emails written by anyone. I felt that the memo (a full text of which is in Chapter 13 on Adam Smith) was critical evidence of Adam being intimidated by the FBI and therefore lying to save his skin, but Judge Holwell did not agree.

In the memo, John Pernell states that the FBI told Adam that "If he did not plead guilty and cooperate, he would not see his children until they had reached 20, and that if the 5 or so trades he is being charged with are not necessarily correct as being executed with inside information. It did not matter. If it weren't these, there could be other counts he could be charged with." Not only did the judge not allow the memo into evidence, but he prevented John Pernell from talking about Adam Smith committing perjury on the witness stand and being intimidated by FBI Agent Kang. This was quite a setback for the defense. It seemed that Judge Holwell had different standards for the prosecutors than for the defense.

Rob Hotz, a lawyer with Akin Gump, followed John Pernell on the witness stand. Rob was one of six lawyers present during two sets of interviews with Adam Smith in January 2010 and July 2010. Adam stated in both interviews that in all his years at Galleon, he had not seen any evidence of insider trading. Now, just seven months later as a cooperating witness for the government, he reversed himself, a complete turnaround of facts. It was clear—Adam was scared and was now lying. The testimonies of John Pernell and Rob Hotz, both credible witnesses for my defense, as well as Adam Smith's own internal emails, highlighted Adam's current state of mind.

The most charismatic defense witness was Geoff Canada. Geoff was CEO of the Harlem Children Zone (HCZ), a charter school system he founded and developed with the ultimate goal of helping children and their families break out of the cycle of generational poverty. I was hooked from the moment I first met Geoff and toured HCZ. For the first time, I saw the tremendous and deeply impactful work he was doing with the children from Harlem. I was truly inspired by his work and his commitment, and over the years, he also become a personal friend. The judge allowed Geoff's testimony, with the provision that he could not talk about my donations to the HCZ. Geoff testified that he had known me for seven years and that we had hit it off right away. He said that my wish "to level the playing field for kids everywhere" had led to my involvement with HCZ. The prosecutors wisely had no questions for Geoff.

A few years later, my family and I went to the Galapagos, travelling to the different islands by boat and experiencing the places where Darwin first came up with his theories of evolution. My children had been thrilled to swim with the penguins and sand sharks and see the giant turtles and iguanas—all of which were totally indifferent to the human beings present. I wanted the children from HCZ to have a similar educational experience, and my intention had been to send a group of children from HCZ to the Galapagos in an ongoing experiential learning program. We were only able to do this for two years until my arrest.

Geoff was instrumental in developing my charitable initiatives and strategy. During a vacation in Sri Lanka, I witnessed the tsunami that hit the island, on December 26, 2004. The next day, my younger sister and I drove six hours north of Colombo to visit the orphanage we had been supporting. The orphans' parents had been killed in the civil war in Sri Lanka and the children were between three and seven years old. The orphanage was near the beach, and unable to outrun the fury of the sea, all the children had been killed. Only a few scattered clothes and shoes remained on the beach. I broke down. Why did God allow this to happen to these kids? First, they had lost their parents and now they had lost their lives. I returned to Colombo and helped raise money to build houses for those affected by the tsunami.

I returned to New York despondent. I questioned my work hedge fund industry. I was lost. I told Geoff Canada I wanted to quit my job and work with underprivileged children. Geoff advised me to keep doing what I was doing, making money, and to continue helping the underprivileged. Since then, I have tried to do this in a more substantial way.

As Geoff was testifying, memories of the orphans came to my mind. These memories continue to haunt me even to this day. Everything that I have endured pales in comparison to what those innocent kids endured in their brief lives.

Geoff also testified that I was generous and that he never had to ask me for money. For inexplicable reasons, the judge informed the defense that neither they nor Geoff could elaborate on the extent or magnitude of my giving to HCZ. The reality was that I had donated more than $10 million to HCZ. This would have undermined the prosecutors' claim that I was greedy.

We had planned to have a few Galleon analysts testify after Geoff, including Steve Granoff and Eric Rothdeutsch. Steve followed Google and independently established a price target of $550. Eric followed ICST when it was acquired by IDTI. ICST was his top pick at that time. We would have loved to have had our AMD and ATYT analyst Nadeem Janmohamed testify as well. But he was reluctant to get involved. He was scared. Prosecutors often threaten witnesses with drastic consequences if they testify for the defense. If defense lawyers did this, it would be considered witness tampering and an obstruction of justice, and they might get disbarred, but different rules exist for the different sides.

Each of these analysts would have testified that they did their research and arrived at their recommendations and stock price independently. And not once did I ask them to fabricate any emails as Adam Smith falsely testified. Additionally, they would have testified that my trading was entirely consistent with their written recommendations.

Imagine, then, my complete and utter disbelief when John Dowd informed me that he was not going to call *any* of the Galleon analysts to speak on my behalf. John's rationale was that we had introduced a lot of evidence through the prosecution's witnesses clearly showing that information was public and didn't need numerous additional witnesses which might tire out the jury. John was technically correct, but he had no appreciation for the people connection with the jury. Each analyst could have been asked three questions:

Did he ask you to fabricate any emails? No.

Did you arrive at your research independently? No.

Did he ever veer from your recommendations? No.

But by their very nature, the prosecution witnesses were hostile to the defense and dismissed all the public information they were shown as speculative. I did not agree but felt I had to comply as John Dowd had more experience with his strategy.

Rick Schutte, president of Galleon, was the next defense witness. Rick joined Galleon as a portfolio manager of the Galleon Explorers fund. When we shut down Galleon in October 2009, I had an investment of $25 million in the Galleon Explorers fund. When Rick started his new fund in 2010, with the concurrence of my lawyer John Dowd, I moved that investment into Rick's new fund. I also had an investment of $25 million in Galleon International run by David Lau. When we closed Galleon International, David Lau started his own Asian fund and similarly, I moved that $25 million to David's new fund. Having worked with both Rick and David, I was confident in each one's ability for investing and managing funds.

Rick Schutte was the ideal person to testify about Galleon and its research efforts. Prior to becoming president, Rick had been the director of research at Galleon and had put into place many of the systems and methods that our analysts were expected to follow. He was also a courageous and steady guy who was not easily intimidated by the prosecutors.

On the witness stand, Rick went into great detail about our research process, and he demonstrated that the Galleon analysts' reports supported all the trades in question. He described our daily morning meetings, with sixty to seventy of our Galleon investment professionals. We had encouraged a level of transparency that was unprecedented, including letting existing and potential investors sit in at these meetings. The analysts were subjected to a methodical and disciplined process requiring in-depth backup details. Rick further testified that analysts routinely met with the companies they followed and wrote weekly reports due by 5:00 p.m. each Friday. He remarked that at morning meetings, I asked more questions than anyone else and was always the best prepared person in the room.

Rick successfully countered an important argument about my supposedly illicit conversation with Rajat Gupta. Rick testified that he was present at the meeting with Gary Cohen and testified that Cohen had very openly talked about all the topics that Rajat and I had discussed two days prior as a preparation for the meeting. Rick also testified that he distinctly remembered my asking our financial services analyst to calculate the impact of the decline on ICBC's stock price on Goldman Sachs, which connected to the supposedly infamous "they are going to lose $2 per share" call to David Lau.

Rick's testimony, together with that of John Pernell and Rob Hotz, coming just a week after the Adam Smith testimony, totally undermined Smith's accusations. Even the progovernment press was impressed with Rick Schutte. They reported that Rick came across as "measured and mature and someone to be believed."

However, my team made an accidental but critical error. John Dowd neglected to inform the jury upfront about my investment in Rick's new hedge fund.

In their cross-examination of Rick, the prosecutors pounced on this issue, implying to the jury that Rick's testimony was somehow tainted because I was an investor in his fund. The situation was laden with irony. The prosecutors, who themselves had offered plea bargains and Get-Out-of-Jail-Free cards to the three main cooperating witnesses, were now implying that Rick had an incentive to lie because I was an investor in his new hedge fund.

Even now, even after all the theatrics and misrepresentation, I was again surprised at how low they would stoop to mislead the jury.

Knowing that Rick's testimony had badly damaged Adam Smith's credibility and exposed his lies, a worried government PR machine went into high gear. A colleague shared an elevator at the day's end with some of the press along with Ellen Davis, the public relations director for the U.S. attorney. While in the elevator, Davis instructed the press to highlight the fact that Rick wasn't a credible witness because of my investment in his fund.

Sure enough, the next morning, the press faithfully followed Davis's bidding. In particular, Chad Bray, a *Wall Street Journal* reporter, opined that the defense had been blindsided by the prosecution bringing up the investment.

Enraged by the WSJ article, John Dowd went into one of his by now-frequent temper tantrums. He sent an email to the WSJ reporter stating that "this is the worst piece of whoring journalism I have read in a long time. How long are you going to suck [U.S. Attorney Preet Bharara]'s teat? All to hurt a decent, honest witness, [whom assistant U.S. Attorney Reed] Brodsky could not lay a glove on. It did not work. The jury was not impressed by the worst cross examination ever delivered. So, in the style of Preet, try to smear him by working the sycophants in the back of the Courtroom. He learned from Schumer in the Senate…Preet is scared sh[**]less he is going to lose this case so he feeds his whores at the WSJ. What a disgrace for an otherwise great paper."

Of course, the *Wall Street Journal* and other media promptly printed Dowd's email verbatim on June 20, 2011. I was appalled by John's lack of professionalism, belligerent tone, and vulgar word choice. At that time, I made the decision to fire him as soon as the case was over. I wanted nothing to do with him. It was enough. Terry Lynam became my lead lawyer.

Our fifth and final witness was Gregg Jarrell, who was examined by Terry Lynam. Professor Jarrell had been chief economist at the SEC and was now professor of finance at Simon Graduate School of Business at the University of Rochester. He had published dozens of articles on economics and finance in academic journals, as well as the popular media. He had testified as an expert witness in about forty cases for the defense and, *importantly, for the Justice Department as well.* He was and continues to be a respected authority on stocks and the markets.

Professor Jarrell spoke about how information is routinely leaked in the market and how professional investors look for clues, such as increased trading volume as well as options activity, as signs of a corporate takeover. He testified that he had studied the government's allegations and accordingly, he and his team had reviewed over 1.1 million Galleon trades 2003–2008. Focusing just on my trades, he said that in that period I had traded a staggering $173 billion worth of stock: about $34 billion a year or $141 million every day! These statistics put in perspective the dollar amount of the trades in question. The government allegations covered less than 0.25 percent of my trades.

DECEPTION #3: $63 MILLION PROFITS FROM ALLEGED INSIDER TRADES

THE STOCKS IN QUESTION RESULTED in $63 million in profits and $67 million in losses. The prosecution focused only on the profits. Not a word was uttered on the losses that, in fact, netted $4 million. Professor Jarrell looked at the news stories, analyst reports, emails, instant messages, and internal Galleon research reports for each trade in question. He and his team demonstrated irrefutably that for each of the original thirty-four stocks, the information that was allegedly inside was *already in the public domain.*

Rick Schutte's testimony showed that my trading was grounded in rigorous analysis by the Galleon analysts. Professor Jarrell's testimony demonstrated that *all of the alleged nonpublic information was indeed public.*

John advised me against testifying. In general, defense lawyers do not want their clients to testify under oath because if there is even the slightest discrepancy in their testimony, the prosecution can and will charge them with obstruction of justice and perjury.

Although I understood John Dowd's concern, I was confident I knew the facts and details inside out and would not have been easily rattled or intimidated by the occasion or any of the prosecutors. Although we had done an excellent job explaining each of the individual trades, I was the only one who could fully explain the context and the actual texts of the wiretaps.

I heeded John's advice and did not take the stand. Consequently, most of the interpretation of the wiretaps, their context—and, indeed, the entire case—had been presented to the jury by the government, which used its three highly motivated, cooperating witnesses to paint the picture for the jury. Although my defense was able to question the government witnesses, it was not able to defend me as effectively as I would have done had I taken the stand.

Now it was time for the closing arguments, typically the most important part of the trial. Both the prosecution and the defense have the opportunity to present their arguments to the jury. The burden of proof is on the government, and accordingly, the prosecutors go first, followed by the defense. In what is yet another unfair advantage for the government, the prosecutors have one last option for a final rebuttal: an opportunity for a final argument and a chance to set the tone for the jury deliberations.

CLOSING ARGUMENTS

THE PROSECUTORS DECIDED TO DIVIDE the closing arguments between their two senior lawyers. However, John Dowd was accustomed to being the lead and did not seek to share the critical closing argument with Terry Lynam. I now realize that John expected my case to be his crowning achievement. He wanted the glory of the win to be his alone. I worried that he might not have the physical and mental energy to carry such a heavy burden by himself and asked if he would be able to do it on his own. It was an academic question; the answer was yes.

The prosecutors started their summation by misstating the facts and dramatically suggesting that I had led others to break the law. However, anyone who had attended the trial knew that the testimony of Anil Kumar and Rajiv Goel was tainted by their fear of punishment for cheating on their taxes for several years. Furthermore, Adam Smith had been charged with trading on inside information at his new firm, Rose Lane Capital, and was exchanging his fabricated testimony about me for his freedom. None of these cooperating witnesses' real crimes had anything to do with Galleon or me, yet I conveniently served as their Get out of Jail Free cards.

Some of the prosecution's assertions were truly outrageous. Even though Rajiv Goel had testified that he did not remember what he had told me about Intel and whether it was good or bad, the prosecutor miraculously "knew" exactly what Goel told me in a call that was not even recorded! In his theatrics for the jury's benefit, the prosecutor *imagined* what Goel told me: "Goel said that things are looking better, things aren't so bad; I told you it was bad before but things are getting a bit better; that's the three-minute call with Rajaratnam."

The prosecutor also alleged that I created an email trail with two other Galleon employees but could not point to a single email because none existed. He repeated Anil Kumar's lies that I had asked him to buy a prepaid phone so that we could communicate secret information but could not tell the jury what the phone number was—because there was none. The prosecutor ignored the fact that it was *my* phone, not Kumar's, that had been tapped and that I had used the same number for over ten years.

The prosecutors used simple language that everyone, particularly the jury, could easily understand. It was pure street theatre, and the jury was attentive. Despite being full of lies and suppositions, the prosecutor's summation was succinct, crisp, and engaging.

Next, it was John Dowd's turn. He started powerfully, thunderously telling the jury, "We showed you the complete picture of what happened and not the tiny sliver that the government would present. We showed you how Raj worked hard for Galleon investors, how he dug for information and made smart investment decisions. We showed you the whole universe of facts that surrounded every one of Raj's trades." He reminded the jury that, "Mr. Schutte told you how Raj asked more questions than anyone else at the morning meetings. He told you how Raj was the best prepared person there. He told you it was obvious that Mr. Rajaratnam had read all of the analysts' research and reports."

John then attacked the government's case. "The government's case rests on the fictional idea that information can't ever become public until a company issues a press release about it. But we have shown you that in the real world, information can become public in all sorts of ways, whether a company wants it to or not and whether the company has made a formal announcement or not. The government can't stand it. In the real world, there are billions of people talking to one another. This is the media age, the age of the internet, blogs and email, and instant communications. In the real world, public companies are operating and functioning and communicating with the press, with investors, with competitors, with distributors and with government agencies." Very little of import ever remains private for long.

John continued. "What duties did Raj have? He had a duty to ask questions. He had a duty to conduct research. He had a duty to review his analysts' reports. He had a duty to talk to company representatives just as analysts do. He had to take advantage of attractive investment opportunities for his clients. And Raj had a duty to ask questions and a duty to act on the answers he got. One of the government witnesses from Intel told you that an analyst's job is to ask questions and push for information and triangulate the information to reach conclusions about a company. That's was Raj's job. That was his duty and Raj had the right to assume that the people he spoke to respected their own duties. Raj wasn't talking to children. He was talking to the most sophisticated businesspeople in the world. And he was allowed to assume that the information they shared with him was information they were allowed to share with him. Remember Raj never even saw all these confidentiality policies the government has shown you. These policies didn't define Raj's duties. They defined other people's duties. Raj did what he was supposed to do as the steward of his investors' money. He sought as much information as he could. Ladies and gentlemen, that's the real world. That's what people like Raj do, and that's not a crime."

Next, John vigorously attacked the credibility of the three government cooperators and pointed out the many contradictions in their testimony. "You cannot convict unless you believe the word of Anil Kumar, Rajiv Goel, and Adam Smith. We have proven to you that every one of these three men lied inside and outside the courtroom. We have proved that they are getting a free pass from the government for their own crimes in return for their testimony against Raj. That's why they are here. That's why they said all these things, because the prosecutors hold the key to the jailhouse for these three men. They might spend twenty-five years in prison and they might not spend a day. None of them has been sentenced yet, and the prosecutors decide whether the government is going to help them at sentencing or not. Let me be blunt. Anil Kumar, Rajiv Goel, and Adam Smith testified the way they have testified because they have been coerced by the government. It's not pretty, but it's that simple."

John had cross-examined Anil Kumar himself and could not hide his disdain for him. He said, "The first words Mr. Streeter (the prosecutor) said to you during this opening statement were 'greed and corruption.' Then the government called Anil Kumar, who might be one of the greediest and most corrupt people you have ever met in your life, a man who made millions of dollars a year but squirreled away millions more in off-shore accounts to avoid paying his taxes, a man who giggled his way through testimony about all the times he lied and cheated his friends and his business partners and the IRS. You think Anil Kumar was funny. I didn't. You should be offended that the government is asking you to believe Anil Kumar, because Anil Kumar might be the most dishonest person you've ever met in your life."

Then John went through the whole litany of lies that Anil Kumar had said under oath including those related to Mindspirit, Pecos Trading, Manju Das, fake affidavits, fake bank statements, fake doctor's notes, and fake tax forms. John told the jury, "We're talking about a grown man, who is a senior partner of McKinsey, the largest consulting firm in the world, and he gets on the stand and says 'Raj made me do it.' That might be what a third grader would say, but not a grown man, and it defies common sense and that's nuts."

It was almost five in the evening when the judge adjourned the court. We were to resume the rest of the closing arguments the next day. John had spoken for about two hours and had been excellent: energetic, articulate and sharp. But he could not sustain the level of energy.

The long trial and late nights were catching up with John. When the trial resumed the following morning at 9:45 a.m., he appeared tired and worn out. He had no energy. Age had caught up with him. He was slow and ponderous, speaking in monotonic length of my trading in the different individual stocks for over five hours. The mind-altering monotony of his arguments sent more than a few jurors went into narcoleptic slumber. As the day wore on, John became even more visibly fatigued than he was when he began. He had underestimated the physical and intellectual stamina needed in a long criminal trial. His last big criminal trial had been seventeen years ago, when he was fifty-three years old.

After a brief rebuttal by the prosecutors, it was time for the judge's instructions.

JURY INSTRUCTIONS

JUDGE HOLWELL READ OUT JURY instructions slowly and methodically, a process that lasted almost two hours.

He read out loud each of the over fifty pages of instructions. Even to a professional investor like me, the instructions were not just puzzling, they were confusing. How would the jury begin to understand such complex and confusing directions? Just as they were wading through all the information that had been presented through the three-month trial, the judge took another two full hours to instruct them as to how they should think about or interpret the information in arriving at their ultimate decision to acquit or find me guilty. The judge's instructions on insider trading were also inconsistent with the rulings of other circuit courts and judges.

For example, the jury instructions stated that "Information is not material nonpublic information if it was either a) publicly available through sources such as press releases, SEC filings, trade publications, analysts' reports, newspapers, magazines, television, radio or word of mouth or, b) not material because it was not information that a reasonable investor would have considered significant in deciding whether to buy, sell or hold securities and at what price to buy or sell."

This was relatively straightforward, and based on this I would have to be acquitted on every charge. Professor Jarrell and Rick Schutte had testified and demonstrated that all the alleged tips were already in the public domain.

But then the jury instructions went on to note that "On the other hand if the information is not generally available and the company would not make it available in response to a request, then it is nonpublic rather than public." This is in direct contradiction to what it stated earlier. For instance, if an obscure website publishes a rumor about a company, this could be considered nonpublic information, whether or not it happened to be true. The jury was then told, "Remember, whether the information is public or nonpublic is an issue for you to decide."

But how would a jury interpret information from a technically nonsecret source, for example a sell-side analyst or a Chinese blog? This information is "not generally available," but it is still out there in the public domain even though the company had not disseminated it because it had not been in its interest to do so. Before Apple introduces a major new product, they may not have announced its new features. However, product details may already be widely discussed on a variety of tech blogs.

The situation was made even worse as Judge Holwell continued with his instructions: "Bear in mind that the law requires only that the information be a factor in the decision to buy and sell. It need not be the only consideration, if inside information was a factor, however small."

Upon hearing the jury instructions, the jury went to its room to begin deliberations, and the judge retired to his chambers. The defense was assigned a room on the seventeenth floor as well. We were asked to stay around in case the jury made a decision. The jury deliberated for twelve full days, which was longer than what most people expected. My defense lawyers maintained that longer the deliberation, the better it was for the defendant. I paid no mind to that: it was pure speculation. Throughout the trial, during the break, my lawyers had discussed the body language of the twelve jurors, attempting to draw conclusions from their posture and movements. It was about as reliable as reading tea leaves.

We spent twelve days waiting in the defense room, each day spent in anticipation of a decision by the jury. We were all required to be present at court in the event the jury arrived at a decision. There were at least six or seven people around at all times: two or three from Akin Gump, including John Dowd and Terry Lynam, two from Shearman & Sterling, the lawyers for the Galleon management company, as well as our PR guy and a few other junior lawyers. I calculated that the lawyers were costing me about $50,000 a day to hang out and wait for the jury to come to a decision. It was yet another reminder that going to trial to defend oneself in the U.S. is an expensive and relatively complex choice, and a key reason for the fact that most people actually have no choice but to accept a plea—even when they are innocent.

The waiting period was tense. John Dowd, Terry Lynam, and I had worked closely together for the past eighteen months. They had assisted me in a time of dire need. For that, I will always be grateful. John Dowd had done his best as had Terry Lynam. Dowd was an able lawyer who believed fervently in the right of all to representation. Like me, he was a warrior. We had collected a lot of information, but when it was time to win the war, he did not use much of it wisely. Worse, he relied only on his own counsel to make all the strategic and tactical decisions. He was not open to any idea other than his own, a significant flaw for a defense where so much of the content was complex and needed an agile and nuanced touch. Terry Lynam, on the other hand, was also an excellent lawyer who had the capacity to recognize and immediately incorporate good ideas from the team.

In the end, our defense strategy was less effective and suffered from the rigid adherence to a single-minded way of thinking.

Finally, on the morning of May 11, 2011, we were informed that the jury had made its decision. We made our way to the courtroom. The judge came in first. The jury followed behind him, filing in one by one. Each one looked somber. It was not a good sign for me. The jury foreman stood up and handed the charge sheet to the judge. After reading the single page, the judge passed it onto the court marshall, who then read the jury's verdict out loud.

The jury found me guilty on all fourteen counts.

None of us believed the government had made its case beyond a reasonable doubt. Each of their witnesses, while trying to incriminate me, had been exposed as liars. I was found guilty in a case where the spectrum of evidence pointed to my innocence.

Outside the courthouse, there were hundreds of media people. Word that the jury had reached a verdict had spread quickly. They were waiting. On the way down, I asked John not to make any statement. Unfortunately, as had become the norm with him, he was not prepared to listen to anyone.

He seemed as concerned about his own public image as with the case. He even regarded his performance at our trial as a victory. Deeply misguided, he told the waiting reporters that we had, in fact, won twenty to fourteen (referring to the twenty charges that were dropped out of the thirty-four stocks in the superseding indictment.) Delusional. My battle would continue, but without John.

SENTENCING

THE GOVERNMENT TOOK ALMOST HALF a year to arrive at their sentencing decision. There was a lot to do, and my going to jail was only part of the agenda. A lot went on during those months.

The government tried to use the quiet time to turn me. The government prosecutors approached my lawyer Terry Lynam to ask, "Why doesn't Raj help himself and talk to us?" Terry understood the code: "Help Raj help himself—cooperate with us." Help them convict Rajat Gupta and they would lighten my sentencing. Anathema. To me, the idea was anathema. They were asking me to help myself by falsely incriminating someone else. Appalling. Not an option. I instructed Terry Lynam to convey the message.

In the meantime, the three prosecutors were also busy updating their résumés. Their victory in the Galleon case could and would be parlayed to lucrative partnership positions at prestigious New York law firms. Partners at New York's premier law firms in New York make seven-figure salaries. I was their ticket to riches. Each achieved his goal.

Reporters were busy writing feature articles. A few began writing books. The nation was hungry for details, and the press continued feeding the beast.

The sentencing guidelines for insider trading cases are largely based on the amount of money alleged to have been made illegally. Based on *all* the government allegations, the Galleon funds made $63 million in profits and lost $67 million, for a net loss of $4 million. But the government now argued that the judge should exclude the losses incurred and use only the gains. Incredibly Judge Holwell agreed with the government.

In our presentencing report, we took the belated opportunity to inform the judge about my background and my charitable efforts. Throughout the trial, at John Dowd's behest, I had sat silently, passively, my voice heard only on the wiretapped recordings. Judge Holwell had not allowed testimony about the extent of my charitable giving. He had had no opportunity to get to know me beyond the trial. In the report, we finally had that opportunity, including to point out that I had given over $50 million to many charities.

The judge also received supporting letters from over 250 people. They were from Galleon employees, friends, business associates, and family. The letters poured in from around the world. They were immediate and heartfelt. I was deeply touched.

The sentencing date was finally set. October 13, 2011. Almost five months to the day of the guilty verdict. Almost two years to the date of my arrest. We made our way to court on a bright fall morning. The usual large numbers of reporters and photographers were already gathered. But this morning, they were restrained. Quiet. No jostling. They opened a path to allow us a clear walkway to the courtroom.

The courtroom was overflowing—family, supporters, observers. The prosecution made its case, asking for the maximum sentence of twenty-four years. Terry Lynam followed, arguing for a much shorter sentence. Before the judge delivered the sentence, he asked me whether I had anything to say. I shook my head. I said no.

At this point, having been found guilty, many defendants do a U-turn, confess criminality and apologize for their behavior—pleading for mercy in the hopes of a reduced sentence. I was not prepared to do that. I would not admit guilt for crimes I had not committed.

I wondered whether Judge Holwell grasped that he presided over a system that was implicitly unfair. Did he understand that he presided over a system where people were unjustly sent to prison? One day in the future, perhaps.

Judge Holwell sentenced me to eleven years in prison, a fine of $10 million, and a forfeiture of $53 million (later in a civil suit, the SEC would fine me an additional $94 million for the same alleged crime). I showed no emotion. This was only phase one of the battle. We were going to appeal. I understood we had two very strong arguments: the illegal wiretaps and the prejudicial "however small a factor" jury instructions.

On December 5, 2011, I self-surrendered on schedule to the Devens Medical Center, intending to file a full appeal. I continued to trust the justice system and accepted the steps in the process.

That morning, I said goodbye to my parents. My mother took me aside and asked me whether there would be a mattress and would I get food? I smiled and nodded. That's all you need, she said. A bed and food. With these, she knew that I could handle anything and told me to keep my head held high. I smiled again. The same words echoing from all those years ago when she would hug me goodbye at the end of every holiday and as I prepared to return to boarding school.

Within forty-eight hours of being at Devens, I knew that I could handle it. I had come full circle. Devens reminded me of all the boarding schools I had attended. The living conditions were spartan, each day was regimented, and supervisors monitored all our movements. I was prepared for this.

CHAPTER 19

THE GREAT PREET-ENDER

Of all the characters in my insider trading drama—heroes, villains, innocent bystanders—no one achieved more prominence than Preetinder Bharara, the United States Attorney for the Southern District of New York who publicly and loudly claimed responsibility and credit for my prosecution and conviction. It is safe to say that our names will, in most circles, be forever intertwined in history. In hindsight, the intersection of our lives is one of those accidents of history, a pure coincidence that would reshape each of our respective worlds.

On October 14, 2009, the day before my arrest, I had no idea who Preet Bharara was. He was irrelevant to my life. And that is an understatement. I was fifty-two years old. I did not have a personal attorney. Frankly, I knew very few lawyers either professionally or socially. I had only a vague awareness of the criminal justice system—I did not know the difference between the district attorney, the United States attorney, or any of the other various prosecutors, top or bottom. I had followed the O. J. Simpson trial like the rest of America, and that was largely the extent of my interest in the legal world.

All of this would change with my arrest. Very publicly and very much by his own design, my chief antagonist into the legal world would be Preet Bharara. As I was being led in handcuffs toward the courthouse by the arresting FBI agents, the media photographers tipped off by Bharara were in position to capture each step and to be broadcast across the globe. Bharara himself stood before a rapt press gaggle and wove a fantastic tale of my supposed financial crimes and intrigue. He thundered that my arrest, "should serve as a wake-up call for Wall Street." In the immediate aftermath of the 2008 financial industry collapse and resulting recession, Main Street America was angry, very angry. Bharara swooped in to serve as their crusader. Just months later, as I prepared my defense in earnest, Bharara's face would grace the cover of *Time Magazine* under the headline, "This Man Is Busting Wall St.: Prosecutor Preet Bharara collars the masters of the meltdown."

These were heady times for Bharara. But with the benefit of hindsight, it was all a mirage—it was, in fact, a real fraud.

First, a bit of background on Bharara that was lost in the hyperbole of my arrest and its aftermath. Preetinder Singh Bharara was born in Firozpur, India, in 1968 and immigrated to New Jersey with his family in 1970. Like so many first generation Indian-Americans of that era, Bharara enjoyed academic and professional success, graduating from Harvard College, then Columbia University Law School, and working at two law firms before joining the SDNY United States Attorney's Office as a line assistant.

Here, Bharara's legal career appears to have plateaued. His tenure as a prosecutor was decidedly unspectacular. He spent five relatively nondescript years in the U.S. Attorney's Office, focused on routine federal narcotics cases and largely reheated, historic Mafia prosecutions of old mobsters. According to many who worked with him during this tenure, Preet was neither a star nor identified as having any leadership material. Nice guy, mediocre attorney, good sense of humor, enjoyed a cocktail or two with his friends—no more, no less.

Perhaps reading the writing on the wall, Preet left SDNY after only five years, having neither built nor participated in any major cases himself. He headed to Washington, D.C., joining New York Senator Chuck Schumer's staff at the recommendation of a SDNY colleague and former Schumer aide. Here, by all accounts, Preet thrived. This job did not require careful, rigorous legal analysis or intellectual thought—instead, it was the rough-and-tumble world of politics, public relations, and theater. Schumer himself is a legendary press animal and Preet learned at his feet. He gained Schumer's trust and cultivated his own media contacts and networks while at the Senate with Senator Schumer.

Soon, everything would break in an even better direction for Preet. Barack Obama upset John McCain in the 2008 presidential election, thereby cementing Schumer, New York State's senior senator, as a New York kingmaker. And Schumer rewarded Preet, tapping him over countless more qualified and established New York attorneys to be the new United States attorney for the Southern District of New York. Preet was confirmed into this position on August 13, 2009, just two months before my arrest. It was a tremendous turn of events for Bharara, an unforeseeable and glorious return to SDNY after his nondescript departure just a few years before.

Bharara was walking into a challenging situation. By the fall of 2009, public rage at the American financial sector was at a fever pitch. The ruinous recession loomed over the entire economy. The Occupy Wall Street movement and similar protests demanded that the government hold the Wall Street institutions and executives responsible for the recession accountable. SDNY, widely recognized as the premier prosecutor office in the nation and at the epicenter of the American financial world, was on the clock to answer this public call. Bharara entered his new office and was greeted by this historic moment.

Moreover, the government was reeling from the embarrassment of having completely missed one of the greatest financial frauds of recent memory. Bernie Madoff had been a long-standing and high-profile financier in New York for decades. Despite countless warnings and red flags over the years, SDNY and the SEC had glossed over the possibility that Madoff was in fact operating a large-scale Ponzi scheme. With the collapse of markets in the fall of 2009, Madoff was unable to keep the charade going. He confessed his wrongdoing to his sons, who reported him to the government. When approached by the FBI in response, Madoff immediately admitted his misconduct and quickly pled guilty. Numerous investors were defrauded and collectively lost billions of dollars managed by Madoff. The government had no good answers for its regulatory dereliction over so many years.

Against this backdrop, Bharara looked to be the wrong man for the job. He arrived woefully unprepared for this task and the challenges that he faced. Bharara had no training in investigating or prosecuting financial conduct. His brief and unspectacular tenure as an assistant United States attorney involved interviewing old and feeble former mobsters or low-level narcotics traffickers. He had no experience or understanding of the complex financial products implicated in the recession or any understanding, sophisticated or otherwise, of how large financial institutions—be they banks, private equity firms, leveraged buyout firms, or hedge funds—operated. Or, frankly, what they even did on a day-to-day basis.

But here, Bharara's good fortune would drown out his lack of any legal skill. Completely unbeknownst to Bharara, his predecessor at SDNY, Michael J. Garcia, and his securities unit had commenced a covert investigation into Galleon and my trading back 2007. The premise for this effort was, of course, deeply flawed and in violation of virtually all DOJ guidelines. It had been prompted when FBI agents confronted Roomy Khan about her renewed criminal conduct, wholly independent of Galleon, and she had again sought to implicate me to avoid her own consequences. This scam of Roomy's had worked in 2000 when she was first confronted with her wrongdoing at Intel. Although unable to provide any proof of her allegations, the government nonetheless gave her credit as a cooperator and she avoided jail. Now in 2007, she had breached her prior cooperation agreement by committing further crimes—crimes again that had nothing to do with me or with Galleon. This breach, under any normal rules and protocols, would have barred her use yet again as a government cooperator. In my case, the "rules" were moot. The government's zeal to pursue Galleon and me allowed them to fabricate reality, a rationale. The government, under SDNY Michael Garcia, invited her further cooperation. Undergirded by Roomy's proactive cooperation, the government submitted its false affidavit and secured a wiretap of my cell phone. The government collected almost a year of surreptitious recordings of my phone calls throughout 2008.

Fast-forward to Bharara's introduction as SDNY U.S. attorney in August 2009. The public call for vigorous prosecutions of the financial industry perpetrators of the Recession had reached a fever pitch. And Bharara had no experience or knowledge to lead any such efforts. But then, I inadvertently made a fateful decision that would give Bharara the life preserver he so desperately needed. I decided to travel to surprise my wife for our wedding anniversary with a trip to Geneva, where I had proposed marriage so many years ago. The irony of course is that trying to celebrate the best decision of my life—launching the remarkable life that my wife and I have created together—would be the decision that would start this most challenging period for me and save Bharara's career.

• • •

My plan to celebrate our wedding anniversary had two components. First, I would fly to London to attend the premiere of the movie *Today's Special* featuring comedian Aasif Mandvi. I have always loved new experiences much more than shiny toys or material items, and the chance to participate in the excitement of a film launch seemed like good fun. From London, I would fly to Geneva, where I would meet my wife and celebrate our anniversary on the same dinner cruise where I had proposed to her. We would return to the U.S. together.

Little did I know that the FBI was tracking my movement. And when it saw the records of my one-way airline ticket purchase, alarms apparently went off that I was fleeing. Bharara had now been in place as the U.S. attorney for approximately two months. So even if he knew little about the previous investigation, the FBI concerns about my purported "flight" would have been elevated to him. A competent prosecutor and investigative team would have, of course, looked even a bit further and seen the rest of my itinerary anticipated a return to New York. And they would have realized that my elderly parents, who had physical limitations, and my three school-age children all lived with me in New York, thereby making the prospect of my absconding to Europe or anywhere else absurd. But Bharara and his crack team could not apparently figure this out. So instead, they decided to rush and arrest me.

But upon my arrest, as I would soon learn, the game changed dramatically in Bharara's favor. The questions of the propriety of the criminal charges against me, which would have required legal acumen and financial industry knowledge that Bharara simply did not have were pushed into the background. Instead, Bharara was savvy enough to play to his strengths—a press campaign and politicking. And so began the Preet Bharara Show.

As I was being arrested in the early morning hours of October 16, 2009, in front of my wife and young children, Bharara was orchestrating a politically astute campaign that would make Senator Schumer proud. First, the perp walk. Bharara and his personal press office—Bharara had greatly expanded the SDNY press team as his first act of business—had worked the phones, tipping off all his cultivated press contacts to ensure maximum coverage of my arrest and transport to the courthouse. This created a made-for-television snippet: a hedge fund founder being walked down the street in handcuffs at the height of the Occupy Wall Street movement. Second, Bharara held a press conference and presentation, complete with demonstratives, handouts for the press, and a colorful and emphatic assertion of my guilt. Bharara had carefully planned this, mastered his talking points even if he had little to no idea of the underlying investigation, the financial terms sketched out for him, and the actual evidence. He trumpeted the wiretaps and forcefully emphasized the use of the word "edge" on these calls to be my code for material, nonpublic, and illegal information. Third, Bharara deftly and directly connected this prosecution to the public outcry for action in response to the financial crisis. My arrest, he pressed with the flourish of a master showman, would be a "wake-up call for Wall Street." And at his side, SEC Director of Enforcement Robert Khuzami added, "Raj Rajaratnam is not a master of the universe, but a master of the Rolodex."

Opportunity had presented itself to Bharara, a chance to launch his tenure as U.S. attorney with a signature, high-profile prosecution and simultaneously comfort the public that his office would hold Wall Street accountable for the financial collapse that had jeopardized the American economy. And Bharara would cast himself as the superhero leading the charge. The media was enthralled. He was, in this introduction, charming and forceful, with a knack for colorful, turns of phrase. Bharara gained the publicity and press adulation that he had learned to value in the political world of Washington, D.C., and that he so craved. And when *Time Magazine* placed him on the cover of their magazine, proclaiming that, "This Man Is Busting Wall St.: Prosecutor Preet Bharara collars the masters of the meltdown," Bharara had arrived. He had turned my arrest into a national, if not a global, event and positioned me as the archvillain in his crusade to right Wall Street. It was an opportunity that he seized. And his execution was, in a word, brilliant.

It was also completely and utterly false.

Consider the *Time Magazine* cover as a symbol of Bharara's calculated corruption. Not a single aspect of the magazine cover, which most certainly was done in close conjunction with Bharara's press team, was true. Bharara was not "busting" Wall Street with the insider trading prosecution against me. And the idea that in doing so, he was somehow "collar[ing] the masters of the meltdown" is preposterous. This subtitle had Bharara's unmistakable fingerprints on it, echoing the press conference gimmick that I was the "master of the Rolodex." Both were absurd.

No one—not even the most dyed-in-the-wool prosecutor or regulator—has ever suggested that insider trading had anything to do with the 2008 financial "meltdown" or collapse. Many prominent market participants and academics question whether insider trading prohibitions have any beneficial impact on the market. Bharara's effort to use my prosecution to blunt the critique of his office's inaction as to the financial crisis is blatantly fraudulent. But it was an integral part of his public relations strategy and spin.

On a separate note, one must wonder what former United States Attorney Michael Garcia and the line prosecutors who investigated my case must have thought upon watching Bharara's public spectacle. After all, there is no question that the investigation into Galleon and me—wrongheaded though it may have been—was done independently of Bharara. And yet, at no point in his endless self-promotion did Bharara pause long enough to admit that he inherited this work, instead grasping for all credit possible for himself.

And Bharara's grandstanding on the date of my arrest was wildly improper as well. In coordinating my perp walk, hyperventilating about the "evidence" in his press conference, and seeding the press with stories of my alleged wrongdoing, it was in fact Bharara who was violating his obligation, the law, and countless DOJ policies. It is a bedrock principle of the American justice system—if not *the* central principle—that the accused is innocent until proven guilty beyond a reasonable doubt. Bharara, in his quest for self-aggrandizement, had turned this presumption on its head. He had declared to the world forcefully that I was guilty on his say-so.

Bharara's coming-out party was at my expense. And he had accomplished quite a bit for himself. He ingratiated himself with the press, ensuring years of largely fawning coverage with a series of strategic leaks and interviews. Bharara's favorite reporters would serve as an extension of his office's own press efforts to smear my reputation in advance of trial. Bharara succeeded in chilling countless witnesses who knew the falsity of his allegations but had no interest in getting drawn into his media circus. Some of my closest colleagues and friends hesitated when approached by my counsel as part of our investigation, instead seeking counsel who inevitably urged caution under the circumstances. And Bharara distracted for the time from the reality that they had not built cases that actually explored the cause of the financial crisis.

Over time, Bharara was forced to backtrack—quietly, of course—from certain aspects of his behavior around my arrest. Although Bharara told the world that he had cracked the code on my alleged insider trading by figuring out the meaning of the phrase "edge," those more knowledgeable about the securities industry told him afterward that he simply had it wrong. "Edge" was a common phrase used in the financial sector, and hedge fund space in particular, to convey the lawful value of a market participant's ideas. Countless times, my colleagues, counterparties, analysts, and others would talk about the "edge" that they had on their analysis of a particular equity based on their lawful research. This, of course, was news to Bharara, the financial services neophyte. Bharara slowly eliminated his emphasis of

"edge" as code in his public statements and by the time of my trial, no reference was made by his prosecutorial team about "edge.

Bharara was later forced to retreat from his highly conclusory press
conferences. Challenged in subsequent cases for his aggressive press strategies, Bharara was sternly rebuked by District Court Judge Valerie Caproni
in *United States v. Silver*, in which Judge Caproni took Bharara to task for
his extrajudicial comments. As a result, Bharara later began adding the
phrase "as alleged" to his accusations of individuals charged with crimes,
belatedly recognizing the constitutional presumption of innocence that he
had ignored in my case. And as for the perp walk, this became a roundly
criticized practice. Even Bharara, after leaving office, seemed to acknowledge
that this was an inappropriate tactic.

But this comeuppance for Bharara would fall into the category of too
little, too late for my case. Bharara had used my arrest to pivot from an
unqualified financial sector novice, unfit for the moment, to a media sensa-
tion. All as we veered headlong toward trial.

•●•

For all of his fanfare and bluster in connection with my arrest, Bharara
was almost entirely absent for the actual prosecution of my case. While the
government and our team worked together and often disputed the contours
of the case, Bharara had exactly no role in any of the substantive discussions.
Unless, of course, there was a camera or microphone present.

Meanwhile, the consequences of the financial crisis were still being felt
by the nation. So Bharara's lack of involvement in my case would have made
sense had he rededicated himself and his office to investigating and prosecuting its causes, as the public had clamored for him to do. Instead, Bharara
sought only to leverage my case for more publicity. Bharara focused with a
laser-like precision only on building insider trading cases in the financial
sector—which again, had no real value on the public market and industry concerns.

But Bharara realized that he had struck political and publicity gold with insider trading cases. They were relatively simple to bring, requiring negligible investigation. Take trading records. Find some connection, no matter how attenuated and often through numerous intermediaries, between the trader and an "insider"—an employee at a publicly traded company. Then bring charges and publicize aggressively. Bharara's office charged dozens and dozens of different individuals, pressuring guilty pleas, cooperation, or convictions at trial. Rinse and repeat.

As the public attention grew, Bharara's gloating knew no bounds. He and his press team celebrated their insider trading "winning streak," turning the very serious business of federal criminal prosecutions and the awesome responsibility that comes with it to just another box score in the sports page. Taking a page out of the personal injury legal world, Bharara advertised his own success aggressively.

And to say that Bharara did not engage in any of the legal issues in my case at all in the pretrial phase does not mean that he was not paying attention. Maximizing the opportunity that my case presented for Bharara required that he secure my conviction at any cost. To do so, Bharara, working hand in glove with the FBI, kept a steady line of communication with the press, leaking story after story to keep up the pressure on me. As I would learn, to my surprise, the government has very limited disclosure obligations in a criminal case. Although they produced to us the materials that they had received from Galleon (which we obviously already had), they were not required to identify witnesses, trial exhibits, or statements that would be used in their case against me. And they fought tooth and nail to resist our requests that they do so in the interest of fairness. So our trial team took to scouring the press on a daily basis because we learned a fair amount about the government's case from "anonymous sources" quoted routinely in the mainstream press. One reporter, Susan Pulliam of the *Wall Street Journal*, was so obviously the recipient of Bharara's leaks that the defense bar referred to her as "AUSA Pulliam."

An indication as to how little Bharara actually knew about my case became obvious around the time of the wiretap decision. Bharara made the novel use of the wiretap in my case a focal point of his press campaign. He celebrated "his" innovative use of this law enforcement tool, of course gliding conveniently past the fact that it was his predecessor Garcia, not Bharara, who sought the wiretaps. And while the impropriety of the wiretaps and the government's false representations to secure it was hotly litigated, Bharara was blissfully unaware. In the weeks leading up to the crucial wiretap decision, Bharara many public appearances celebrating the wiretap as though its approval was a foregone conclusion. And when the decision came out— denying our motion to have the wiretaps thrown out but sharply criticizing the government, Bharara was surprised and furious. According to sources in his office at the time, it was only when Bharara read the court's opinion that he realized for the first time how narrowly the government escaped disaster in its problematic prosecution of me.

As my trial commenced, Bharara was not content to let his prosecutors, the ones who had worked to build and present the case, upstage him. Bharara brought his wife to court (one of the prosecutors, Andrew Michaelson, also bizarrely brought his family) as though my trial was some type of party. He also made a habit of coming to the trial at various points, conspicuously making a point of meeting with the prosecutors in the well (the area reserved for attorneys participating in the trial) of the courtroom. Sitting close to these "strategy sessions," watching Bharara, it was clear that he was adding no value, instead just posing to be seen.

•●•

My ARREST IN 2009, AND trial and sentencing in 2011 in many ways marked the high point of Bharara's run as SDNY U.S. attorney. In those three years at the start of his tenure, Bharara was able to create a facade of himself as a Wall Street reformer and rising star. He was routinely mentioned as a potential attorney general and even a candidate for political office, rumors that he actively planted and cultivated. In interviews, Bharara opined that the job he would really like is one he "could never get"—obviously referring to the presidency of the United States, which requires any candidate to be born in the United States.

Bharara also courted public acclaim in a way unseen in the normally buttoned-up world of public service. He leveraged his media contacts and newfound celebrity status to make appearances at the *Vanity Fair* Oscar party and other entertainment events. Remarkably, he met with and opened the SDNY offices (where countless highly sensitive files and secret grand jury material are maintained) to actor Paul Giamatti and the directors of the Showtime series *Billions*, which dramatized the hedge fund world and glamorized the investigations into insider trading. Bharara was seemingly ubiquitous, routinely invited to speak at public events and a fixture late into the night at the cocktail parties that followed, usually surrounded by a throng of young admirers.

Slowly but surely, the bloom started to come off the rose for Bharara beginning in 2014. His slide began nearly three years after my conviction, so I followed much of it from my government-provided accommodations in Devens Federal Medical Center.

Bharara was presumably feeling his oats, given his much-hyped string of insider trading convictions. These prosecutions and the media attention that Bharara cultivated around them largely drowned out the complete absence of any prosecutions relating to the financial crisis. His office had convicted me. It had then convicted Rajat Gupta. And, seeking to wring every last ounce of publicity from their wiretap, he then charged my brother Rengan just days before the statute of limitations would have run on any potential indictment. Rengan was in Brazil and, according to sources close to Bharara, the government did not expect Rengan to appear and defend himself. This would be a "show" indictment, one that generated publicity but required little work.

Bharara, however, miscalculated. Upon learning of the sealed indictment from a *Wall Street Journal* reporter, Rengan retained counsel and promptly flew to New York to self-surrender. The government, embarrassed by the journalist's mistake, which revealed the government's leaking, moved to have the indictment unsealed and tried desperately to coerce Rengan into pleading guilty. Rengan did not budge. Armed with the full support of my legal team and the copious research and analysis that we had conducted, Rengan proceeded to trial.

The government did not understand its own case or Rengan's trading, which was inconsistent with the purported illegal inside information. On the eve of trial, it voluntarily dismissed several of the counts or allegations against Rengan. Worse yet, it no longer had any control of its cooperating witnesses from my trial. Both Rajiv Goel and Anil Kumar had been sentenced to terms of probation; the government had no threat to shape their testimony this time. But it had no other witnesses. So Goel testified, admitting that he did not even know Rengan. Kumar also testified and was even more damaging; he contradicted his testimony from my trial and that of Rajat Gupta's and undercut the government's allegations against all of us. At the close of evidence, the senior and respected presiding Judge Naomi Buchwald dismissed additional charges, leaving only one count for the jury to consider.

On July 8, 2014, Rengan was acquitted. All twelve jurors determined that the government had failed to prove its case. Tellingly, this was diametrically opposed to my jury's conviction of me on the very same charge. Bharara was furious, his much-celebrated "winning streak" broken. He released a statement, opining that "[w]hile we are disappointed with the verdict on the sole count that the jury was permitted to consider, we respect the jury trial system whatever the outcome, and we thank the jury for their services." That Bharara took the moment to take a dig at Judge Buchwald's midtrial dismissal of two counts while cleverly omitting the four counts that Bharara himself had dropped just before Rengan's trial reeked of pettiness. But it would only be a precursor to the real fireworks.

On July 17, 2014, a few days after Rengan's acquittal, the U.S. Attorney's Office held a departure dinner for two of its longer-tenured prosecutors, who were heading back to private practice. These dinners were a staple of the U.S. Attorney's Office culture, good-natured affairs where current and former prosecutors and often judges who were also alumni gathered to break bread, enjoy cocktails and conversation, and listen to roasts that were humorous and irreverent in nature, but always cloaked in an overall warmth.

It was the tradition that the sitting U.S. attorney was the host of the event and typically offered his or her own remarks. Bharara, more so than many of his predecessors, reveled in these events. He fancied himself to be witty and in fairness was an adept public speaker with a penchant for one-liners. However, on this evening, he was clearly in no mood for the lighthearted banter that would be the norm. After his deputy Richard B. Zabel spoke, poking fun in a self-deprecating manner at the office for its recent defeat in Rengan's trial, Bharara took the microphone. His remarks had no such self-awareness. Instead, Bharara offered feeble excuses for the loss to Rengan's lawyers and, to the amazement of the nearly 150 attendees, delivered a profanity-laced tirade against Judge Buchwald, suggesting ironically enough that she did not understand the basic rules of evidence. As one attendee put it, "Preet was pretty nasty," and others, including sitting judges and other prominent members of the defense bar, were struck by his churlish and wildly inappropriate remarks.

Bharara's tireless self-promotion was attracting a wider, more powerful audience. In 2014, when then-Attorney General Eric Holder announced his intention to step down, Bharara lobbied aggressively for the position. But the White House was, by all accounts, wary of Bharara. It instead nominated Loretta Lynch, the United States attorney for the Eastern District of New York, the office that Bharara and the Southern District considered to be its chief rival. President Obama's remarks on November 9, 2014, in announcing Lynch's nomination took an unmistakable shot at Bharara.

> Loretta might be the only lawyer in America who battles mobsters and drug lords and terrorists, and still has the reputation for being a charming "people person." (Laughter.) That's probably because Loretta doesn't look to make headlines, she looks to make a difference. She's not about splash; she is about substance.

The headline-seeking Bharara's hopes for a bigger public platform had been thwarted, undone by his own hubris.

This would not be the last disappointment for Bharara as the year ended. In a crippling blow to Bharara's self-styled war on Wall Street through hedge funds, the Second Circuit upended his dubious insider trading initiative. On December 10, 2014, in *United States v. Newman et al.*, the Second Circuit appeals court reversed the insider trading convictions of the defendants and opened the door for challenges to several of Bharara's other celebrated insider trading cases. Again, the panel of respected jurists was unsparing in its critique—if not outright ridicule—of Bharara's legally thin approach. The *Newman* roundly rejected the government's theory that a recipient of MNPI (the tipper) who did not know the source of the information (the tippee) or that there was any corruption or improper benefit provided to the source could still be held criminally liable. It also confirmed that mere friendship between a tipper and a tippee did not by itself constitute an improper benefit.

The circuit's opinion emphasized that, "[a]lthough the government might like the law to be different, nothing in the law requires a symmetry of information in the nation's securities markets." With dripping condescension, the appeals court observed the "doctrinal novelty of [the government's] recent insider trading prosecutions, which are increasingly targeted at remote tippees many levels removed from corporate insiders."

For me personally, the *Newman* decision meant everything and yet nothing at all. It was a complete vindication of something that I had been saying all along—namely, in our industry, traders are deluged with opinions on investment strategies by various people, all claiming high levels of confidence and certainty, many engaged in pure puffery. This is the lifeblood, I presume, of day traders and unsophisticated investors. But not our firm. Galleon was a multibillion-dollar hedge fund driven by our research. We listened to some of those individual voices in the ordinary course of life, much the same way sports fans talk about sports, but we did not rely on them. And we most certainly did not try to corrupt them with payments or anything of the like. The evidence at my trial had made that clear, but the government had successfully argued to the jury that the law required much less. And now, the Second Circuit had told the government that it was wrong.

The *Newman* decision should have rendered void the entirety of my conviction. As but one example, the government had never alleged—nor could they—that I knew any of Roomy Khan's alleged insider sources of information or that she had allegedly corrupted them. Google's Shamarra Hussain and Polycom's Sunil Bhalla are people I first learned about after I had been arrested and to this day, I have never spoken with and know nothing about either of them. The government had argued at trial that it did not need to show any evidence that I was aware of their existence or that Roomy had allegedly paid them to violate their fiduciary duties to their respective companies. The government was wrong and the jury was therefore misled. But although my lawyers laid this out in clear and incontrovertible detail in what is known as a habeas petition—a submission after a conviction is otherwise final—the courts declined to revisit my case, presumably on the theory of letting sleeping dogs lie.

But for Bharara, the Second Circuit's rebuke was real. In belittling the "doctrinal novelty" of Bharara's approach, the appellate court had pointed out Bharara's emphasis on his supposed policy goals as a basis for insider trading prosecutions instead of the law. This, of course, is consistent with Bharara's career focus on politics, rather than legal analysis. And it also underscores his emphasis on publicity and the court of public opinion over the hallowed traditions of legal precision that should be the foundation of any criminal prosecution.

Real lives were implicated by Bharara's folly. While my case was either too far removed or too celebrated to be revisited, the same was not so for others. David Newman and Anthony Chiasson, the named defendants in the Second Circuit case, were exonerated and a verdict of not guilty ordered. The government abandoned its pursuit of Michael Steinberg, a former SAC Capital trader, allowing for his prior conviction to be vacated. Other insider trading defendants benefitted similarly and the new government prosecutions were slowed. Bharara's winning streak had come spectacularly undone.

Bharara, perhaps sensing the fall of his insider trading initiative, had pivoted to more familiar terrain—the world of New York State politics. His office had charged Sheldon Silver, one of the most powerful leaders in the state's political world, with accepting bribes in an undoubtedly high-profile prosecution. Of course, not content to let the charges speak for themselves, Bharara had gone on a speaking tour to announce the allegations publicly on the rubber-chicken circuit throughout New York. Bharara had now aimed his insider trading publicity model at the world of public corruption.

But the chickens were slowly but surely coming home to roost for Bharara. On March 30, 2015, Bharara and other members of his prosecutorial team were sued in their personal capacity by David Ganek, founder of the $4 billion hedge fund, Level Global. Level Global had been raided for insider trading amidst widespread media publicity in November 2010, a month after my arrest. Bharara's office had sought and received on an ex parte basis from the District Court a warrant to search the Level Global offices. In typical fashion, Bharara had orchestrated maximum press coverage of this gambit, ensuring front page coverage through his network of eager reporters and news outlets. Although no charges were brought against Ganek, he was forced to liquidate the fund while dealing with irreparable damage to his reputation arising out of the press firestorm.

Ganek realized later that Bharara's office had fabricated claims about Ganek's personal involvement in the FBI affidavit submitted to support the Level Global search. It was no different than the falsified information that the government had provided in connection with the wiretap application in my case. At first, this posed little concern to the government. Prosecutors and law enforcement typically enjoy unqualified immunity shielding government officials from all but the most egregious violation of legal rights. The government moved quickly to dismiss the case against Bharara and his colleagues. In this instance, however, senior and respected District Court Judge William Pauley took a very different view. Judge Pauley rejected Bharara's motion to dismiss, instead opining that, "[d]iscovery is now appropriate to ascertain whether this case is about a simple misunderstanding or whether something more troubling was afoot." It was clear, that under Bharara's watch, the government was losing the benefit of the doubt that it had long enjoyed with the bench.

As it would turn out, Judge Pauley was not alone in doubting the integrity of the Southern District under Bharara, and a new turn of events would further highlight these concerns. Senate Majority Leader Silver and his counsel were not amused by Bharara's press tour around the unproven allegations against him. They worried about the impact that Bharara's incessant media onslaught would have on Silver's ability to defend himself. Accordingly, Silver sought to dismiss the indictment, citing Bharara's inappropriate public remarks as improperly prejudicial. These were the very same concerns that we had raised years earlier.

On April 10, 2015, District Court Judge Valerie Caproni, like Judge Pauley a highly regarded, no-nonsense jurist, rebuked Bharara in a different vein. In a stern, published opinion by District Court Judge Valerie Caproni in *United States v. Sheldon Silver*, the District Court reprimanded Bharara for his publicity blitz against the New York State majority leader who had been accused of public corruption.

> The U.S. Attorney, while castigating politicians in Albany for playing fast and loose with the ethical rules that govern their conduct, strayed so close to the edge of the rules governing his own conduct that defendant Sheldon Silver has a non-frivolous argument that he fell over the edge to the defendant's prejudice," Ms. Caproni wrote in her decision. "In particular, the court is troubled by remarks by the U.S. Attorney that appeared to bundle together unproven allegations regarding the defendant with broader commentary on corruption and a lack of transparency in certain aspects of New York State politics.

Judge Caproni made her disdain for Bharara's conduct clear, punctuating her opinion by stating that "criminal cases should be tried in the courtroom and not in the press." For me, this admonition would be years too late. But it would serve to chill Bharara's behavior going forward, restoring greater integrity toward a fair process.

There was one more shoe that would drop for Bharara. On May 19, 2016, the Southern District under Bharara indicted William "Billy" Walters for violation of the insider trading laws. This was a revival of the government's insider trading initiative, slowed by the fallout from the *Newman* decision and the vacated charges that followed. And the Walters prosecution had all the promise to be a splashy, headline-inducing case. Walters was a renowned sports gambler, the type of colorful character that would make for ready media fodder. As a plus, professional golfer and household name Phil Mickelson was implicated in the allegations, although uncharged for his trading consistent with the inside information allegedly received by his sometimes golfing partner Walters. As Walters proceeded toward trial, his lawyers pressed District Court Judge P. Kevin Castel, alleging extensive leaks by the government resulting in extensive press coverage prior to the formal lodging of charges. Worse yet, Walters' counsel argued that the leaks had been a part of the investigative strategy, to prompt Walters and his confederates to discuss the press reporting on wiretapped phones, thereby generating additional "dirty" calls to warrant further wiretaps. Walters asked for the indictment to be dismissed.

The government reacted swiftly and unequivocally. It denied any leaks and derided the accusations by Walters' counsel as nothing more than a "fishing expedition." In support of its opposition, the government submitted a sworn affidavit by the then chief of the securities unit, so appointed by Bharara himself, attesting to the rigorous internal investigation undertaken and the confirmation that no leaks by anyone associated with the government had occurred.

Judge Castel ordered a hearing, which he later conceded that he had done in an abundance of caution while presumptively crediting the government's defense. As part of that hearing, he ordered the government to turn over certain internal communications and documents. And in doing so, Judge Castel inadvertently pulled the curtain back on Bharara's press strategies.

Forced to gather materials despite its earlier claims at exhaustive internal inquiries, Bharara and his office were forced to admit prior to the court-ordered disclosure that law enforcement leaks to the press had in fact occurred. The government admitted in a January 4, 2017, ex parte submission to the court that, "[i]t is now an incontrovertible fact that FBI leaks occurred, and that such leaks resulted in confidential law enforcement information about the Investigation being given to reporters." Moreover, the government offered that it "believe[d] that the appropriate course is for the court to assume that a Rule 6(e) violation occurred and proceed to consider the issue of remedy."

Eager for a scapegoat, the U.S. Attorney's Office pointed the finger at senior FBI Special Agent David Chaves as the "leaker" and advised the court that Chaves had admitted as much. According to the government, "Chaves admitted to providing confidential information to reporters without the knowledge or consent of the USAO." But Bharara denied any wrongdoing, stating in its submission that, "[t]he available information uniformly indicates that the USAO was not a source of confidential information provided to reporters about the Investigation. Members of the USAO, at all levels, were distressed by the leaks."

However, the documents provided to the Court—only when ordered to do so—paint quite a different picture. Internal emails made public reveal that as far back as 2014, Bharara, his deputy Zabel and the head of the New York FBI office were in regular communication about the issue of press leaks and secret engagement between the government and journalists. As the *Wall Street Journal* aptly pointed out in an April 19, 2017, editorial:

> There's also emerging evidence that something was rotten in Mr. Bharara's operation....According to emails revealed in the Walters case, Mr. Bharara knew about the leaks pouring out of the FBI's white-collar unit, including to reporters at the Journal. He called it 'outrageous and harmful' in a 2014 email, but as far as we know, he did nothing to stanch the leaking."

If anything, the *Wall Street Journal* understates the gravity of misconduct. All of this information was hidden from the court originally when Bharara had his office dismiss the questions of leaks out of hand and instructed his chief of the securities unit to file a false affidavit in support of this lie. SDNY, which claims to be the premier investigative office in the land, represented to the court that it had conducted an exacting review internally and found no misconduct. It was only when forced by court order to produce the underlying documents revealing the truth that the government changed its tune.

As is the case in most of the instances where Bharara's dishonestly was ultimately revealed, there were no consequences. Just as David Ganek's complaint was ultimately dismissed and his business never restored and just as Newman, Chiasson and Steinberg's reputations were forever tainted, Billy Walters would receive no justice. Judge Castel, for all of his stated indignation, denied the motion to dismiss the indictment despite the leaks. The chief of the securities unit was never sanctioned for his false affidavit to the Court. And Special Agent Chaves was never prosecuted. Remarkably, he has moved on to a career as a corporate compliance executive and speaker on the public circuit.

When I learned of all this, I had to chuckle. We had long raised these very same concerns about leaks throughout my prosecution and had been met with the same pearl-clutching denials from the government. Special Agent Chaves was one of the key FBI special agents handling my case. Bharara and Zabel were the point people for the public during my trial. I felt again vindicated, despite the lack of any consequence. I had been right to stand on my principles.

· • ·

BHARARA'S MOST RECENT CAREER TURN only confirmed all of our suspicions about him. Denied the opportunity for further progress within the DOJ, Bharara stayed on as the U.S. attorney for the Southern District for the entirety of President Obama's two terms. The surprise election of Donald J. Trump as United States president would under normal circumstances mark the end of Bharara's tenure. After all, it was the long-standing tradition of the DOJ that upon the inauguration of a new president, Democrat or Republican, each of the ninety-two United States attorneys across the nation would tender their resignation and allow the incoming president the opportunity to select, either all at once or in phases, his or her own candidates for the positions. Especially given the change in party and the antipathy that Trump expressed about the Southern District of New York and Bharara's friend and former U.S. Attorney Jim Comey, the rumor mill was rife with the potential replacements for Bharara.

But Bharara had another card to play. On November 30, 2016, just after Trump's election, Bharara met with the president-elect in his Trump Tower residence. After this interview, Bharara emerged and announced to the press that he would continue to serve under soon to be President Trump as the SDNY U.S. attorney. He did so apparently without any concerns over or criticism of Trump's controversial statements or positions on the campaign trail. President-elect Trump did not ask for the resignations of any of the sitting U.S. attorneys at the time. Bharara was the only one who made a highly publicized trip to Trump Tower and the only one to seek media attention for staying on.

But this would be a short-lived arrangement. On March 11, 2016, now President Trump sought the resignations of forty-six U.S. attorneys appointed by President Obama. Forty-five of the U.S. attorneys complied, as per tradition and expectation, without any fanfare. Only Bharara created a press spectacle. True to form. Bharara refused to resign and instead took to Twitter to proclaim, despite no one asking, that, "I did not resign. Moments ago, I was fired." So launched the rebranding of Preet Bharara, media personality and devout Trump antagonist.

Most former U.S. attorneys follow one of two paths—either they redouble their efforts at public service, moving on to other positions in government, or they go to private practice at a law firm, advising and shepherding clients, corporate and individual, through the legal world. Bharara did neither. Instead, he launched a podcast dubbed *Stay Tuned with Preet Bharara* on a fledgling media venture called Café. Bharara, who was by all accountants independently wealthy as a result of his brother's successful internet venture years ago, would give up any pretense of being a practicing lawyer to launch himself headlong into the world of media celebrity.

Bharara has thrown himself headlong into his media world. He has a carefully curated Twitter account, which includes the self-aggrandizing tag line, "Banned by Putin, fired by Trump. Former US Atty, SDNY." (Bharara was one of eighteen government officials barred from entry into Russia in response to perceived political prosecutions; Bharara is the only one of the eighteen who publicly markets this status.) His Twitter account is littered with daily one-liners or sentence fragments documenting his thoughts for his followers. He conducts a weekly podcast interview, often with well-known celebrity guests. But most prominently, Bharara has positioned himself as a voice in the Trump resistance, wailing at each of the considerable outrages of the past four years and decrying the absence of "justice." He has become a talking head on cable news program, seemingly ready at a moment's notice to offer his opinions on topics of the day, especially with respect to all things Trump.

Bharara's transparent grasp for relevance and public adulation continues to be a source of my bemusement. Bharara focuses so much of his energy seemingly decrying Trump's flawed character and dishonesty. Yet Bharara proactively sought to work for Trump as a part of his administration before being asked to leave with others. Even worse, on October 19, 2017, Bharara, in response to reporting that Trump was interviewing new candidates for the vacant U.S. attorney positions, tweeted that, "It is neither normal nor advisable for Trump to personally interview candidates for US Attorney positions, especially the one in Manhattan." Bharara then made the rounds on the talk shows, explaining that any prosecutor appointed should have the independence, in case that they would need to lead investigations into Trump in the future. Perhaps Bharara had already forgotten his own interview with Trump to retain his SDNY position. Or, more likely, Bharara conveniently ignored it to pursue more clicks and eyeballs.

What is telling is what Bharara did not do. Despite his constant refrain about the dangers of the Trump administration and the threat to the rule of law, Bharara did not once roll up his sleeves and serve as a lawyer for any of the countless constituents in need of legal services during these fraught times. One did not see Bharara advising clients separated from their families. One did not see Bharara representing any of the whistleblowers who were under siege from Trump. One did not even see Bharara commit time or energy to the Mueller team or either impeachment effort. Instead, Bharara was more than content to enjoy life as a quasi-celebrity, building his media brand and profit.

In hindsight, based on my experience, it should all have been so predictable. After all, I had a front-row seat to Bharara's love of the limelight, his self-adulation, and his theatrics. He came to the U.S. attorney position as a creature of politics. And, perhaps in a warped way to his credit, he had not changed to fit the dignity of the position and the office but instead had changed the position and the office to fit his interests and skills.

There is a fitting coda to my Bharara experience. To my surprise, I learned recently that Bharara had organized a "task force" to explore and make suggested revisions to the insider trading law. Not surprisingly, he tacked his own name to the group, calling it the "Bharara Task Force on Insider Trading." The group is composed of Bharara's former prosecutors and regulators at the U.S. Attorney's Office and the SEC that pursued insider trading prosecutions, Judge Jed S. Rakoff who presided over my civil insider trading cases and others and is an outspoken friend and admirer of Bharara, and one academic. The task force includes exactly zero market participants or seasoned defense lawyers.

The Bharara Task Force on Insider Trading published their findings on January 27, 2020. In its executive summary, the Task Force reports that:

> For too long, insider trading law has lacked clarity, generated confusion, and failed to keep up with the times. Without a statute specifically directed at insider trading, the law has developed through a series of fact-specific court decisions applying the general anti-fraud provisions of our securities laws across a broadening set of conduct. As a consequence, the law has suffered—and continues to suffer—from uncertainty and ambiguity to a degree not seen in other areas of law, with elements of the offense defined by—

and at times, evolving with—court opinions applying particular fact patterns. The rules of the road have been drawn and redrawn around these judicial decisions, and not always consistently across the country or over time. Although there have been attempts in the past to codify the law to bring greater certainty and clarity to the offense of insider trading, none has succeeded. This has left market participants without sufficient guidance on how to comport themselves, prosecutors and regulators with undue challenges in holding wrongful actors accountable, those accused of misconduct with burdens in defending themselves, and the public with reason to question the fairness and integrity of our securities markets.

I did a double take when I read this. *After* prosecuting me and scores of other individuals for violating insider trading laws, *after* vilifying us in the press, *after* ripping many of us from our families, *after* forcing the expenditure of millions upon millions of dollars to defend ourselves, *after* taking credit for "collaring the masters of the meltdown" with his insider trading initiative...Bharara and his task force concede that "insider trading law has lacked clarity, generated confusion, and failed to keep up with the times"?

A disproportionate number of Bharara's targets were South Asians.

TARGETING SOUTH ASIANS

Was Preet Bharara deliberately targeting South Asians? And why? The fact of the pattern was not lost on many observers and became the particular topic of conversation among the South Asian expatriate community in the U.S. I have been asked this question many times and each time my answer is the same: "I would like to think not."

However, the fact that the prosecutors identified three additional senior Silicon Valley executives—each of them South Asian—as targets in Rengan's plea-bargaining negotiations does cause me to pause and take note.

In December 2013, the speculation of Bharara's targeting of South Asians reached fever pitch in India and among the Indian expatriate com-

munity in the United States. Preet Bharara arrested a female Indian diplomat, Devyani Khobragade, India's deputy consul general in New York.
The charge was that Khobragade underpaid her domestic worker. Bharara
tossed aside proper diplomatic protocol. Rather than requesting a meeting at the federal offices with Ms. Khobragade and her attorney, Bharara
arrested her as she was dropping off her child at school. She was then
strip searched as well as cavity searched—ridiculously degrading and completely unnecessary for an alleged misdemeanor of underpaying a domestic employee. Public opinion spiked against Preet Bharara. There was no
turning back.

In an email to her colleagues that was later published by *The Indian
Express*, Ms. Khobragade said, "I must admit I broke down many times as
the indignation of repeated handcuffing, stripping, and cavity searches,
swabbing, held with common criminals and drug addicts were all being
imposed on me despite my incessant assertion of immunity."

"The Devyani case is amazing because of the manner in which she was
apprehended and incarcerated. What is more remarkable is that Manhattan
is home to hundreds of UN officials, consular officials, and wealthy Wall
Street types who have undocumented nannies and who exploit their staff in
many ways," says Arjun Appadurai, a Paulette Goddard professor of media,
culture, and communication at New York University.[48]

What is more amazing is that Bharara remained unfazed. He stood firm
in his belief that the prosecutor's job is to bring anyone who breeches the law
to justice "no matter how powerful, rich, or connected they are."

In his lack of repentance, Bharara also displayed a profound and ironic
lack of awareness about his own self-serving hypocrisy. Bharara embraced
Anil Kumar despite his knowing that Anil Kumar paid his domestic help,
Manju Das, just five dollars a day while evading taxes for millions of dollars
through a complex web of offshore accounts. The shifting sands of principles and standards in the world of Preet Bharara remain astonishing.

Even the foreign minister of India at that time, Salman Khurshid,
called the Khobragade incident "a conspiracy rather than an act of gigan-
tic stupidity," concluding that there was "no need to take Preet Bharara

or his comments seriously." The Indian media, none of them beholden to Bharara, were outraged and had no reservation in referring to him as India's Uncle Tom.

In an op-ed column in Firstpost, the editor, R. Jagannathan, suggested Bharara was being used by U.S. authorities to victimize Indians. "The Americans practice sophisticated racism," he wrote. "Thus they will use a Preet Bharara to target Khobragade (or Rajat Gupta or Raj Rajaratnam) so that it looks like Indian-Americans are implementing the law and hence not racist." Jagannathan ends by saying, "At the very least, we should target Preet Bharara for humiliating an Indian diplomat and make sure he never enters this country again."[49]

Many Indians also remember the ordeal of Krittika Biswas, daughter of an Indian diplomat posted in the Indian consulate in New York. In February 2011, Bharara arrested Krittika at school for cyber bullying. She was marched out of school in handcuffs and forced to spend twenty-eight hours in a detention cell. It was later found that another student was responsible for the crime.[50]

In his pursuit of insider trading cases, a disproportionate number of those people charged were of South Asian origin. One of them was Sanjay Valvani.

Although I did not know him, the tragic case of Sanjay Valvani hit particularly close to home for me. By 2016, by the age of forty-four, Valvani had risen from a humble upbringing in an immigrant South Asian household to become a talented and highly regarded portfolio manager at Visium, an $8 billion hedge fund in New York.

Bharara's office indicted Valvani on June 15, 2016, saying he could face up to eighty-five years in prison for his alleged insider trading. *Business Insider* reported on the media jumping "all over the story...news photographers snapped pictures of him as he left the courthouse in downtown Manhattan." Although he believed he had done nothing wrong and pleaded not guilty, the article noted that Valvani was distraught because "he was being professionally isolated and he worried about the impact the charges would have on [the 170 or so] Visium employees." Visium shut down on June 17, 2016. A friend of Valvani's remarked, "Once you're accused on Wall Street, even if you win your case, you're toxic. No one will talk to you."[51]

For Valvani, described as a "kind, soft-spoken and humble" father of two, the ordeal proved to be too much. On June 20, 2016, his body was found with a suicide note reiterating his innocence.

CHAPTER 20

THE FIGHT CONTINUES

My journey, which began at dawn on a cold October morning in 2009, is now largely ended. I learned firsthand the failure of America to live up to its promise when it comes to its justice system. Justice has sadly devolved into an aspiration only. What is actually delivered through the system is something far less and imposes a far greater cost to individual defendants trapped within the government's crosshairs. The carnage and cost in terms of human capital to the nation will continue unabated until the country rises up and demands reform.

Although there has been a lot of bipartisan support for criminal justice reform, a disproportionate amount of the attention is focused on police brutality. This is important, but what is missing from the conversation results in another form of brutality: prosecutorial misconduct and overreach.

There is a lot to be done. I offer, with the résumé of having lived through the experience of being accused, tried, convicted, and incarcerated under the brightest of lights, my suggestions as to specific proposals that would immediately start to restore fairness—justice—to the process.

The United States system of investigation and prosecution in establishing justice is unique in the world. We have politicized the role of the prosecutor at the federal, state, and county levels. Nowhere else are prosecutors (or judges) elected. Prosecutors in other countries around the world are civil servants. In the U.S., prosecutors are not just elected, they are appointed in a general partisan manner. The job is a ladder with the promise of higher office at every step, as evidenced by the fact that nearly every senator or congressman who ever practiced law once served as a prosecutor. Winning becomes more important than doing justice. Voters vote for winners, not justice doers.

I am inspired by the prospect for change. In our partisan times, the issue of criminal justice reform does seem at least to have the attention of a bipartisan coalition, sometimes making strange bedfellows, but bedfellows nonetheless.

There are many things that can be done immediately.

1. *DOJ prosecutors must be prohibited from pretrial public comment.*

The foundation of the American justice system, understood universally, regardless of age, gender, or creed, is that the accused is "innocent until proven guilty." The Sixth Amendment codifies the precept into the Constitution. The concept has been embraced unequivocally by all United States courts as the premise from which all criminal law emanates.

Watching the announcement of a litany of charges in high-profile cases, the presumption of innocence is, however, hardly evident. To the contrary, prosecutors roll out highly choreographed press conferences, offering one-sided, colorful distillations of the government's allegations. These accusations are amplified by the eager press corps trumpeting the government's sound bites for public consumption. Prosecutors warn with practiced solemnity of maximum potential sentences, impact on the community, and the fundamentally moral wickedness of their targets. At the very most, the presumption of innocence is given a sotto voce nod by the prosecutors and their press at the very end, if at all.

The harm, as I experienced firsthand, is profound. The show of force by the government intimidates potential defense witnesses. They are understandably cowed by the prospect of dissenting. The press coverage feeds upon itself, increasing the psychological harm on defendants and families including, often, their children. In the modern age, where all information reported is a click away, this coverage is instantly available to the public—all of whom are potential jurors—thereby immediately threating the constitu- tional right to a fair trial. There is not a soul who believes a juror does not immediately type the defendant's name into Google, no matter what warn- ings to the contrary are given by the court.

There can be no dispute about the need for a formal prohibition on pretrial comments from the government. They serve no proper purpose. Not a single one of a prosecutor's statements to the public or ensuing press coverage is evidence. Because the defendant is presumed to be innocent, the government's claims of deterrence are wholly without merit. In fact, the public repetition of the allegations is nothing more than a tactical smear. Even worse, the allegations and insinuations become catnip to the improper ambitions of prosecutors. The Preet Bharara story, taken Rudy Guiliani and others before him, lay this bare.

This prohibition can be properly cabined. If the government secures a conviction at trial, the prohibition should lift. The defendant would no longer be presumed innocent. At that point, the government can advise the public of its work, based on evidence that it actually introduced at trial, vetted by the courts, and tested by the defense. This change requires no delay—the DOJ can adopt this rule and it must.

2. *The prosecution should be required to promptly identify witnesses and exhibits that it intends to use.*

This too is a simple reform to put into place. The current rules of crim- inal procedure require startlingly little of the government, simply document production shortly after lodging charges. But critically, "discovery" is done with no organization or structure. Everything is dropped on a defendant and his legal team, leaving them to sift through it all and guess at the govern- ment's intentions. The government is required to disclose trial witnesses and exhibits but given until the very last possible moment to do so. In fact, it is considered an act of benevolence when judges require such disclosure even a few weeks before trial.

In the modern day, this is simply unworkable for the average defen- dant. In my case, the government produced libraries full of electronic data collected. We had hours and hours of wiretaps to pore over, transcribe, and analyze. The government had years to review this material—if indeed they did—before bringing charges. We were faced with the constant time pressure of an impending trial.

The government should be required to record—via audio and video—all statements made by potential and actual cooperating witnesses. This simple modification would solve many problems of unfairness in the system. It would allow the government to satisfy its existing obligations of turning over all *Brady* material, meaning information including witness statements that is inculpatory of the government. It would ensure no errors in transcription by improperly motivated prosecutors and agents—a problem we saw repeatedly in reviewing their notes, produced at the last minute. Recording statements would also force witnesses to be truthful from the moment they began to meet with the government, rather than allowing their testimony to be molded by prosecutors looking to strengthen their case.

I know that certain defendants and even government witnesses (in my case) pled guilty specifically because they did not have the resources to push back against the government tsunami. It is not realistic to assume reform that will eliminate these legal costs, but they can be constrained reasonably if the government is asked to be open about its proof earlier in the process.

Again, there is no good reason for the government to object in the normal case. (There are cases involving violence, where perhaps there is a better argument to delay disclosure of witness lists, but that prophylactic is already in place in the rules.) Other than tactical advantage, the government should be prepared to move forward quickly and share the basis for their publicly made accusations. This will also allow defense counsel to investigate in a more meaningful way to ensure that the information is accurate or needs to be corrected. If the government's intention is to expose the truth, this pressure testing is a valuable addition to the process. Only if the government's focus is on winning should the current system of trial by surprise from witnesses never before heard be permitted to continue, which leads me to my next observation.

3.   *The government's use of cooperating witnesses should be modified—slightly but meaningfully—to incentivize truthful testimony.*

One of the true eye-openers to me during my prosecution was the government's cooperation process. From the time of my arrest to the eve of my sentencing, the government sought my cooperation against other targets and promised great benefits if I were to flip. I never did. The reason was simple: I will never bear false witness against another. For me, this is not a matter of religion; this is a matter of principle.

As I began to learn, however, the government has manufactured a structure that makes truth telling a much harder choice for most people. A defendant who is charged with a crime or facing the potential of charges has only three real choices: cooperate, plead guilty, or go to trial.

In white-collar cases, the government makes clear to defense counsel that option number one—cooperation—is the only option that virtually guarantees the avoidance of jail time and the minimization of legal fees.[52] Either of the other two choices requires risk and financial expense. For even the very honest, this is temptation at its highest level. Giving into this temptation is something that a defendant can justify as putting family first, preserving financial stability, and securing future certainty. In other words, very little of this decision is based on the pursuit of justice—it is the pursuit of self-interest for the defendant, but most importantly, for the government.[53]

Worse yet, the government has designed a wickedly clever system to hide this reality from the jury at trial. The government requires a defendant to proffer or admit to their own wrongdoing and that of others. In doing so, the government makes clear to defense counsel that this audition to be a cooperator will be successful only if the government believes the defendant to be admitting his or her wrongdoing and further believes that the defendant can assist the government. In most cases, the targets for a defendant seeking to cooperate are clear from the outset. In my case, the defendants knew full well that they had to "admit" to insider trading in order to establish "plausibility" by the government, and the defendants had to "assist" the government by inculpating me. Only if they did so would the government accept them as cooperators and extend the benefits. If accepted, the defendants would be required to plead guilty to select charges, immunized for all other wrongdoing, and later be sentenced in a proceeding where the government would be joining the defense counsel in extolling the cooperation efforts of the defendant to ensure a most favorable sentence.

These benefits are never disclosed. Worse yet, these facts are actively hidden from the jury. In SDNY, the prosecutors go many steps further. They do not allow cooperating defendants to be sentenced until after they have testified at trial as expected. Why is this? Plausible deniability. This practice allows a defendant to testify accurately that he or she does not know what sentence they will ultimately receive. While technically true, the government and the defendant both know that in white-collar cases, the defendant will not serve a moment in prison. The judges themselves participate in the choreography. They must participate in this process to encourage future cooperation and allow the government to continue to build cases. It is theater, not a process.

Here is the reality of my case: Rajiv Goel, Anil Kumar, Adam Smith received no jail time, despite acknowledged crimes wholly independent of the allegations against me. Ali Far received no jail time, despite admitting to the government that he had lied. Roomy Khan received only one year of jail time in an extraordinary circumstance because she lied so many times and on so many occasions. For Far and Khan, the government so distrusted them by the end that they did not call them as witnesses at my trial but still vouched for them at their sentencings.

Sentencing cooperating defendants immediately and prior to their trial testimony is inherently consistent with the idea of pursuing justice. The sentencing process for the cooperating witnesses would operate exactly as it currently does. The defense counsel would make presentations to the sentencing judge about the cooperator to seek a minimal sentence. And the government would describe to the sentencing judge the cooperator's efforts and assistance. Once the judge sentenced the cooperating witness, he or she would then still be able to testify at trial but there would be no incentive to please or ingratiate the government any longer—instead, the cooperating witnesses who were so qualified because of their truthfulness would be able to testify truthfully. Under the current system, the cooperating witness must worry that the government will not like their testimony and will therefore not be supportive at the future sentencing. This serves no purpose other than strategic advantage for the government to procure false testimony.[54]

4. *The court and, if necessary, bar disciplinary committees, must vigilantly police prosecutors and law enforcement.*

The single biggest disappointment in my experience was the realization that the government and the accused play by two very different sets of rules. In addition to standing on principle, I proceeded to trial because I was raised not to shy away from a fair fight. This, however, was nothing like a fair fight. From the press conference to the dump of documents to the games played by the prosecution in terms of the charges and evidence, the disadvantages were obvious and significant. All of this is compounded by the sheer optics of a prosecutor representing "the United States of America" as they all so earnestly pointed out to the jury before literally pointing to me repeatedly sitting in a courtroom chair as being guilty.

Unfair, but that I can tolerate. What I cannot tolerate is the intentional misrepresentations. The law as written does not allow for prosecutors, law enforcement, and the government's witnesses—all of whom are extensions of the government—to make misrepresentations to the court in their statements or their submissions. Yet in my proceedings, the government through all three sets of individuals lied early and often in pursuit of a conviction.

Examples abound; here are a few:

a) The court recognized the government's wiretap application was rife with sworn misrepresentations made by FBI Agent Kang,

b) Lead prosecutor Reed Brodsky repeatedly mislead the jury in his remarks,

c) The U.S. attorney falsely denied press leaks which were later revealed,

d) Anil Kumar provided almost wholly contradictory testimony in three separate trials under oath at the behest of the government.

The list of misrepresentations and lies goes on for pages.

In different and varied ways, other defendants in criminal cases have suffered similar violations at the hands of the government, sometimes more extreme and sometimes less so. There is one constant: the government is virtually never sanctioned. Ever. At best, courts admonish the government and urge it to do better. And then when they fail to do so, courts continue to do nothing.

Doing justice means for everyone involved. Just as a defendant, if convicted, is sanctioned for their wrongdoing with incarceration, fines, public humiliation, and often all three simultaneously, so too prosecutors and other law enforcement agents should be sanctioned for their wrongdoing. And in appropriate circumstances, all possible sanctions including incarceration, fines, and public humiliation should be on the table.

If anything, the deterrence served by doing so would be greater and more important to the public than the actual punishment. Allowing the government to engage in misconduct impales the public trust and is likely to be repeated against other citizens. The government, by design, is a recidivist waiting to happen. If not held to the very highest of standards, as they claim to embrace, the consequences have been and will continue to be severe.

The answer to this problem is already in place. Courts have the inherent power to craft the appropriate sanction for the government when it engages in wrongdoing. Because the bar is already so low in that virtually no sanctions are ever levied, even a minor but concrete punishment by the court will serve to immediately chill future misconduct.

Happily, for me, the issue is gaining traction as the litany of wrongful prosecutions come to public attention. Momentum is building. In my humble opinion, it is time for courts to lead. Judges sit above the fray. They are unlike the press, who have commercial motivations. They are distinct from the defense bar, with no preexisting relationships with the government. They don't have to balance multiple client interests. They are certainly set apart from law enforcement agents themselves not wanting to violate the blue wall. Judges in federal courts have lifetime tenure specifically to be independent and to act without fear or favor. With respect to prosecutorial misconduct, the courts must lead.

To understand where the justice system should—*must*—go, one needs to keep in mind the disparities endemic to this process. Defendants—innocent or guilty—are human beings and deserve to be treated respectfully and fairly. The time-honored language of our justice system including the presumption of innocence, the blindness of justice, the pursuit of truth as the cornerstone of all proceedings, the sanctity of sworn testimony and oaths, all promise to protect even those accused from the machinery of show trials or star chambers. The custodians of this process are the judges and the prosecutors. By acknowledging and doing nothing about the misrepresentations and the "doctrine of novelty," the judges violated their own canon.[55]

In an ideal world, the prosecutors would live up to their self-proclaimed integrity and honor. I am sure many do. But when they do not, it is incumbent on the judges to protect the system. Sadly, this is not the state of affairs now. I lived this experience. I can only hope for meaningful reform so others will not have to.

CHAPTER 21

REFLECTIONS

I doubt I will ever express gratitude for this experience, and yet because of it, I like myself better. Getting through that initial and momentary wall of despair, I realized I had gained a sense of peace and awareness that opened me and set me free. Through every step of this journey, I felt a fierce determination to fight for my innocence. I was raised by my father never to throw the first punch, but if punched, never to back down. His advice sustained me through every day of this journey. I never felt victimized. I now understand how the U.S. justice system is structured to grind people down. I have now shifted my focus to exposing this system where there is literally no accountability for prosecutorial overreach and FBI misconduct.

Once ensnared in the criminal justice system, I learned that fighting for your innocence in America is not for the faint of heart or soul. The fight consumes everything—your heart, your body, your soul—and your bank account. The process tests you to the core. Also, in my case, the old adage that when you go through difficulty, you really know who your friends are proved to be absolutely true. While I am estranged from some of my former so-called friends, many remained close and have become closer. These friendships have strengthened with great and affirming solidarity. It was this support—the support of my family and friends—that gave me the internal fortitude that continues to sustain me. Many former friends were ones who advised me to cop a plea, cooperate with the government, and to cut my losses. I realized how little these "friends" knew me.

I have also been asked why was I so "naive" about my business dealings with Rajat Gupta and Anil Kumar, specifically with regard to New Silk Route. I have thought about it. NSR was the primary reason why they entered my orbit. The reality is during that period, Anil Kumar and Rajat Gupta were just two of between one hundred and 150 people with whom I interacted on a weekly or biweekly basis. I found the private equity mandate of NSR to provide growth capital to South Asian companies, including in Sri Lanka, to be appealing. It also passed our core litmus test of being additive to Galleon. My participation in NSR was intentional. At the same time, we were also building out our Galleon crossover fund and the Galleon Africa and Middle East fund. Both these funds were operational—with capital, investment analysts, and traders—and were growing smoothly. Once I realized that Anil Kumar and Rajat Gupta were constantly asking for more without yet demonstrating any benefit to Galleon, I moved quickly to separate myself from them. I liquidated Galleon's equity stake in NSR. Voyager was shut down. When Anil Kumar did not perform in the India Book, I shut that down as well. Not every business idea or venture succeeds. Not every person delivers on what they promise. The key is to act decisively and to move forward.

INVESTING

INVESTING IN THE STOCK MARKET was the core of my professional life. I loved waking up and going to work. It was exhilarating managing the vast spectrum of daily issues that defined my life as a portfolio manager, the mundane to the sublime. I was often under extreme pressure. I had to process and make decisions on multiple streams of information. Everything for me was about anticipation and instinct. Success in the market over a period of time generates a certain amount of self-esteem; consistent success breeds consistent self-confidence. When we lost money, I was crushed; the losses threw a pall over everything. I asked endless self-reflective questions.

What could I have done differently? What had I done wrong? These questions repeated themselves in an endless loop in my mind. Perhaps I could have read one more report, done just a bit more due diligence, been more challenging of my analysts' thought process, studied one more analysis. I detested losing. It tore me up.

In terms of investments, I tried to learn from my mistakes. At the end of each year, I systematically looked at the top twenty-five losers in my fund to identify any pattern in my trading so that I could avoid the same mistakes going forward. Ironically, in 2007 and 2008, the two years before I was arrested in October 2009, AMD was the one stock in which I lost the most money—$26 million and $67, million respectively. Remember, this is the same company about which Anil Kumar swore under oath that he was feeding me inside information during the very same period.

Professionally, I have achieved far more than I could ever have expected. The incredible excitement, the insurmountable tension, and yes, the sweaty palms—the pure adrenaline rushes of my daily life are now memories in the rearview mirror, a past life growing smaller by the minute. I never did anything just for the money. Money itself was never the goal. Money affords freedom. The freedom of spirit. The freedom to travel the world with family and friends, to support the underprivileged through charities that were always important to me and which I continue to do even through today.

THE GALLEON CASE

I HAVE SPENT COUNTLESS HOURS analyzing why I lost the case. Where could things have been different. With the benefit of hindsight, a few things are now clearer to me:

1. *The Judge accepting the falsified FBI affidavit and subsequent illegally obtained wiretaps as evidence.* Despite formally observing that the government "acted with reckless disregard for the truth" when it submitted the sworn wiretap affidavit containing extensive false statements and omissions, Judge Holwell allowed

the wiretaps into evidence and to be used as "snippets" of "truth" taken entirely out of context.

To many, it appeared that he did not have the fortitude to overcome the visceral and popular sentiment that I was already found guilty in the media to suppress the wiretaps as required by the law. Others speculated that prior to the trial, Judge Holwell had already determined that I was guilty and suppressing the wiretaps would cause the case to collapse. Ironically, Judge Holwell, later admitted, "Wiretaps can make anything sound suspicious."

After he left the bench and entered private practice, he spoke at a legal conference on November 16, 2012: "It's difficult to overstate how damaging wiretap evidence can be to a jury. Playing a recording in front of a jury of you calling your mother to ask what you're going to have for Sunday dinner sounds criminal."

2. *The Jury of one's peers.* My jury had no experience in the stock market. They were made up of twelve good people, but not one had the domain knowledge to make decisions about the nuances of the case. They were novitiates to Wall Street, and my trial was their classroom. They were thrown into a situation where they had to quickly learn the rules of a complicated environment where decisions were made in real time and millions of dollars invested daily. The jury instructions of fifty pages are a case in point and were simply too complex for anyone to understand. The instructions were incomprehensible even to me, a professional investor in the stock market. If I could not understand them, I have no doubt the jury couldn't either.

3. *The government built an eloquent and compelling case supported entirely of falsehoods.* The government's arguments were succinct, clear, easy to understand, and played to populist sentiments. Neither the jury nor the public understood the markets or the intricacies. They had no basis to question the bold statements of the prosecutors. The fabricated narrative of Anil Kumar was accepted as the truth by the jury and the media, even though the

facts and records clearly contradicted him. With clever coaching from prosecutors, Anil was able to look woefully forlorn on the stand, whereas in reality, his demeanor bordered on the arrogant. As a result, the gap between what the jury was told and what really happened was enormous. In short, the jury was misled. The deep flaws in the U.S. justice system enable and encourage cooperating witnesses to perjure themselves freely with no accountability.

4. *The defense.* The defense focused entirely on stocks and did a terrific job on the individual trades. Unfortunately, we failed to provide the full economic and market context for my trading decisions. We failed to tell an emotionally compelling story. And we were overshadowed by the false testimony of the three cooperating witnesses.

John Dowd's strategy was to present an overwhelming amount of detail to show that all the conversations on the wiretaps were already in the public domain. He placed detailed emphasis on highlighting all the many instances where information about a particular company was obviously public—newspapers, public forums, chat rooms—instances where "nonpublic information" was clearly public. He brought in expert academic testimony. Dowd had no doubt whatsoever that we would win an acquittal just on the sheer volume of repeated data points proving the information I was trading was public. The drumbeat of information proved to be information overload. Many jurors nodded off to sleep many times during his six-hour summation.

5. *More witnesses should have testified for the defense.* Rick Schutte was the only Galleon employee who testified. John Dowd's strategy of having Rick Schutte testify instead of me was an academically solid one.

Conventional wisdom says that in most cases the defendant should not testify for fear of being trapped by prosecutors and then charged with an additional count of perjury, but this was a unique case in the sense that the wiretaps were critical and we needed to explain them. Unlike Anil Kumar or Rajiv Goal, I did not cheat on my taxes by having secret offshore accounts; cheat my employers by moonlighting; or, cheat others. I had nothing to hide. And I would have done a better job.

However, I did not get the chance to speak. The jury did not get the chance to hear me. My own words. I was a silent observer, relinquishing the opportunity to shape my own story. They were given nothing to counter the overwhelming amount of negative publicity the trial generated about me. I may as well have been Darth Vader during the six weeks of the trial. It is a fact. There is no way to describe the sheer volume of information that went into every decision I made to buy and to sell. Only I could have explained the fact that not a single decision was frivolous. No decision was based on the words of a single man or woman. Just as I faced the jury with six weeks of stoic silence in the courtroom, every evening they "relaxed" to headlines blaring condemnation and vitriol about me. Evil and corruption personified. The media's portrayal of me was villainous. I was the singular instrument responsible for the entire financial crisis.

If I were to have testified, at the very least, I would have put the wiretaps in perspective. John believed otherwise. He considered my testimony unnecessary. He assured me that the government had not proved its case beyond a reasonable doubt. He placed his confidence in himself.

The one juror who spoke to the press after the trial said that the jury would have liked to hear from me. Had I testified, I could have easily highlighted the many times when my trades were in opposite direction to the alleged tip or inside information. I would have stressed that while I talked to many people, all of my trades (100 percent) were consistent with the written recommendations of our analysts.

Additionally, it would have been helpful for the Galleon investor relations team to step up. We passed up opportunities to expose the lies of Anil Kumar and Adam Smith. We could have bolstered Rick Schutte's testimony and negated Anil Kumar and Adam Smith's narratives. We could have also reinforced Rick's testimony of the real Galleon, its operations in reality—how we did business, how we did our research, and how we made trading decisions—all of which would have explained and justified the investment decisions I made.

Despite John Dowd's hard work, tenacity, and passion in defending me, we could not overcome the false narrative of the three cooperating witnesses and disingenuous and specific use of the wiretaps by the prosecutors.

In the wave of alleged insider trading cases between 2009 and 2013, eighty-five people were charged. Every single defendant who went to trial lost. The rest pled guilty.

Walter Pavlo, a nationally recognized expert on white-collar crime, wrote insightfully about this issue in the December 19, 2012, issue of *Forbes*. In "Can White-Collar Defendants Get a Fair Trial?" Pavlo, quoting the famed white-collar defense attorney Barry Slotnick, averred that "People have been so injured in their lives economically that they may not be able to dismiss white-collar defendants," no matter how innocent. Slotnick believes we have a tainted jury pool, an entire society with a bias against anyone with a coat and tie. He says, "These cases are amazing in that everyone who goes to trial for a financial crime is being found guilty."

Pavlo goes on to assert what I have noted earlier, that the jury instructions given by a federal judge are very complicated, especially to a jury that typically consists of blue-collar workers who have little knowledge of the inner workings of finance. Studies have shown that jurors who are economically stressed may harbor a deep resentment against corporate America. Pavlo writes, "When the average wage in the U.S. is around $50,000, it is difficult for jury pools who reflect the general population to relate to the dollars involved...The prosecutors are keen to present evidence against defendants of high-priced cars, homes, bar tabs and vacations. It plays well." Pavlo concludes, "If you're one of those thinking about taking your case to trial, don't discount the mood of the country, and it is a sour mood."[56] Studies have shown that in the U.S., those who take a case to trial and subsequently lose get a sentence that is on average twice as long as those who simply plead guilty and do not cooperate. This is known as the trial penalty, the extra time that federal defendants get if they exercise their right to a trial and lose.

GREED

THE PROSECUTORS AND THE MEDIA made Greed a central theme in the Galleon case even though the evidence demonstrated that I did not directly benefit from the alleged trades. I learned however that in high-profile cases, there are very few clean hands. Although the media loves to infuse greed on those who work on Wall Street, they turn a blind eye to that greed which is more insidious and dangerous because it goes unchecked.

There is greed for power reflected in Preet Bharara's actions and words as he positions himself for higher office in the tradition of a few former U.S. attorneys who have unscrupulously used the backs of Wall Street as stepping stones for their mayoral and even presidential ambitions. Preet Bharara targeted an outlier industry like the hedge fund industry, which employs relatively fewer people and has less political leverage than mainstream finance firms, and took an elastic view of insider trading and deceived the jury.

Astoundingly, in the April 30, 2014 issue of *New York Times Magazine*, Preet Bharara acknowledges that he "didn't touch Wall Street's real players—the top bankers." The former prosecutor (and U.S. attorney) was almost sheepish about the insider trading cases when the article's author (Jesse Eisinger) spoke to him, saying "They made our careers, but they don't change the world." In fact, several former prosecutors in the office told Eisinger that going after bankers was never a real priority. "The government failed," another former prosecutor said. "We didn't do what we needed to do."[57] Preet's agenda was Preet. Simple and straightforward.

After my trial, the three prosecutors in my case left their government posts for high-paying jobs as partners of law firms. All of them had no problem making the transition from denouncing supposed greed in the financial markets to focusing on their own greed in how much money they could make as partners of leading law firms.

- The lead prosecutor, Jonathan Streeter, accepted a senior job as equity partner in the white-collar criminal defense practice of New York law firm Dechert, LLP.

- Prosecutor Reed Brodsky joined Gibson Dunn as a partner.

- John Michaelson, the SEC lawyer who initiated the case, misleading everybody about the Polycom "smoking gun" instant message from Roomy while knowing full well that there was no contact between us thereafter, joined Boies Schiller Flexner as partner after trying *only one case: Galleon.*

They and their new employers are no doubt peddling their skills as former prosecutors to future defendants charged with insider trading.

These were not the only beneficiaries from my case:

- Robert Khuzami, the SEC enforcement chief at the time of my arrest, the cohost together with the U.S. Attorney Preet Bharara of the media extravaganza on the day of my arrest, and the one who called me the "master of the Rolodex" used his own Rolodex to obtain a senior partnership position at Kirkland & Ellis, a leading law firm, at a reported salary of $5 million a year.

- Agent Kang was rewarded for his lies, false wiretap affidavits, and witness intimidation by a being promoted to a bigger, higher-paying job at FBI headquarters in Washington, D.C.

- Judge Holwell left the bench soon after my case to start his own private practice, Holwell Shuster & Goldberg. Judges are appointed for life and seldom leave the bench. But as the judge who presided over one of the first high-profile insider trading cases, he must have determined that his services would be in demand and could be very profitable. After just one case, *Galleon,* he became an expert on insider trading and has been widely quoted by the media on various aspects of the topic.

This experience has also taught me much about human nature and how people react so differently when faced with adversity. Rajat Gupta and Dani Chiesi stood their ground and fought for their innocence. Rajat Gupta went to trial. Dani Chiesi ran out of money and pled guilty, but she did not cooperate to get a lesser sentence. Both were sentenced to jail for their decision not to cooperate. The prosecutors were bent on destroying those who refused to cooperate.

Cooperating witnesses like Anil Kumar would sell anyone to save their own skin. Not only did he lie blatantly in his testimony against me but also turned against his own mentor Rajat Gupta. Adam Smith was scared and lied his way out of trouble. Rajiv Goel, while not lying outright, suffered convenient "lapses of memory" at critical times. Anil Kumar, Rajiv Goel, and Adam Smith were all rewarded with no jail time and served only probation.

The performance of the mainstream media was another disappointment. In too many instances, reporters, who should act as watchdogs for the public, were asleep or did not understand what was going on and just parroted whatever the prosecutors said, acting like stenographers. The prosecutors used the press to influence public opinion. In its greedy quest for advertising dollars and book sales, the media distorted the truth and fabricated sensational stories.

Although popular media sided with the prosecutors, the legal and academic sentiment was very different. Many legal scholars were sufficiently disturbed by the government's lies in the wiretap affidavit and Judge Holwell's decision to give the prosecutors a free pass that they wrote legal articles analyzing Holwell's actions. During my appeals process, eight ex-judges wrote an amicus brief on my behalf. Professor Robert Blakely, who is widely regarded as the chief architect of Title III of the 1968 Wiretap Act, voluntarily wrote an amicus brief on my behalf stating that the wiretaps should have been suppressed. Others, such as Nobel Prize-winning economist Milton Friedman, took the view that insider trading should not be a crime. These scholars continue to be deeply concerned about the legal precedents set by allowing the government to misrepresent facts and to use devious means to achieve "justice."

Every day, federal prosecutors strong-arm defendants into pleading guilty and punish those who do not plead with lengthy sentences—by definition undermining the fairness and credibility of the system. These prosecutors operate with impunity. They are almost never punished for any wrongdoing.

From the onset of my experience, the FBI and its Agent Kang played outside the lines. They lied on the wiretapped affidavit; intimidated potential witnesses; and to further their false narrative, constantly leaked information to the press. In fact, in 2017, Kang's partner in investigating insider trading, FBI Agent David Chaves, admitted to leaking information to the *Wall Street Journal* and the *New York Times* in another high-profile insider trading case involving top golfer Phil Michelson and Waters. Agent Chaves was investigated, but predictably, Agent Chaves was never reprimanded. Insider games continued unchecked.

Like most Americans, I viewed the FBI as the world's finest law enforcement agency. My experiences have changed my mind. Running up to the November 2016 presidential elections, Americans have grown increasingly skeptical of the FBI as they learned that former FBI Director James Comey and Deputy Director Andrew McCabe either admitted to or were accused of opportunistically leaking information. President Trump fired them both.

The federal law enforcement apparatus, the DOJ and the FBI, will stop at nothing to land the ultimate target of their investigation. They reward cooperators and convict and imprison all those who, on principle or out of loyalty, refuse to cooperate.

An editorial in the *New York Times*, November 8, 2013, tells a sad story:

For what may be the first time on record, a former prosecutor in Texas is going to jail for failing to turn over exculpatory evidence in a murder trial. The 10-day jail sentence for the prosecutor, Ken Anderson is insultingly short: The victim of his misconduct, Michael Morton, an innocent man, spent nearly 25 years in prison.

Mr. Anderson deliberately withheld evidence that would have exonerated Mr. Morton. Mr. Anderson, who later became a judge, pleaded no contest. He was disbarred from the court, stripped of his law license, and sent to jail—for a mere 10 days. "But because prosecutors are so rarely accountable for their misconduct," the editorial continues, "the sentence is remarkable nonetheless."

The editorial goes on to say that "prosecutorial misconduct is far too common and the remedies for it, if any, usually come long after the harm has been done. Criminal defense lawyers have actually called for judges to issue a standard written order reminding prosecutors of their ethical duty."[58]

As the previous chapters have demonstrated, my experience with the American court system has gone through many peaks and valleys. One of the toughest days was the passing away of my father while I was in prison. He was a true gladiator, a fearless person, and a man of extreme kindness and generosity and compassion. If he was your friend, he was your friend forever.

I have been asked many times, "Do you regret going to trial? Should you have just copped a plea despite being innocent?" My sentence would have been a lot shorter and a lot less costly.

In the fall of 2017, my wife and three children arrived for a visit. My eldest child, a daughter, was then a law student. She is now a practicing attorney, and she followed my case closely throughout law school and into her professional life. She said spontaneously, "Dad, I'm so glad you didn't plead guilty. I'm so glad you fought because you didn't do anything wrong. Even though we would have had you home sooner if you'd pled guilty and did not go to trial." I looked at my other two children. Both nodded, vigorous in their agreement. I looked at my wife. She said nothing, but I knew she was thinking the same thing. For the first time since my arrest years before, my eyes swelled up with tears. These three children matter to me most in the world. They each looked directly at me. For years, they had stood right by me. And here they were, older, wiser, and still feeling no regret. So many emotions and no words to describe any of them. I thought about everything that they must have gone through at such tender ages. My family conducted themselves with courage, fortitude, dignity, and realism. In every instance, they faced many more challenges than I.

What I dealt with pales in comparison to their exposure at an altogether vulnerable moments of their lives. I will carry the words of my children with me for the rest of my life. All three of them gave me a precious gift at that moment that nobody can take away from me.

I have no regrets.

ENDNOTES

1   Jesse Eisinger, "Why Only One Top Banker Went to Jail for the Financial Crisis," *The New York Times Magazine*, April 30, 2014, https://www.nytimes.com/2014/05/04/magazine/only-one-top-banker-jail-financial-crisis.html.

2   Christie Smythe, "Murky Laws Complicate Insider Trading Cases, Ex-Prosecutor Says," *Bloomberg*, December 5, 2012, https://www.bloomberg.com/news/articles/2012-12-05/murky-laws-complicate-insider-cases-ex-prosecutor-says.

3   *United States v. Rajaratnam*, No. 09 CR 1184 RJH, 2010 WL 4867402, at *18 (S.D.N.Y. Nov. 24, 2010).

4   *Id.*, at *17.

5   Josh Cohen, "Is Title III Dead? The Future of Wiretap Challenges in the Wake of Rajaratnam," *The Champion NACDL*, September/October 2013, https://www.nacdl.org/Article/Sept-Oct2013-IsTitleIIIDeadTheFutureofWiret.

6   (id 2518(1)(c):

7   (id 2518(1)(c):

8   (2010 WL 4867402 at *17).

9   Preet Bharara, "Report of the Bharara Task Force on Insider Trading," The Bharara Task Force on Insider Trading, January 2020, https://www.bhararataskforce.com/executive-summary.

10 Kimberly Kindy, David S. Fallis, and Dan Keating, "Lawmakers Reworked Financial Portfolios After Talks with Fed, Treasury Officials," *Washington Post*, June 2012.

11 Richard Painter, Testimony before the Subcommittee on Government Operations of the Committee on Oversight and Reform, U.S. House of Representatives, September 14, 2020.

12 "U.S. Senators' Stock Picks Outperform the Pros'," *Wall Street Journal*, October 26, 2004; "Abnormal Returns from the Common Stock Investments of the U.S. Senate," *Journal of Financial and Quantitative Analysis*, December 2004.

13 Christie Smythe, "Murky Laws Complicate Insider Cases, Ex-Prosecutor Says," *Bloomberg*, December 5, 2012.

14 Mike Taibbi, "Analysis of the Great American Bubble," *Rolling Stone Magazine*, May 11, 2012.

15 Mike Taibbi, "Why Isn't Wall Street in Jail?" *Rolling Stone Magazine*, February 16, 2011.

16 Interview, August 2010.

17 Court of Appeals for the Second Circuit, October 15, 2015.

18 "Judge Says Preet Bharara and Co. Maaaaaybe Violated Hedge Fund Manager's Constitutional Rights," Dealbreaker.com, March 10, 2016.

19 Galleon Records.

20 Galleon SEC 13F Filing.

21 Galleon Records.

22 Galleon SEC 13F Filing.

23 Khan 2001 Criminal Case Docket Entry 22.

24 Khan 2001 Criminal Case Docket Entry 7.

25 Smith Testimony, 3/30/11.

26 (id 2518(1)(c):

27 Josh Cohen, "Is Title III Dead? The Future of Wiretap Challenges in the Wake of Rajaratnam," *The Champion NACDL*, September/October 2013,

https://www.nacdl.org/Article/Sept-Oct2013-IsTitleIIIDead
TheFutureofWiret.

28 (id 2518(1)(c):

29 FBI Agent Kang, Wiretap Application.

30 (2010 WL 4867402 at *17).

31 (2010 WL 486742 at *9–10).

32 "Past, Present, and Future of Insider Trading Law Examined at Columbia
    Law School Conference," Columbia Law School, November 28, 2012,
    https://www.law.columbia.edu/news/archive/past-present-and-future-
    insider-trading-law-examined-columbia-law-school-conference.

33 Richard Holwell. Interview. "Richard Holwell: Why Raj Rajaratnam Got
    11 Years in Prison," *PBS Frontline*, September 23, 2013, https://www.
    pbs.org/wgbh/frontline/article/richard-holwell-why-raj-rajaratnam-
    got-11-years-in-prison/.

34 Robert Blakely brief, 2010.

35 Josh Cohen, "Is Title III Dead? The Future of Wiretap Challenges
    in the Wake of Rajaratnam," *The Champion NACDL*, September/
    October 2013, p. 14, https://www.nacdl.org/Article/Sept-Oct2013-
    IsTitleIIIDeadTheFutureofWiret.

36 Richard Holwell. Interview. "Richard Holwell: Why Raj Rajaratnam Got
    11 Years in Prison." *PBS Frontline*, September 23, 2013, https://www.
    pbs.org/wgbh/frontline/article/richard-holwell-why-raj-rajaratnam-
    got-11-years-in-prison/.

37 Josh Cohen, "Is Title III Dead? The Future of Wiretap Challenges
    in the Wake of Rajaratnam," *The Champion NACDL*, September/
    October 2013, https://www.nacdl.org/Article/Sept-Oct2013-IsTitleIII
    DeadTheFutureofWiret.

38 Brady letter from government to Galleon defense counsel dated 2/9/11.

39 Dowd's closing arguments, April 21, 2011.

40 Robert Blakely brief, 2010.

41 Josh Cohen, "Is Title III Dead? The Future of Wiretap Challenges in the Wake of Rajaratnam," *The Champion NACDL*, September/October 2013, https://www.nacdl.org/Article/Sept-Oct2013-IsTitleIII DeadTheFutureofWiret.

42 Dowd closing arguments, April 21, 2011.

43 Galleon Records.

44 Transcript 3/16/2011, page 861.

45 FBI 306 Interview, December 17, 2009.

46 Rengan's trial transcript, pages 807, 887, 895, 896, 1014, and 1036.

47 *The Billionaire's Apprentice* by Anita Raghavan, page 360.

48 Ayesha Singh, "The Vengeful Indian," *The New Indian Express*, January 5, 2014.

49 First Post—December 18, 2013, R. Jagannathan.

50 Indira Kannan, "Devyani Khobragade case: Meet Preet Bharara, the Indian-American prosecutor who brought down Rajat Gupta and took action against the diplomat," *India Today*, December 18, 2013.

51 Rachael Levy, "Behind the Life and Death of a Star Money Manager Accused of Insider Trading," *Business Insider*, September 29, 2016.

52 "[T]he informer is a vital part of society's defensive armor." (*McCray v. Illinois*, 386 U.S. 300, 307 (1967).

53 "This court has long recognized the serious questions of credibility informers pose...We have therefore allowed defendants broad latitude to probe [informers'] credibility by cross examination and have counseled submission of the credibility issue to the jury with careful instructions (*Banks v. Dretke*, 540 U.S. 668, 701-02 (2004).

54 "A prosecutor who does not appreciate the perils of using rewarded criminals as witnesses risks compromising the truth-seeking mission of our criminal justice system. Because the Government decides whether and

when to use such witnesses, and what, if anything, to give them for their service, the Government stands uniquely positioned to guard against perfidy. By its action the Government can either contribute to or eliminate the problem. Accordingly, we expect prosecutors and investigators to take all reasonable measures to safeguard the system against treachery. (*United States v. Bernal-Obeso*, 989 F.2d 331, 333-34 (9th Cir. 1993).

55 "Code of Conduct for United States Judges," https://www.uscourts.gov/judges-judgeships/code-conduct-united-states-judges.

56 Walter Pavlo, "Can White Collar Defendants Get a Fair Trial?" *Forbes*, December 19, 2012.

57 Jesse Eisinger, "Why Only One Top Banker Went to Jail for the Financial Crisis," *New York Times Magazine*, April 30, 2014.

58 "A Prosecutor is Punished," *New York Times*, November 8, 2013.

Works Cited on Jacket

Jesse Eisinger, "Why Only One Top Banker Went to Jail for the Financial Crisis," *The New York Times Magazine*, April 30, 2014, https://www.nytimes.com/2014/05/04/magazine/only-one-top-banker-jail-financial-crisis.html.

Christie Smythe, "Murky Laws Complicate Insider Cases, Ex-Prosecutor Says," *Bloomberg*, December 5, 2012, https://www.bloomberg.com/news/articles/2012-12-05/murky-laws-complicate-insider-cases-ex-prosecutor-says.

Id.

United States v. Rajaratnam, No. 09 CR 1184 RJH, 2010 WL 4867402, at *18 (S.D.N.Y. Nov. 24, 2010).

Id., at *17.

Id., at *17.

Id., at *10.

Josh Cohen. "Is Title III Dead? The Future of Wiretap Challenges in the Wake of Rajaratnam." *The Champion*, September/October 2013, p. 14, https://nacdl.org/Article/Sept-Oct2013-IsTitleIIIDeadTheFutureofWiret.